Burying the Past

Burying the Past

Making Peace and Doing Justice after Civil Conflict

Nigel Biggar, Editor

GEORGETOWN UNIVERSITY PRESS / WASHINGTON, D.C.

Georgetown University Press, Washington, D.C. 20007
©2001 by Georgetown University Press. All rights reserved.
Printed in the United States of America
10 9 8 7 6 5 4 3 2 1   2001
This volume is printed on acid-free, offset book paper.

Library of Congress Cataloging-in-Publication Data

Biggar, Nigel.
    Burying the past : making peace and doing justice after civil conflict / edited
by Nigel Biggar.
        p. cm.
    Includes bibliographical references and index.
    ISBN 0-87840-821-5 (cloth : alk. paper)
    1. Restorative justice. 2. Reconciliation.   3. Civil war—Case studies.
I. Title.

JC578.B49 2001
303.6'4—dc21
                                                            00-061751

Contents

Acknowledgments

This book has its origins in a conference that was held in September 1998 at St. Antony's College, Oxford, under the title, "Burying the Past: Justice, Forgiveness, and Reconciliation in the Politics of South Africa, Guatemala, East Germany, and Northern Ireland." The conference would not have happened without the support of a wide range of organizations whose generosity deserves to be recorded here. The following provided funding, some of which has been used to produce the present volume: the British Academy, the British Council (Lima), the British Embassy (Cape Town), the Foreign and Commonwealth Office (Human Rights Department), the Friedrich Ebert Foundation (London Office), the Joseph Rowntree Charitable Trust, the Life and Peace Institute (Uppsala), the Northern Ireland Office (Central Community Relations Unit), and the World Council of Churches (Geneva). The Faculty of Theology at the University of Oxford gave its official backing; and Blackwell's Bookshop and Oxford Analytica supplied material help. Special thanks are owed to Dr. Ian Linden, Director of the Catholic Institute for International Relations, London, for his ready encouragement, advice, and assistance.

Most of all, however, I am grateful to Virginia Dunn-Biggar, who was responsible for the administration of what was widely acknowledged to be an exceptionally well-run conference. She also shared the responsibility for producing the final manuscript of this volume.

Nigel Biggar

Contributors

NIGEL BIGGAR is Professor of Theology in the Department of Theology and Religious Studies at the University of Leeds, where he directs the Institute for the Advanced Study of Religion, Ethics, and Public Life. He is the author of *Theological Politics* (Oxford: Latimer House, 1988) and of articles on Northern Ireland in the Belfast press.

ALEXANDRA BARAHONA DE BRITO is Senior Research Associate with the Institute for Strategic and International Studies in Lisbon. A Luso-American Foundation Visiting Fellow at the Center of International Studies at the University of Princeton in 1999, she is the author of *Human Rights and Democratization in Latin America: Uruguay and Chile* (Oxford: Oxford University Press, 1997) and coeditor of *The Politics of Memory and Democratization* (Oxford: Oxford University Press, 2000).

JEAN BETHKE ELSHTAIN is Laura Spelman Rockefeller Professor of Social and Political Ethics at the Divinity School in the University of Chicago, a Fellow of the American Academy of Arts and Sciences, and a former Guggenheim Fellow. Her recent books include *Augustine and the Limits of Politics* (Notre Dame: University of Notre Dame Press, 1995), and *New Wine and Old Bottles: International Politics and Ethical Discourse* (Notre Dame: University of Notre Dame Press, 1998).

TUOMAS FORSBERG is Director of the Finnish Institute of International Affairs, and coauthor of its report, *The Role of Truth Commissions in Conflict Resolution and Human Rights Promotion: Chile, South Africa, and Guatemala* (Helsinki: Finnish Institute of International Affairs, 1998).

BRANDON HAMBER coordinates the Transition and Reconciliation Unit at the Centre for the Study of Violence and Reconciliation in Johannesburg, South Africa, where he also coordinated the Centre's project on the Truth and Reconciliation Commission. A Visiting Fellow at the Initiative on Conflict Resolution and Ethnicity (INCORE) at the United Nations University and the University of Ulster in Northern Ireland (1997–98), he is editor of *Past Imperfect: Dealing with the Past in Northern Ireland and Societies in Transition* (Derry/Londonderry: INCORE, 1998). He is a clinical psychologist by profession.

TERENCE McCAUGHEY is Senior Lecturer in Irish at Trinity College, Dublin, where he also lectures in the School of Biblical and Theological Studies. An ordained minister in the Presbyterian Church and a former President of the Irish Anti-Apartheid Movement, he is author of *Memory and Redemption: Church, Politics, and Prophetic Theology in Ireland* (Dublin: Gill and Macmillan, 1993).

HUGO VAN DER MERWE is Senior Researcher at the Centre for the Study of Violence and Reconciliation in Johannesburg, South Africa, and is coeditor of *Conflict Resolution: Theory and Practice* (Manchester: Manchester University Press, 1993).

MARTHA MINOW is Professor of Law at Harvard Law School and author of *Between Vengeance and Forgiveness: Facing History after Genocide and Mass Violence* (Boston: Beacon Press, 1998).

DONALD SHRIVER is President Emeritus and Professor of Applied Christianity at Union Theological Seminary, New York, and author of *An Ethic for Enemies: Forgiveness in Politics* (New York: Oxford University Press, 1995).

RACHEL SIEDER is Lecturer in Politics and Coordinator of the Rights and Justice Programme at the Institute of Latin American Studies in the University of London. She is author of *Customary Law and Democratic Transitions in Guatemala* (London: Institute of Latin American Studies, 1997); editor of *Central America: Fragile Transition* (London: Macmillan, 1996) and of *Guatemala after the Peace Accords* (London: Institute of Latin American Studies, 1998); and coeditor of *Negotiating Rights: The Guatemalan Peace Process, 1987–96* (London: Conciliation Resources, 1997).

MARIE SMYTH is a Research Fellow at the Initiative on Conflict Resolution and Ethnicity (INCORE) at the United Nations University and the University of Ulster in Northern Ireland, where she directs a project titled Community Conflict Impact on Children. Previously she founded and directed The Cost of the Troubles Study. She is coauthor of *Northern Ireland's Troubles: The Human Costs* (London: Pluto Press, 1999) and *The*

State of the Place: Northern Ireland after the Good Friday Agreement (London: Pluto Press, 2000).

STEF VANDEGINSTE, a lawyer by training, conducts research at the Centre for the Study of the Great Lakes Region of Africa at the University of Antwerp. In 1996 he worked for the U.N. Development Programme as Governance Programme Officer in Kigali, Rwanda, and in 1995 and 1998 he was a delegate of Amnesty International in research missions to Burundi.

CHARLES VILLA-VICENCIO, Professor of Theology at the University of Cape Town, South Africa, was Director of the Research Department of the Truth and Reconciliation Commission, which was responsible for the production of the TRC's final report. Among his publications are *A Theology of Reconstruction: Nation-Building and Human Rights* (Cambridge: Cambridge University Press, 1992), and *The Spirit of Freedom: South African Leaders on Religion and Politics* (Berkeley: University of California Press, 1996). He is coeditor of *Looking Back, Reaching Forward: Reflections on the Truth and Reconciliation Commission of South Africa* (London: Zed Books, 2000).

Introduction

Discussion about the transition of states from authoritarian rule to democracy, and of ways of dealing with a violent and repressive past, is currently fashionable. Moreover, it has already generated a considerable body of literature. So why should we add this volume to it?

There are, in fact, several reasons. First, notwithstanding its fashionable status, the topic remains a very important one, and deserves widespread and sustained attention. Burying the political past is something that has affected, is affecting, and will affect the lives of millions of human beings, for better or for worse. Therefore, any attempt to glean more wisdom from past experience for present and future endeavor in this area can only be worthwhile.

Second, the topic is a complex one, and needs attention from a range of different perspectives. This volume combines several distinct approaches. Part I examines central ethical concepts—such as justice, retribution, and forgiveness—and their interrelationships. Part II considers the different dimensions or levels of burying the past, including those of institutions, national and international; local communities; and individual psychology. Part III concentrates on the different historical experiences of five countries on three continents: Chile, Guatemala, South Africa, Rwanda, and Northern Ireland.

Third, although the pages that follow contain a diversity of perspectives and opinions, there are many, albeit unwitting, points of contact. For example, the chapters on concepts refer to several of the historical cases that are treated more thoroughly in Part III; and the chapters on those cases make various uses of the concepts analyzed in Part I. In other words, what is contained here is not just a collection of disparate voices (valuable though that might be); it also comprises an implicit conversation, important elements of which are made explicit and developed in the Concluding Remarks chapter.

Fourth, this book was produced in the immediate aftermath of South Africa's innovative and controversial Truth and Reconciliation Commission (TRC). One of its special concerns, therefore, is to evaluate the achievement of the TRC. Accordingly, this is the focus of three of the thirteen chapters that follow (those by van der Merwe, Hamber, and Villa-Vicencio), while several others devote considerable attention to it (e.g., those by Biggar, Shriver, Elshtain, and Minow).

Finally, the present volume was composed in the United Kingdom in the aftermath of the Good Friday Agreement and in the (bumpy) course of the "peace process" in Northern Ireland. Another of its specific concerns, therefore, is to see what useful light might be shed on that process by analyzing relevant concepts, considering the different levels of the task, and drawing from the experience of other parts of the world. Accordingly, the final chapter (by McCaughey) is devoted to Northern Ireland, and two others give it substantial treatment (those by Biggar and Smyth).

In sum, *Burying the Past* makes a distinctive contribution to the current discussion in its combination of moral philosophical analysis with historical and social scientific description; in its deliberate attention, not just to international law and truth commissions, but also to the process of reconciliation at the level of local communities and individual psyches; in the international variety of historical experiences that it considers; and in its particular concerns to evaluate South Africa's TRC and to throw light on the task of burying the past in Northern Ireland.

Beyond this general justification, a further, specific one needs to be made. Part III consists of five chapters, each devoted to giving a critical account of attempts to bury the past made in one particular national context. Given that there are far more than five countries with relevant experience, what has governed our selection here? Northern Ireland was chosen because the question of how to bury the past there is a very live one, because it comprises an urgent European case in which people from other parts of the world have taken a keen interest, and because it is of special concern to the editor. The choice of South Africa was made, obviously, because of the innovative and controversial way in which it has sought to negotiate its way out of the past and into the future through the TRC—a way that many have found illuminating, and some exemplary. Then, since South Africa's TRC was constructed with deliberate reference to earlier truth commissions in Latin American countries, it was important to include a chapter on one of those. Chile was chosen because the detention of General Pinochet had recently given rise to public debate about whether the pursuit of justice in this case might indeed jeopardize democratic peace; and also because it had instantiated a novel use of international law to help bury a national past. A chapter was assigned to Guatemala because it represents a situation where the political constraints on doing justice have been more severe than elsewhere. Finally, Rwanda was selected, partly because there the constraints are as much logistical and economic as political, and partly because its chosen way of settling the past offers an instructive contrast to that adopted by South Africa. In brief, there are positive reasons for the choice of each of the national cases represented here. The negative reason for excluding others is simply that the five chosen comprise a diversity of context and experience that is sufficient to stimulate a range of illuminating comparisons and contrasts.

PART I

Concepts

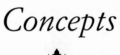

CHAPTER 1

❧

Making Peace or Doing Justice: Must We Choose?

Nigel Biggar

The Dilemma

On the afternoon of Saturday 15 August 1998, a bomb planted by a dissident Irish republican group, the self-styled "Real IRA," exploded in the town center of Omagh in Northern Ireland, injuring hundreds of civilians and killing twenty-nine. The following Friday, the front cover of the British satirical magazine, *Private Eye*, featured Bertie Ahern, the Irish *taoiseach*, and Tony Blair, the British prime minister. Ahern says to Blair, "We'll hunt the killers down," to which Blair responds, "And then we'll let them out." The words put into Blair's mouth alluded to the Good Friday Agreement, which had been concluded about four months previously between the British and Irish governments and the representatives of the political parties in Northern Ireland; and according to which paramilitary groups such as the IRA had committed themselves to peace in exchange for the early release from prison of their members.

Strictly, *Private Eye*'s satire was unfair (but then satire usually is). The republican perpetrators of the Omagh atrocity were not covered by the terms of the Good Friday Agreement, which provided for the early release of paramilitary prisoners on condition that they belonged to an organization committed to peace. Nevertheless, the satirical exchange between Ahern and Blair nicely captures one of the most controversial issues raised by attempts to find a way forward out of civil conflict—in Northern Ireland, South

Africa, or wherever: namely, the tension between the moral demands of justice and the political requirements of peace.

This is not just an academic issue, but one of considerable political importance; for insofar as people regard a political settlement as unjust, they will not support it; and if enough people regard it as unjust, it will cease to be viable. In Northern Ireland, for example, British unionist support for the Good Friday Agreement and the consequent "Peace Process" is precarious; and one of the reasons for this is that many unionists regard the early release from prison of members of the IRA convicted of terrorist crimes to be immoral. In South Africa many feel similarly about the Truth and Reconciliation Commission's granting of amnesty to those guilty of acts of torture and murder, provided only that their deeds were politically motivated and that they made a full public confession of them.

The issue of the tension between making peace and doing justice after civil conflict, then, is of political importance as well as academic interest. It is the main aim of this essay to argue, with special reference to Northern Ireland and South Africa, that the tension is in fact much less severe than some suppose; and that it is a serious misrepresentation of the Good Friday Agreement and of the work of the Truth and Reconciliation Commission (TRC) to describe them simply as trading justice for peace.

Bypassing the Dilemma: The Policy of Forgetting

Before I try to make that case, however, I must first address the proposal that the tension between peace and justice is better bypassed than negotiated; that the doing of justice in the aftermath of civil conflict is impossibly fraught, and should simply be dropped; and that the past and its unredressed grievances are best buried by deliberately forgetting them, by sweeping them under the carpet, by drawing a thick line between past and present, turning around and walking resolutely off into the future.

This policy, were it to work, would have the advantage of not raking over old coals, kindling fading resentments and suspicions, and igniting fresh wrangling over the "truth" about the past and about how much responsibility should rest on whose shoulders. And there is some historical evidence that, at least in certain circumstances, such a policy of forgetting does seem to work. Timothy Garton Ash has offered as instances the examples of post-World War II France and post-Franco Spain.[1]

There is also some evidence that alternatives to the policy of forgetting can be counterproductive. Ash notes, for example, that the current German policy of permitting those informed upon in the former East Germany access to their State Security Service files has resulted in the rupture of relationships and the leveling of unjust accusations. Likewise, in a poll that was published in July 1998, 74 percent of white urban South Africans, and 62 percent of blacks, reckoned that the operations of the Truth and Reconciliation Commission had done more to stir up old resentments than lay them to rest.[2]

Before I try to interpret this evidence, let me declare that I have a strong prejudice against trying to bury the past by deliberate forgetting; and for three reasons. First, some may be able to forget; but not, I think, the victims. Second, if government does not attend to the victims and their injuries, then it fails in one of its most basic political duties; for protecting and upholding victims of injury is one of the basic raisons d'être of the state. And third, grievances without redress tend to fester. Festering, they help to infect future generations with an indiscriminate hatred of the perpetrators and their descendants—and also with an endemic mistrust of the state that, having failed in its duty to vindicate victims past, seems ready to tolerate the injury of victims future. Such hatred and mistrust, then, constitutes an unstable mixture that, under certain conditions, is liable to explode and to rupture the half-forgetful present with the unfinished business of the past. Recent examples of this can readily be found, I think, in Northern Ireland and in Bosnia. And, again, Ash has pointed out the case of postcommunist Poland, where the failure to "purge" high places of former communists suspected of collaborating with the secret police led to the fall of a government and still disturbs Polish politics.[3]

So there are three reasons for my prejudice against a policy of forgetting. But can my prejudice withstand the evidence? How can it make sense of the counterexamples I've mentioned?

On South Africa, I could respond to the findings of the recent poll by saying that attempts to dig out the truth are always bound to be disturbing; but they may still be the only way to lay stable long-term foundations for the future. Bringing the truth to light is but the first step in a long process of reconciliation that will take generations to complete. And if that is true of South Africa's Truth and Reconciliation Commission, it may also be true of Germany's policy of access to the Stasi files.

But what about the examples of France and Spain? Not being an historian of these countries, I do not have the competence to judge what their historical experiences signify for the issues before us. But if the relevant historical expertise were present, I would interrogate it along these lines. First, how true is it to say that these countries have pursued a policy of forgetting? In France, for example, the end of World War II was immediately followed by a period of rough reckoning—the *Épuration* (or "Purge"). Surely a policy of forgetting after a period of reckoning is one thing, and a policy of forgetting instead of reckoning quite another.

But even if it were true that a policy simply of forgetting had been pursued, there are still questions to be asked with a view to making important distinctions. What kind of forgetting has been practiced? Presumably, a forgetting of the perpetrators and their crimes. But what of the victims and their injuries—have they been forgotten, too? This distinction is important because remembering the victims and what they have suffered is an important part of doing justice—as I shall explain shortly.

Beyond inquiring about the precise nature of a policy of forgetting, we also have to ask whether or not it is—or was—successful, and what it is that we mean by "success" in this matter. Presumably, we mean a certain level of political stability. But how enduring must this be? On this point, it is notable that Ash himself admits that the policy of forgetting pursued in France was not entirely successful.[4]

If, in the end, we conclude that we have found a case where a policy simply of forgetting has been "successful," then we have the further task of asking what this implies. Does it imply that a policy of forgetting should always be pursued in the aftermath of civil conflict, or only in certain cases? And, if the latter, then what are the characteristics that differentiate these cases from others?

So, there are seven questions I would pose to the example of postwar France and post-Franco Spain or any other case (e.g., post–civil war Ireland) that seems to recommend a policy of forgetting. The rest of what I have to say assumes a negative answer to the sixth question. It assumes that there are at least some cases where the past should not be buried simply by forgetting, where the tension between making peace and doing justice should not be relaxed by abandoning all attempts at the latter. In these cases, we have to try to bury the past and its lingering grievances, not by sweeping them under the carpet, but by laying them to rest; that is, by doing some kind of justice.

But here, of course, is where the tension arises, and where the attractions of deliberate forgetting seem powerful. For trying to do justice in cases of injury is normally thought to involve punishing the perpetrators. But if the injury has occurred in the political context of a civil conflict, then the perpetrators are likely to see their deeds as justified by their intended service of law and order, or democracy, or national liberation, or socialism, or whatever; and they are likely to regard attempts to punish them as the continuation of war by judicial means. So, at this point, attempts to do justice begin to threaten the negotiated peace, the fragile accommodation that managed to bring civil conflict to an end. What, then, shall we choose? A peace built upon the public suppression of the victim's memories, or a justice that risks bringing war back to life again?

Negotiating the Dilemma: Reconsidering Justice

That is the dilemma on which the rest of this essay will dwell. I shall argue that it can be negotiated; that, in fact, it need not present us with a simple choice between peace and justice; and that, in the cases of South Africa and Northern Ireland, the making of peace has involved the doing of some considerable justice. In order to launch this argument I must first open up the question of what we understand criminal justice to be.

My assumption is that it is common to think of criminal justice primarily, even wholly, in terms of the punishment of the perpetrator. But this is a mistake, for justice is primarily not about the punishment of the perpetrator, but about the vindication of the victim.

What do I mean by vindication? What kinds of nonpunitive justice does it involve?

The first thing it involves is recognizing the injury as such, and thereby acknowledging the dignity of the victim. To suffer an injury and have it ignored is to be told, effectively, "What happens to you doesn't matter, because you don't matter"; so to have it acknowledged is to have your dignity affirmed. Here what I have in mind is the comment made by Archbishop Desmond Tutu about the significance of the local hearings of the TRC's Committee on Human Rights Violations; namely, that these were occasions when those who had hitherto been treated like rubbish, could stand up and have their stories heard.[5] So the first step in vindicating the victim—and the first act of justice—is to recognize the significance of the injury and thereby the dignity of the injured.

The second step, obviously, is to give the victims support, material and psychological, and to seek to repair the damage as far as possible.

The third step in vindication is to seek to establish the truth of what happened, why it happened, and who was responsible. The importance to the victims of getting at the truth is something that I have found striking, and rather puzzling. It struck me first when I saw the film version of Ariel Dorfmann's play, *Death and the Maiden*. This is set in a South American country (presumably Chile, since Dorfmann is Chilean), where a woman, Paulina, realizes that her neighbor, Roberto, is the man who raped and tortured her in prison during the previous military regime. She kidnaps him and puts him on trial in her living room. The subsequent interrogation reaches this climax:

Paulina: . . . I'm not going to kill you because you're guilty, Doctor, but because you haven't repented at all. I can only forgive someone who really repents, who stands up amongst those he wronged and says, I did this, I did it, and I'll never do it again.

Roberto: What more do you want? You've got more than all the victims in this country will ever get. What more do you want?

Paulina: The truth, Doctor. The truth, and I'll let you go. . . .[6]

The importance of getting at the truth also struck me when watching film footage of the session of the TRC's Committee on Human Rights Violations where Joyce Mthimkulu, whose son Siphiwo was murdered by the police, says this: "If they can just show us the bones of my child, I'll be grateful. Where did they leave the bones of my child? Where did they take him? Who handed him over to them? What did they do to him?"[7]

The same point struck me again when listening to a relative of one of the victims of the bombing of the PanAm flight over Lockerbie, whose mission in life seemed not so much to get the perpetrators punished as to make the British Government make public what it knew about the case.[8]

In each of these cases, the predominance of the desire for the truth on the part of victims is striking.[9] But it is also puzzling. Because what, exactly, does discovering the truth achieve? What difference does it make?

Here are some suggestions. In a case where the fate of a loved one is uncertain, the discovery of the truth liberates relatives from the excruciating limbo between lingering hope and full-blown grief. The discovery of the truth also helps the victim to understand her suffering, to tie down and delimit its significance—and suffering that we can somewhat comprehend is usually easier to bear. Further, the public identification of the perpetrator subjects him to social pressure to accept responsibility for the injury he committed, and thereby himself to recognize the dignity of the victim.

Further still, if the perpetrator was the servant of a regime wont to violate human rights in pursuit of its political ends, then the making public of the truth about his crime will help to discredit the old regime, and thus help reassure actual and potential victims that the political future will not be a repeat of the past.[10]

Thus far my main point has been that criminal justice is primarily about the vindication of the victim, and that there are ways of vindicating the victim that do not involve the punishment of the perpetrator: namely, by recognizing the injury, supporting the victim, and discovering the truth.

Now I want to consider whether the punishment of the perpetrator, while not the primary aim of criminal justice, is nevertheless part of it; that is, whether the vindication of the victim does not, among other things, involve some kind of punishment. My answer is, Yes it does, provided that we understand punishment in a certain way.

Basically, we should think of punishment as being teleological or goal oriented[11] within retributive limits. On the one hand, punishment is retributive insofar as it is a response to someone who has committed a crime (and not simply a means of utilitarian social engineering); insofar as it asserts the principle of fairness by imposing penalties designed to annul the advantages over others that the criminal unfairly seized by his crime[12]; insofar as it expresses the degree of opprobrium with which the community regards the crime; and, therefore, insofar as there is some conventional or symbolic proportion between it and the penalty.

On the other hand, punishment is not retributive in the sense of annulling the crime itself, because that is impossible. It is true that, in cases of damage to property, reparation or compensation together with "damages" (for the denial of use and mental distress) can go some way toward reversing the effects of the injury; but the victim's consequently heightened sense of vulnerability, not to mention the breach of trust between the criminal and his community, nonetheless persist. Further, where damage to the person is concerned, the only compensation possible is monetary; in which case, as Sir Walter Moberly put it, "the annulment is *ersatz*. . . ."[13] Nigel Walker, formerly professor of Criminology at Cambridge University, puts it more vigorously: "As anyone who has been mugged or raped is aware, this [the concept of punishment as the annulment of crime] is nonsense. Victims can be compensated, but not unraped or unmugged."[14] What is true of rape and mugging is, of course, true a fortiori of torture and murder.

So, punishment should be thought of as retributive in some senses, but not in others. Further, within these retributive terms it should also be thought of as aiming to realize certain good states-of-affairs: the prevention of the repetition of the crime by, for example, incarcerating the criminal; the restoration of the victim's *status quo ante* as far as possible by compelling the criminal to make reparation or compensation and to pay damages; the reassurance of victims, actual and potential, and the deterrence of would-be criminals, by publicly expressing the community's active opprobrium; and the repentance of the criminal, both for his own sake and for the community's,[15] by conveying to him the fact and degree of that opprobrium.[16]

Before we proceed any further, let me summarize the main features of the account of criminal justice that I have just given.

First, I've implied that it is divisible. There are separable parts of criminal justice. One can do some without doing others.

Second, criminal justice is primarily about the vindication of the victim, then about the protection of potential victims, and then (and partly therefore) about the reform of the perpetrator.

Third, victims can be somewhat vindicated and protected without punishing the perpetrator at all.

Although, fourth, the full vindication of victims will require such punishment.

Fifth, the point of this punishment is the vindication of actual victims, the protection of potential ones, and the reform of the perpetrators. Punishment necessarily involves the suffering of the perpetrator, but that is not its point; in other words, it is not vengeful.

However, sixth, it is retributive, but not in the sense of aspiring to annul the crime by imposing suffering on the perpetrator "equal" to that criminally inflicted on the victim. Rather, punishment's retributive character lies in its being a response to someone who has actually broken the law (and not being inflicted on an innocent for some utilitarian purpose); and insofar as the penalties that it imposes are designed, as far as possible, to annul the relative advantages unfairly seized in the criminal act and/or to express the community's opprobrium.

So there is my theory of criminal justice.[17] Now let me bring it to bear on the main issue before us—the extent to which we have to choose between meeting the political demands of making peace and meeting the moral claims of doing justice. The question that arises here is this: Does the theory that I have outlined help to reduce the tension between the political demands and the moral claims, and therefore enlarge the scope for doing both? I believe that it does, and I shall now seek to explore how it does so in terms of the "peace processes" in South Africa and Northern Ireland.

The Case of South Africa

In South Africa the chosen route from civil conflict to a peaceful future has been by way of a Truth and Reconciliation Commission. One of the most controversial features of the TRC was its power of granting amnesty to those who made a full public confession of injuries they had perpetrated, and that were politically motivated. Repentance and reparation by perpetrators were not required. This means that many people have been allowed to get away with deeds of torture or illegal killing, without being sentenced and punished—and without so much as an apology. To this extent peace has indeed been bought at the price of justice.

On the other hand, the amnesty granted was not a blanket one. The condition of political motivation permitted the commissioners to reject applications in cases where the means used were disproportionate to the declared political end, and which were therefore more reasonably attributable to racism or sadism.

Further, the requirement that amnesty applicants make confession of their deeds in public—and the public here, thanks to broadcasting, was nationwide—exposed them to the opprobrium of (at least) large sections of the national community, albeit not in the ritual form of receiving a judicial sentence. In some cases, the trial of making public confession and suffering public exposure moved applicants to public repentance.

Further still, since the public confessions of agents of the apartheid regime disclosed the state- or government-authorized nature of many of the violations of human rights, they have helped to discredit the regime in the eyes of many of its more passive supporters, to bolster support for a genuinely new regime, and to reassure actual and potential victims that the future will not be a repeat of the past. It is true that the granting of amnesty was not made conditional upon the applicant making reparation to his victim; and therefore that this way of bringing home to the perpetrator the damage he had done, and so of encouraging him to repent, was let go. Nevertheless, through its Committee on Reparation and Rehabilitation,[18] the TRC was able to make recommendation to the president for appropriate reparation to victims by the state.[19]

Finally, through its Committee on Human Rights Violations, the TRC offered some victims the opportunity to tell their stories, not only in public, but in the context of a legally authorized, quasi-judicial institution. It thereby gave them a measure of acknowledgment and validation of their dignity by the state.

The Case of Northern Ireland

In Northern Ireland, as I have already indicated, one of the most controversial elements of the "Peace Process" has been the provision in the Good Friday Agreement for the early release of paramilitary prisoners. This has been controversial because many in Northern Ireland, especially unionists, regard it as trivializing the victims' injuries. It should also have been controversial—although, to my knowledge, it has not been—because of its indiscriminate nature: that is, because it applies equally to all members of qualifying organizations, whether or not their crime was the shooting of an armed soldier or the indiscriminate bombing of a pub packed with civilians.

On the other hand, the injuries suffered by victims are taken seriously by the national community, insofar as the British government has put in place a system of reparation and support.[20]

Further, in many cases, the perpetrators of their injuries have been convicted and sentenced for their crimes, which means that these have been exposed to public opprobrium, and their victims assured of vindication by the state. Additionally, in that the Good Friday Agreement provided only for the release of prisoners, and not their pardon, the public verdict still stands.

Moreover, the perpetrators did serve part of their original sentences, in many cases most of it, before their release; so they have paid a considerable price for the unfair liberties they took—a price that reflects, albeit with unavoidable crudity, an appreciation of the gravity of the injuries suffered by the victims.

Further still, since the changed political circumstances make it highly unlikely that the prisoners, once released, will resort to their criminal ways, this policy does not compromise the dimension of justice that is concerned with the protection of potential victims—all the more so, given that the prisoners are released on a license that is revocable on evidence of reversion.[21]

Conclusion

My conclusion, then, is that both in South Africa and in Northern Ireland, the chosen peace processes have involved the doing of considerable amounts of the different parts of criminal justice, albeit in a manner that has either constitutionally bypassed judicial procedures (as in South Africa) or constitutionally trumped it (as in Northern Ireland).

Some might object that justice in both cases has nevertheless been unacceptably compromised. In South Africa persons guilty of committing or authorizing gross violations of human rights have gone unpunished; and punishment, if not the whole of justice, is certainly part of it. To this a two-fold response may be given. First, punishment is not an end in itself. Some of its purposes have been achieved by other means—the informal communication of public opprobrium, the protection of potential victims, and the repentance of some perpetrators; and another purpose might yet be achieved—the making of reparations to actual victims. Second, all actualizations of justice by human beings in the world of time and space are limited, and it is arguable that no other means available in the circumstances would have achieved more justice than the TRC.[22]

In Northern Ireland, some might object, justice was intolerably compromised in that persons guilty of grave crimes have been released from prison after serving only light sentences. A response to this should begin by noting that sentencing is not a science, and that in most cases the fittingness of a sentence to a crime is bound to be crude and largely conventional.[23] Add to this the fact that in all the crimes under consideration political motives played a part, and one then has a reason for treating them differently from normal cases. Nevertheless, it remains true that the excessive and indiscriminate nature of some of the crimes suggest that sectarian hatred, rather than concern for rational political ends, was the predominant motive, in which case the reason for special treatment diminishes and the compromise of justice at this point increases.

A Theological Coda

Since I am a Christian moral theologian, and not just a moral philosopher, I am bound, before I finish, to consider how Christian belief about the nature of things bears upon the matters before us. I have two points to make.

The first thing to be said is that my predisposition in favor of a constructive, teleological concept of justice owes much to the influence of the Bible, with its concept of justice as interpersonal reconciliation, and especially of the New Testament, where the themes of compassion, mercy, and forgiveness are so prominent. Correlatively, this influence has predisposed me to regard the retributivist rationale for punishment critically.

It is true, of course, that there are plenty of Christians who are retributivists, regarding retribution as the main or even sole aim of punishment, and conceiving it in terms of the imposition of an equality of suffering. Indeed, one of the reasons why unionist support for the Good Friday Agreement is so equivocal is that many unionists are evangelical Protestants, who subscribe to a Calvinist doctrine of the Atonement, which sanctifies a retributivist concept of punishment.[24] Nevertheless, it seems to me that any retributivist who reads the New Testament with an open mind cannot but be unsettled by the recurrence of the themes of compassion, mercy, and forgiveness, and of the prohibition of retaliation, and be pressed to think again upon the question, "What, exactly, is the point of retribution?"

The second way in which Christian belief bears on the matters before us is more directly theological, and has to do with our response to the fact of the limits of human justice. The notion that human justice is limited is, of course, neither novel nor surprising. But the severity of those limits, which become all too clear in the context of thinking about doing justice after a civil conflict that has involved gross and widespread violations of human rights, might well give one pause. Here the natural fragmentariness of human justice is writ larger. Here the political and economic constraints are much more obvious. Certainly, here as elsewhere one may hope to do some justice for some of the survivors, although none for the dead; but here the numbers of dead are so great as to inhibit our customary oversight.

Further, if the ultimate fulfillment of justice is reconciliation (and I believe it is), and if reconciliation requires forgiveness (which it does), and if only the victim has the right to forgive her injurer (which is the case), then, within the world of time and space, full justice in cases of murder is impossible, since the victim, being dead, cannot forgive.[25]

The severity of the limitations that constrain the realization of secular justice raises a series of questions. Can we continue to gaze upon the vast sea of unvindicated dead without hope and yet still with care? Or shall we preserve hope by ceasing to care for the hopeless, rationalizing them as the inevitable "refuse of an [emancipating] historical process"?[26] But would not such rationalizing of the unrelieved suffering of others diminish our own humanity with a certain callousness?[27] How, then, can we acknowledge the mountainous horizon of unfinished—and, secularly speaking, unfinishable—judicial business, and still prevent our commitment to justice from hardening into utilitarian ruthlessness or sinking into despairing inertia?

One answer to these questions lies in the traditional Christian (and Jewish) notion of eschatological hope—hope that, beyond time and space and by the superhuman power of God, the vast majority of victims who have received no justice in this world and the rest who have received only fragments and tokens of it, will yet be fully vindicated. Now, as Max Horkheimer has rightly pointed out, the "monstrousness" of the thought that there is no final justice, no vindication for the wronged dead, does not amount to a cogent argument for its contrary.[28] Nevertheless, if eschatological hope is necessary to render rational and possible an acceptance of the severe limits of secular justice that is not acquiescent but expectant, not resigned but resolute; and if the rightness of that resoluteness seems to us quite as true as anything else we believe in; then that is one reason for supposing eschatological hope to be true, too. And there may well be others.

Endnotes

1. Timothy Garton Ash, "The Truth about Dictatorship," *The New York Review of Books*, 19 February 1998, 35, 40. Ash, perhaps wisely, is equivocal about whether France and Spain furnish us with examples of "successful" policies of forgetting. On the one hand, he judges that "the ancient case for forgetting is much stronger than it is quite comfortable for historians to recall" and cites postwar France as a "successful democ-

racy." But on the other hand he notes that in France the policy of obliviousness followed an initial period of *épuration* (p. 35) and was pursued "at a cost, which often has not shown up until a generation later" (p. 40).

2. Rian Malan, "South Africa's bid to bury its past ends with few truths and little reconciliation," *The Sunday Telegraph*, 2 August 1998, 24.

3. Ash, "The Truth about Dictatorship," 38.

4. See note 1.

5. Recorded in "Getting Away with Murder," a BBC TV documentary about the TRC, which was presented by Michael Ignatieff. Originally broadcast on 1 November 1997 as part of the "Correspondent" series, it subsequently won the Royal Television Society Award and the Golden Nymph and Unda Awards at Monte Carlo.

6. Ariel Dorfmann, *Death and the Maiden* (London: Nick Hern Books, 1991), 44.

7. In "Getting Away with Murder."

8. On "Thinking Allowed with Laurie Taylor," BBC Radio 4, 19 August 1998.

9. The desire for truth does not necessarily supplant the desire for retribution. Joyce Mthimkulu later opposed the granting of amnesty to her son's killers—partly because the political nature of their motivation was dubious, and partly because they showed no remorse.

10. This I take to be implicit in Charles Villa-Vicencio's evaluation of the TRC: "Suffice it to say, that, for all the failures of the Commission, it is largely as a result of its work that few, if any, South Africans can ever again . . . say, 'We did not know'" ("Learning to Live Together with Bad Memories," paper presented at the University of Leeds, 25 November 1999). The point is made explicit in *Reconciliation through Truth*, where Kader Asmal and his coauthors assert that the public establishment of the truth about the old apartheid regime is a vital step toward both bolstering support for the new one and ensuring that it really is different: "In these early years of consolidating democracy, there must be a galvanising and self-critical vision of the goals of our society. And such a vision in turn requires a clear-sighted . . . grasp of what was wrong in the past. . . . An important goal of the [Truth and Reconciliation] commission is to act as a catalyst for swift and thorough disclosure of past horrors, in order to . . . end . . . the steady and corrosive drip of past pathologies into the new order" (Kader Asmal, Louise Asmal, and Robert Suresh Roberts, *Reconciliation through Truth: A Reckoning of Apartheid's Criminal Governance* [Oxford: James Currey; New York: St. Martin's Press, 1997], 6, 26).

11. I say "teleological" here rather than "utilitarian" because, on this account, while punishment aims to promote the welfare of certain classes of human beings—actual victims, potential victims, actual criminals, would-be criminals—it does not pretend to be able to calculate, much less advance, "utility" (i.e., the maximal happiness of the maximal number of people).

12. This rationale is controversial. John Finnis espouses it (*Natural Law and Natural Rights* [Oxford: Clarendon Press, 1981], 260–64). Nigel Walker rejects it (*Why Punish?*

[Oxford: Oxford University Press, 1991], 74–76), noting that Andrew von Hirsch, one of retributivism's most prominent contemporary advocates, eventually abandoned it (ibid., 150–51, n5). Walker is right to argue that not all crimes can be thought of as the seizing of unfair advantages. It is hard to see, for example, what advantages IRA members could be thought to have gained by their crimes, and which could be "annulled" by a prison sentence. Nevertheless, there are other kinds of crime—for example, those involving material gain—which can be sensibly thought of in these terms.

13. Sir Walter Moberly, *The Ethics of Punishment* (London: Faber and Faber, 1968), 188–89.

14. Nigel Walker, *Why Punish?*, 74.

15. An impenitent criminal remains a threat, except in cases where the rationale for his criminal action has been removed by a change in external circumstances (e.g., where the rationale for "terrorist" activity by members of the IRA in Northern Ireland has been removed by the commitment of the republican movement to peaceful, political means).

16. Nigel Walker doubts that the repentance or spiritual improvement of the criminal can be a (or the sole?) reason for punishment, because the latter would lack justification in cases where the offender persists in maintaining the moral rectitude of his action. He also regards as "feeble" the reply to this that one cannot be certain that the offender will persist in this attitude forever (*Why Punish?*, 78). But why is this feeble? Why should the community stop telling the truth to someone, just because they do not appear to be listening?

17. The theory of criminal justice that I am proposing is similar to Charles Villa-Vicencio's theory of "restorative" justice, but differs in being less equivocal about the role of retribution. Although Villa-Vicencio recognizes "what may well be a legitimate basic need for censure and punishment," he is inclined to speak of restorative justice as an "alternative" to retributive justice (as the title of his essay indicates: "A Different Kind of Justice: the South African Truth and Reconciliation Commission," *Contemporary Justice Review*, 1 [December 1998]: 407–28). However, what he means by "restorative justice" is, in fact, a form of criminal justice in which retribution is subordinate to constructive ends.

18. The work of the TRC was divided into three committees: the Committee on Human Rights Violations, the Committee on Amnesty, and the Committee on Reparation and Rehabilitation. For a succinct description of the aims and structures of the TRC, see *Essays on the Truth and Reconciliation Commission*, South African Embassy Information Series, No. 4 (The Hague: Embassy of South Africa, April 1998), 6–8.

19. At the time of writing (October 1999), however, the new government in South Africa was subject to criticism for its slowness to act on the matter of reparations, and for the paucity of the funds it had earmarked for it.

20. Of course, whether this system is sufficiently extensive and generous is a politically moot point.

21. Nothing that I have said here prejudices the claim that more justice remains to be done in Northern Ireland on behalf of nationalists and republicans—for example, that the truth about "Bloody Sunday" (the highly controversial event in 1972 when British troops shot dead thirteen demonstrators in London/derry) should be fully disclosed. However, since complaints against the injustice of the Good Friday Agreement have come mainly from unionist lips, my concern in this part of my essay has been to argue for its justice largely in unionist terms—although, by recognizing that the sincere political motivation behind at least some republican acts of violence distinguishes them from ordinary crimes, I do not adhere to those terms absolutely.

22. Kader Asmal and his coauthors give an extensive list of "sound reasons" why South Africa preferred a Truth and Reconciliation Commission to the holding of Nuremberg-style trials of the officials of the apartheid regime: (1) there was no certainty that "victors' justice" could have been imposed in the political circumstances that obtained; besides, (2) such justice would have been selective and politically opportunistic; (3) a judicial process would have focused too much on the perpetrators at the expense of the victims; and (4) it would have focused on individuals rather than the regime; (5) the conduct of criminal trials would have placed the prosecutorial bureaucracies of the old order in a position of enormous influence; and (6) "the necessity to prove the minutiae of individual cases beyond a reasonable doubt in an elaborate and formal process can establish an uneven playing field in favour of the perpetrator; and it can constipate historical debate" (*Reconciliation through Truth*, 18–20).

23. Nigel Walker: "[N]obody nowadays regards precise commensurability as an achievable aim" (*Why Punish?*, 101–02).

24. For this reason, many religiously serious unionists are irritated by the naming of the accord reached in Belfast on 10 April (Good Friday) 1998 as the "Good Friday Agreement," because whereas (in their eyes) the original Good Friday represented the expensive achievement of God's grace through Jesus' vicarious suffering of just retribution, the Belfast Agreement has offered cheap grace to impenitent criminals.

25. This is a point made by more than one of the Jewish contributors to Simon Wiesenthal's book, *The Sunflower: On the Possibilities and Limits of Forgiveness* (New York: Schocken Books, 1997), including Abraham Heschel (164–66) and Dennis Prager (216–20). It is true that the murdered victim's relatives and friends may forgive the injury done them, and that God may forgive the injury done Him (through the infliction of damage on His creature), but it remains true to say that no one can forgive the injury suffered by the victim except the victim herself.

26. Helmut Peukert, "Fundamental Theology and Communicative Praxis as the Ethics of Universal Solidarity," in James A. Reimer, ed., *The Influence of the Frankfurt School on Contemporary Theology* (Lampeter: Mellen Press, 1992), 233.

27. Peukert makes a similar point: "How can one retain the memory of the conclusive, irretrievable loss of the victims of the historical process, and still be happy, still find one's

identity? If for the sake of one's happiness and one's own identity this memory is banished from consciousness, is this not tantamount to the betrayal of the very solidarity by which alone one is able to discover oneself?" (H. Peukert, *Science, Action, and Fundamental Theology: Toward a Theology of Communicative Action*, trans. James Bohmann (Cambridge, Mass. and London: MIT Press, 1984), p. 209.

28. Max Horkheimer: "The thought is monstrous that the prayers of the persecuted in their hour of greatest need, that the innocent who must die without explanation of their situation, that the last hopes of a supernatural court of appeals, fall on deaf ears and that the night unilluminated by any human light is also not penetrated by any divine one. The eternal truth without God has as little ground and footing as infinite love; indeed, it becomes an unthinkable concept. But is the monstrousness of an idea any more a cogent argument against the assertion or denial of a state of affairs than does logic contain a law which says that a judgement is simply false that has despair as its consequence?" Quoted by Peukert in *Science, Action, and Fundamental Theology*, 209–10.

CHAPTER 2

Where and When in Political Life Is Justice Served by Forgiveness?

Donald Shriver

It is not easy for Americans to speak convincingly about "burying the past." In our national culture, we bury the past only too regularly. We are a future-oriented people, focused on the pragmatics of the "next act" of our personal and public dramas. As Yale historian Carl Becker once remarked, Americans think of the past as the dust kicked up at the back of a moving vehicle. With eyes on the future, we are unregenerate optimists. Ward Just says of us in his novel, *The American Ambassador*, "Like prairie topsoil, optimism was a national resource. . . . America reinvented itself each day; why couldn't the world do likewise?"[1]

A wiser word to his own fellow citizens was spoken by another American novelist, William Faulkner: "The past is not dead and gone; it isn't even past." Faulkner spoke as one belonging to a segment of American society whose members have strong reason to remember that their region lost a war. Defeat, suffering, and irreparable loss engrave the human memory in ways seldom matched by successes and victories. The unsuccessful peoples of the world have the longest memories of historic pain. Among Americans, descendants of African slaves and descendants of those Europeans called "Indians" have long memories indeed. Against them are arrayed many spiritual neighbors of that Chicago housewife who in 1992, complained that there was too much talk about what African Americans had suffered in the past: "It's up to them to paddle their own canoe. [They shouldn't] always think about the fact that they were slaves."[2]

The irony in her remark is that, as a person who allegedly paddles her own canoe, she tells some civic neighbors how they ought to think. In this she inadvertently violates her own philosophy but affirms something vital about human existence: our concern about how others think of us. Human society depends upon some shared understandings of its members and some common agreements on what we should expect of each other. As Professor Gesine Schwan of the Free University in Berlin remarks, there can be no society among humans who "barricade" themselves in their own worlds: "Without a culture of mutual understanding society breaks into fragments."[3]

So how should any of us, as citizens, cope with the injuries done to some of us or to our ancestors in the recent or remote past? Precisely for those who have suffered those injuries, the political world has to take account of the painful past, especially if political powers were the perpetrators of that pain. For their victims, justice to the past is a form of justice in the present and for the future.

What it may mean to "bury the past" in a just and constructive way, rather than in an unjust and destructive way, is the theme of my discussion here. Specifically, I intend to address the question of what it means to serve justice in the process of enacting a certain forgiveness in the push and pull of political relationships.

The Political Context

South Africans will be the first to say that, since 1990, theirs has been no perfect example of collective efforts to recover from the vast damages of apartheid politics. But just as world opinion focused for decades on the stunning evils of that racist political order, so now many look to modern South Africa as a precedent for how a society can both remember and recover from an evil past. If South Africa is not offering us an ideal example of what it means to seek social justice in the very act of seeking social forgiveness and reconciliation, it is at least a bright current light in a murky business.

President Nelson Mandela summarized his own moral-political philosophy of the matter when, in the presence of President Bill Clinton, he said:

It was very repugnant to think that we could sit down and talk with those people, but we had to subject our plan to our brains and to say, "without these enemies of ours, we can never bring about a peaceful transformation to this country." And that is what we did. The reason why the world has opened its arms to South Africans is because we are able to sit down with our enemies and to say, let us stop slaughtering one another. Let's talk peace.[4]

Mandela's political priorities match closely a definition of politics by Sir Bernard Crick:

[P]olitics involves genuine relationships with people who are genuinely other people. . . . They may be genuinely repulsive to us, but if we have to depend on them, then we have to learn to live with them.[5]

Such a definition combines a prominent democratic ideal—tolerance—with a utilitarian necessity—interdependence. We are told from some quarters that social utility and interest are incompatible with high-principled ethics; but, especially for framing an ethic for political life, I side with those philosophers and theologians who keep utility inside the ethical calculus. The Hebrew mind, in particular, was sure that "righteousness" and "blessing" belonged together, that the righteous would covet blessing for themselves and their neighbors, and that blessing was not merely the experience of pleasure but an experience of right relationships. This combination of overlapping, internally related ethical terms can mean, for example, that "the law of the Lord" intends its observers to flourish "like a tree planted beside a watercourse."[6] It means that "doing justice, loving mercy, and walking humbly with God"[7] are not discontinuous personal virtues but dimensions of relationships realized in both interpersonal and social contexts. There is nothing necessarily subethical about the idea of personal or collective self-interest. Much depends on what sort of self one is interested in, what future one covets for oneself in relation to other selves. Political ethics must give Nelson Mandela and every other political leader the scope to consider whether learning to live together is in the interests of all concerned. In South Africa, Rwanda, Northern Ireland, and Bosnia, the alternative has been learning to kill each other. The transition from the latter to the former is the heart of any realistic speech about a just and forgiving way to bury the past.

What Kind of Justice?

Philosophers have a long history of attention to concepts of justice. Very seldom have they inquired about the relation of justice to forgiveness, and when they have done so, they have usually been suspicious of the relationship.[8] Books on justice by theologians are numerous, as are those on forgiveness. But few are the Western authors who have advanced the idea that justice and forgiveness have an intimate relation. At stake in any exploration of the relationship will be choices between varieties of justice matched to varieties of forgiveness. Without attempting to catalogue those varieties here, I want to take some clues chiefly from certain contemporary political attempts to practice a just forgiveness and a forgiving justice. Protecting those terms from being dubbed oxymoronic requires some resort to contemporary history.

Doing Justice to the Truth:
The Public Telling of Stories of Suffering

It is a truism that there is no need to talk of forgiveness if there is nothing to forgive. Not truistic is the hope of evildoers to cover their tracks. Hitler wanted to plow under all evidence of the death camps. Those who tortured African National Congress (ANC) members in the prisons of South Africa taunted them with the assurance that no one would ever hear of their suffering.

Forgetfulness is the enemy of justice, unless one takes refuge in that untrue truism: "There is nothing we can do to change the past." *Au contraire*: we can change our relation to the past, and the first step for doing so is uncovering its dreaded secrets. There can be no final burial of the past before an inquest.

A French journalist, David Rousset, survived several of the Nazi camps including Buchenwald. He wrote about the intention of the perpetrators to bury their crimes beyond any recall:

How many people here [in the camp] believe that a protest has even historic importance? This skepticism is the real masterpiece of the SS. Their great accomplishment. They have corrupted all human solidarity. Here the night has fallen on the future. When no witnesses are left, there can be no testimony. To demonstrate when death can no longer be postponed is an attempt to give death a meaning, to act beyond one's death. In order to be successful, a gesture must have social meaning. There are hundreds of thousands of us here, all living in absolute solitude.

In the context where Jonathan Schell quotes Rousset's words, he also quotes W.H. Auden on the solidarity of art: Through art, "we are able to break bread with the dead, and without communion with the dead a fully human life is impossible."[9] A Yale historian remarked recently that the job of the historian is "the resurrection of the dead," the making of their story so accessible to contemporaries that they cannot doubt that in their own time the dead were as real as we are in our time.

Having now visited the mute memorials of five Nazi camps, including Buchenwald and Auschwitz, I know how indirectly, how pathetically symbolic, have to be our ways of remembering those dead. An execution stake here, a dented tin plate there, a ragged uniform, the ruins of crematoria ovens—postwar Germans have managed faithfully to preserve these tokens of evil in an impressive attempt to remember a past that serves as a warning for their own future and the world's.

The testimony of the survivors, of course, is more vivid. Almost all of them feel special obligations to speak on behalf of the dead as well as themselves. In her eloquent, pain-soaked book on the South African Truth and Reconciliation Commission, Antjie Krog resorts to poetry for expressing this loyalty of the living to their dead companions:

Beloved, do not die. Do not dare die! I, the survivor, I wrap you in words so that the future inherits you. I snatch you from the death of forgetfulness. I tell your story, complete your ending—you who once whispered beside me in the dark.[10]

As they told their own and others' stories before the TRC, victims have frequently said that the very telling has been a step toward their own personal healing and a certain reentry into civic society. Lukas Baba Sikwepere, blinded by the police while in custody, spoke of his appearance before the TRC in these moving words:

I feel what . . . what has brought my sight back, my eyesight back is to come back here and tell my story. But I feel what has been making me sick all the time is the fact that I couldn't tell my story. But now I . . . it feels like I got my sight back by coming here and telling you the story.[11]

To have your story of unjust suffering entered into a public record and thence into future history-writing is to experience an increment of justice—justice to your personal truth that governmental power has tried to muffle. It may be a very incomplete justice, but at least it is a beginning. For forty years after 28 February 1947, the Guomindang regime in Taiwan made it a punishable offense to refer—even in private conversation—to the massacre of some 20,000 Taiwanese civilians during that week by the army of Chiang Kai-shek. In 1988 it finally became legal to speak about the event, and now the curators of a new "2/28 Museum" are beginning to display the extant names, pictures, and other records of those who perished. Their search for all the names will be a long one.[12]

If forgetfulness is the enemy of justice, so also is it the enemy of forgiveness. We imply an erroneous version of forgiveness when we salute the motto, "Forgive and forget." Rather, "Remember and forgive" is the threshold of forgiveness. Kierkegaard was psychologically right when he said,

> Forgetting is the shears with which you cut away what you cannot use, doing it under the supreme direction of memory. . . . When we say that we *consign* something to oblivion, we suggest simultaneously that it is to be forgotten but also remembered.[13]

Perhaps a less paradoxical, more social way of expressing this insight is to say that persons and societies must, for their health, strike a balance between burying the gruesome past and burying themselves in the memory of it. They must remember in such a way that future access to the memory is personally and publicly possible, but so as to drain the memory of its power to continue to poison the present and future. As I have written elsewhere, "The mind that fixes on pain risks getting trapped in it. Too horrible to remember, too horrible to forget: down either path lies little health for the human sufferers of great evil."[14] Personally, to know that your story is now accessible in the books, means that you are no longer alone its sole keeper. Socially, to preserve the record is to post a public warning sign against the repetition of such injustice in the future.

Psychiatrists and recent truth commission experience have demonstrated that neighborly listening to such stories is not popular in any society. It is one thing to believe you know about war from war movies; it is another to listen to real war veterans tell about their experience of that reality. The liberation of listening ears—and their tragic rarity—has been eloquently documented in the recent book by Eric Lomax, *The Railway Man*. Lomax suffered torture in the River Kwai prison camps in Burma, which he could never communicate to wife, family, or friends: "I had to behave all the time as if the past had not occurred. . . . I was still fighting the war in all those years of peace."[15] Thanks to Dr. Helen Bamber, who as a young physician had interviewed survivors of Bergen-Belsen, the dam of repression in Lomax was broken, and at age seventy he finally cut the shackles that had bound him for forty-three years in continual inner imprisonment.

What poisons the inner life of persons also poisons the inner life of societies. Discounting the American prejudice in favor of the future, one might justly say that the world's superspecialists in memory are the peoples of the Balkans. Alternatively, the choice might be the Irish. Someone has said, "The British never remember, the Irish never forget." But that is to suggest the necessary interchange between victims and agents of oppression; first for unearthing memories of injustice and finally for giving them decent burial with all due permanent public memorials. One of these days, one must pray, the list of Irish-British resentments will be well remembered by both peoples: from William the Conqueror, through Cromwell and the Famine, to Bloody Sunday, Enniskillen, and Canary Wharf—all to be really consigned to the past because now fully acknowledged and as fully contrasted with new in-place relationships of the present. Who can doubt that the recent apology of Prime Minister Tony Blair for British irresponsibility in the 1840s over the Irish Famine was another increment of the healing of memories between the two peoples?

In sum, there are two divergent motives behind calls for public remembering, and politicians are morally bound to make some choices between them: Is the purpose of recall to be the nourishing of revenge? Or is it the nourishing of public purpose not to repeat the evil? The justice of truth telling needs the justice of forbearance from revenge.

Refusing Vengeance

In her probing book, *Wild Justice*, Susan Jacoby makes the case for retributive justice as indispensable to social peace, law, and recovery from crimes of the past. As the most extreme form of retribution, vengeance preoccupies countless ancient and modern narratives, from the Greek dramas to the latest news from Kosovo. The Greeks were nervous about the destructive potentials of blood feuds. By establishing its court system, Jacoby observes, Athens sought to tame the wild justice of vengeance by taking punishment out of the hands of victims into the hands of public legal institutions. It is better for the society that the courts punish, says the theory; for in the hands of victims more chaos and less civic peace will result. But punishment there must be, else citizens will never satisfy their gnawing hunger to get their "due."

The problem of defining that "due" is twofold: neither moral principle nor social good permits a retribution that simply repeats the crime, which is the fundamental argument against capital punishment. Second, many crimes leave in their wake losses without remedy. The family of Steve Biko, murdered in prison in 1977, refused to appear before the TRC, fearing that the commissioners would grant amnesty to the murderers. In a court settlement, the family accepted a payment of about US$11,000, small compensation for a human life.[16] Obvious here is the retreat from sheer vengeance and its replacement by measures that are as much symbolic as tangible. Pulling victims and the entire society back from the brink of the chaos of unrestrained vengeance is ancient in the wisdom of most cultures. In its original scriptural context, the rule of "an eye for an eye" was for the Hebrews a first barrier against the propensity of the vengeful to take out a second eye for good measure. The biblical fear of the rampages of vengeance was early embodied in the myth of Cain and Abel, where, after the murder, Cain is sure that "whoever finds me will slay me." No, says the Creator, I am putting a "mark" on Cain, "lest anyone who comes upon him should kill him."[17] So Cain survives to become the first city builder, but one of his successors, Lamech, lays claim to the right of boundless vengeance in his boast to his wives:

I kill a man for wounding me,
young man for a blow.
Cain may be avenged seven times,
But Lamech seventy-seven.[18]

In time such vengeance will destroy many a city. An early historical record of that was set down in the work of soldier-historian Thucydides in his *History of the Peloponnesian War*. From one appalling incident—a tide of revenge that swept through the city-state of Corcyra—Thucydides came to the sober conclusion:

> [M]en too often take upon themselves in the prosecution of their revenge to set the example of doing away with those general laws to which all alike can look for salvation in adversity, instead of allowing them to subsist against the day of danger when their aid may be required.[19]

Whether on the small scale of capital punishment of a single murderer or the vast scale of modern war and its retaliatory destruction of entire enemy cities, the dangers of our vengeful impulses will sober all realistic political leaders as they seek to moderate those impulses in the direction of punishments of evildoing that leave room for personal and social healing. The jury of social science may still be undecided as to how much "satisfaction" comes to victims from the punishment of perpetrators; but in any event, that form of justice must be balanced and infused with a justice that promises a new measure of social peace. In effect, some form of retributive justice must be combined here with some form of restorative justice. The need for such a combination gets painfully expressed by Eric Lomax as he experiences "a cold twinge of satisfaction" at the postwar execution of two perpetrators of his torture:

> I regretted that there were not more of them going to the gallows; I felt that thousands of them were guilty. There was unfinished business between me and the Japanese people as a whole, and a few of them in particular.[20]

The case for retributive justice can be made from the Bible; but a stronger biblical case can be made for an intimate connection between justice and mercy, especially in the teachings of the Hebrew prophets.[21] Norman Snaith remarks that the word for "justice" in Hebrew usage was always "toppling over" into associations with mercy and compassion. Like interests in social life generally, ethical words in Hebrew discourse often qualify, nudge, and

overlap with each other. Politics, ethics, and forgiveness have this in common: in practice they involve "multivalued" choices, the term that Sir Geof-
frey Vickers uses to describe most socially responsible choices. Susan Jacoby
has a version of such choice in her summary of the relation of justice and
love:

> The entire modern argument over the relation between revenge and
> justice turns on [the] question of the equilibrium between memory and
> hope. With moral and legal balance firmly in mind as a social goal, the
> formula, "justice, not revenge" has the same absurd ring as "justice, not
> forgiveness."[22]

I would add that my use of the word "revenge" is more cautious than hers.
I would prefer "justice, not punishment" for her lexicon of absurdities.
Punishment is compatible with forgiveness, but the question remains: What
kind of punishment?

Without denying the many names under which the banner of justice
marches into classical ethical discussion, I can report that there is new,
overdue, and worldwide interest in the concept of "restorative justice,"
which comports closely with a notion of forgiveness in politics. The concept
is sadly lacking in much Western legal tradition, and its advocates are
sometimes accused of sentimentalism and soft-headedness. Especially in the
United States, powered by a certain moralistic strain of Christianity, we are
legally infatuated with the punishment of criminals while neglecting almost
completely the restoration due their victims. So-called primitive societies
seem more alert to the obligations that wrongdoers incur toward victims and
their families. This is the downside of much Western treatment of criminals.
The South African TRC has done the world a favor by putting victims at the
center of their hearings.

Restorative justice mandates second priority for the restoration of the
perpetrators themselves. Punishment that engenders contrition, repentance, and compensatory action in evildoers is worth a lot more careful
research and public discussion, especially in the United States, where the
meaning of the word "penitentiary" has virtually disappeared from public
speech.

That the coming to public light of perpetrators' "legal" crimes through
the work of the TRC constituted a form of punishment, should not be

underestimated. Although the TRC legislation did not mandate that the perpetrators express sorrow for their crimes, many did so, and in the long run public condemnation will continue to constitute a certain due punishment. Can law mandate repentance? The South African parliament thought not, and whether this was political wisdom remains in dispute. Most court procedures in the United States allow for variation in sentencing according to levels of confession and "hardness" in the criminal. Contrition can be faked, but it is ordinary for judges and juries to assess that possibility as they deliberate.

Missing in much of that deliberation is practical attention to the repair of damage to victims. It puzzles me that, in U.S. law in particular, we speak of "paying one's debt to society" in abstraction from concrete debts to victims. As a country with the highest per capita rate of incarceration in the world—a total of almost two million men and women in prison—the American public spends billions on putting criminals behind bars, but very little on compensation to victims. We could control our national addiction to civil tort suits and huge money awards if our criminal courts were more routinely expected to consider compensations for victims as an ordinary procedure in law. Abstract justice can be more expensive than concrete justice.[23]

Abstract justice may also inflict yet further damage on victim, perpetrator, and society at large. We do not know with certainty if the punishment of the perpetrator really does "satisfy" the surviving victims. Vengeance may indeed be a dish best eaten cold; but if Eric Lomax is a fair example, once indulged, a taste for vengeance is hard to satisfy. If many examples in the work of the TRC tell us anything, it is that a taste of reconciliation can bring new surges of health all around. Desmond Tutu tells of the TRC hearing in the Eastern Cape near the site of the Bisho Massacre. Black as well as white police carried out this atrocity. The three most responsible for ordering the killing appeared before the Commission, confessed the details of the crime, and expressed great sorrow for it. As the details came spilling out, said Tutu, the hostility of the audience rose visibly. Anger was in the air. Then, one of the three turned to the audience and said, "We are heartily sorry for this terrible act. We hope that you will find it possible to forgive us." After a pregnant pause, the audience rose spontaneously to their feet and responded in loud applause.[24]

It is quite possible that such an event could only happen in a country like South Africa, whose people are so deeply imbued with certain religious convictions that they turn more "naturally" toward reconciliation than do peoples of different cultures. But there are other examples. One is the example in the United States of the parents of Amy Biehl.[25] Asked by reporters about the amnesty granted to her four young confessed murderers, the parents replied: "It's not really a family issue we're dealing with here. . . . This truth and reconciliation process is about a nation." Soon after, the father added, "It's better to forgive and get back to business"—the business of putting together a fractured body politic, transforming its law and custom so that no longer can any citizen be legitimately tempted to murder in the name of political justice.

It is often said that there can be no peace without justice. In South Africa they seem to know the companion truth: no justice without peace. Democratic politics, at least, requires a principled retreat from the politics of violence and a systematic resort to the politics of debate, civic listening, dialogue, majority rule with respect for minority rights, and nonviolent judicial process. Where this context is lacking, how can courts and legislatures expect that the law will be obeyed? In June 1998 world newspapers carried the terrible story of the murder of James Byrd, Jr., African American resident of Jasper, Texas. The three white men who killed him (by dragging him for miles behind their truck) were apprehended and brought to trial. In the meantime, Mr. Byrd's sister, Mary Nell Verrett, spoke about restorative justice and the social integrity of our racism-beset American history when she said to a reporter:

My brother would have wanted the world to grow from this, and I think it will. Our family has no use for destructive hate. We have done our best to communicate a message my brother would have wanted the world to know: We are all here to stay. It is just as well we learn to live together as one community.[26]

If Americans as a whole are more inclined to vengeful forms of justice in contrast to restorative forms, the same cannot be said about African Americans. Elsewhere I have tried to document the claim that the culture of these survivor-descendants of the greatest atrocity in our history—legal slavery—has more consistently embodied forgiveness than has the culture of any other subgroup of our citizenry. Mary Nell Verrett is an authentic example of the validity of this claim.[27] Her words suggest a third facet of justice that is part and parcel of forgiveness.

The Just Affirmation of the Humanity of Victim and Perpetrator

Our century is littered with the outrages of dehumanization. Those whom we would kill, we first make subhuman. It is a war strategy of vast destructive power. From Auschwitz to Coventry to Dresden to Hiroshima to Phnom Penh to Sarajevo to Soweto to Kigali to Pristina, we have accumulated precedents of mass murder, usually preceded by some synonym for "subhuman" pasted over the image of enemies. We can call this phenomenon "beastly," but that is an unjustified insult to the beasts. To be sure, it takes training to peer through a dark lens long enough to begin to see one's neighbors as essentially inferior to oneself. Harder for most of us, perhaps, is training in the habit of seeing the worst of neighbors as still human like ourselves. To adopt that latter habit is to acquire empathy for the "repulsive" (Crick's word for them), a habit quite different from either sympathy or excuse. To explain and to understand is not to justify; but to empathize is to discover the common humanity that links victims to their perpetrators.

In this respect, Daniel J. Goldhagen did not serve the ongoing cause of reconciliation between Germany and the legatees of World War II when he defined the Germans of that era as peculiarly freighted with "eliminationist antisemitism." The great moral trouble with his theory is that it lets the world—and even the present generation of Germans—off the empirical hook. In a sharp critique of *Hitler's Willing Executioners*, several American Jewish historians have faulted him for failing to make sober comparisons of the Holocaust to other collective crimes in our history. It is not a matter of relativizing the evil of the Holocaust, they say, but of a realistic assessment of widely shared human characteristics. Norman G. Finkelstein wrote:

> Lurid as Goldhagen's account is, the lesson it finally teaches is thus remarkably complacent: normal people—and most people, after all, *are* normal—wouldn't do such things.

Finkelstein goes on to quote the American psychiatrist who supervised the Nuremberg Nazi defendants:

[W]e must conclude not only that such personalities are not unique or insane, but also that they could be duplicated in any country of the world today.[28]

On the face of it, this conclusion is bad news for us all. But the hopeful news is that, for reconciliation between enemies, both may be able to recover from the mental-emotional illness of dehumanization in a discovery that "those people" are people much like ourselves. Another psychiatrist, Robert J. Lifton, provides encouragement for believing that such a recovery is possible. At the end of his monumental study, *The Nazi Doctors*, based on his extensive interviews with men who practiced "medicine" in the death camps, Lifton asks if it is mandatory for him to empathize with these parodies of his own medical profession. By training and by ideology, these doctors learned to exclude the victims of their experiments from the empathy they reserved for some other people. Lifton came to the conclusion that all of us are vulnerable to this "doubling": "Under certain conditions, just about anyone can join a collective call to eliminate every last one of the alleged group of carriers of the 'germ of death,'" which the Nazis attributed to Jews and other *leben-sunwertes Leben* ("life unworthy of life"). The end of his interviews left Lifton with a personal problem: having unearthed the potential of "just about everyone" for refusing empathy to certain other humans, what about his own empathy for the Nazi doctors? The moral challenge here was to be sure that one could empathize without sympathizing or excusing. As the definition of Michael Bosch has it: Empathy involves resonating with the other's unconscious affect and experiencing his experience with him while the empathizer maintains the integrity of his self intact.[29]

Lifton's surmounting of his own resistance to dismissing genocidal members of his own profession as subhuman monsters is a momentous, not so say intimidating moral challenge. His moral conscience doubtless would accord closely with Martin Buber's translation of the Second Great Commandment: "You shall love your neighbor as a person like yourself." But the work of doing so is akin to Max Weber's definition of politics: "slow boring of hard boards."

An extra bonus of this painful reformation of social perception is fundamentally political: it invites our awareness that in many a social conflict there is something to forgive on all sides. Drowning each other's sins in a murk of relativity is not the ethical formula here: distinctive truths, particular restorations, and specific empathies are the ingredients of real, concrete political justice. Such also are the ingredients of a forgiveness in politics infused with a justice that preserves moral integrity. Underneath this formula resides a surmise basic to the awareness that Christians are supposed to bring to politics and that the Apostle Paul expressed when he said: "All have sinned and come short of the glory of God."[30] Robert Frost, not an especially religious poet, was replicating this insight when in his poem, "The Star Splitter," he asked if the citizens of a small town were wise to exclude from their company a man just back from a year in jail:

if we started ruling each other out
for the least sin, we'd soon have no one left to live with,
for to be social is to be forgiving.[31]

I put this insight alongside another from a local court judge in North Carolina who once said to a group of clergy: "Justice is a search. Our forbears cut off the hands of thieves, and we realize that this was unjust. We shouldn't define justice too closely, for then our searching would cease, and we would cease."

We would cease, because the morality that condemns others has this in common with the immorality that harms others: neither fears the dangers of a resulting alienation. The just who make room for forgiveness and the forgiving who make room for justice are aware of that danger. Both have, as their central hope, the eventual healing of fractured human relations.

Endnotes

1. Ward Just, *The American Ambassador* (Boston: Houghton Mifflin, 1986), 123–24.

2. *The New York Times*, 21 June 1992.

3. See Gesine Schwan, *Politik und Schuld: Die zerstörische Macht des Schweigens* (Frankfurt am Main: Fischer Taschenbuch Verlag, 1997). The quotations are from her article on the same theme, "Wo die moralische and psychische Überforderung beginnt," *Die Welt*, 9 January 1999. My translation.

4. *The New York Times*, 28 March 1998, A5.

5. Sir Bernard Crick, *In Defence of Politics*, 2nd ed. (Chicago: University of Chicago Press, 1972), 128.

6. Psalm 1:3 (New English Bible/NEB).

7. Micah 6:8 (NEB).

8. Immanuel Kant is perhaps the most famous modern example. See *Religion Within the Limits of Reason Alone*, trans. Theodore M. Greene and Hoyt H. Hudson (New York: Harper and Brothers, 1960), lxxiv–lxxvi. The spirit and substance of Kantian morality is so pervasively individualistic that it is difficult to know if he took seriously the need for social strategies for social recovery from socially enacted evil. This individualism has characterized much Protestant and Catholic thought about forgiveness. See my book, *An Ethic for Enemies: Forgiveness in Politics* (New York: Oxford University Press, 1995, 1997), 58–62.

9. Jonathan Schell, *The Fate of the Earth* (New York: Alfred A. Knopf, 1982), 162, 167. This book, one of the soberest treatments ever written on the threat of nuclear war, concentrates on the tragedy wherein a present human generation puts into its own hands the power to abolish a human future and thereby a human memory.

10. Antjie Krog, *Country of My Skull: Guilt, Sorrow, and the Limits of Forgiveness in the New South Africa* (New York: Random House, 1999), 38.

11. Ibid., 43.

12. As recently as November, 1998, in the Taiwan Theological Seminary in Taipei, when I spoke of this development, a member of the faculty said to students that this was the first time she had ever been able to share her grief publicly for the death of her favorite uncle in 1947. Middle class, potential Taiwanese leaders were the special targets of this massacre.

13. In *Either/Or*, as quoted by Robert Bretall, ed., *A Kierkegaard Anthology* (Princeton: Princeton University Press, 1951), 28.

14. Shriver, *An Ethic for Enemies*, 119.

15. Eric Lomax, *The Railway Man* (New York: W.W. Norton and Company, 1995), 221–22.

16. See Krog, *Country of my Skull*, 30.

17. Genesis 4:14–15 (NEB).

18. Genesis 4:23–24 (NEB).

19. Thucydides, *History of the Peloponnesian War*, trans. Richard Crawley (New York: E.P. Dutton and Co., c. 1876), 226–67. See an extensive discussion of this incident in my *An Ethic for Enemies*, 18–22.

20. Lomax, *The Railway Man*, 211.

21. Christian readers of the New Testament will know that laws permitting vengeance get considerably overridden by many teachings of Jesus (see Matthew 5:38–39); and that the Apostle Paul derives his theological argument against human vengeance from the Hebrew Bible's words, "Vengeance is mine, says the Lord, I will repay"—that is, leave all vengeance to the divine Last Judgment (Romans 12:19, quoting from Leviticus 19:18 and Deuteronomy 32:35). Reversion to the other, vengeance-permitting texts of the Penta-

teuch are favorites of advocates of capital punishment. How Christians among Americans use these texts, in preference to those of the New Testament, for theological legitimization of capital punishment, is one of the mysteries—and evils—of biblical literalism.

22. Susan Jacoby, *Wild Justice: The Evolution of Revenge* (New York: Harper and Row, 1983), 361–62.

23. This is notoriously the case with what it costs in the United States to carry through an execution. Legal procedures and other expenses connected with executions amount to an average cost of $2 million to $3 million.

24. Tutu's account was part of his sermon at the French Church in Berlin on the occasion of the presentation by the Evangelical Church in Germany of its Bonhoeffer Peace Award to the Truth and Reconciliation Commission, 25 April 1999.

25. Amy Biehl was an American Fulbright Scholar in South Africa. Only a few days before she was scheduled to return to the United States, she was killed by several black youths in the township of Guguleta, near Cape Town.

26. *USA Weekend* [*USA Today*], 24–26 July 1998, 9.

27. See Shriver, *An Ethic for Enemies*, chapter 6, 170–217.

28. Norman G. Finkelstein and Ruth Bettina Birn, *A Nation on Trial: The Goldhagen Thesis and Historical Truth* (New York: Henry Holt and Company, 1998), 98–99. See Goldhagen, *Hitler's Willing Executioners: Ordinary Germans and the Holocaust*, Vintage Books (New York: Random House, 1997), especially 392–93. A more sober, balanced account of the executioners can be found in Christopher R. Browning, *Ordinary Men: Reserve Police Battalion 101 and the Final Solution in Poland* (New York: Harper Collins, 1992).

29. Robert J. Lifton, *The Nazi Doctors: Medical Killing and the Psychology of Genocide* (New York: Basic Books, 1986), 500–03.

30. Romans 3:23 (NEB).

31. *The Poetry of Robert Frost*, ed. Edward Connery Latham (New York: Holt, Reinhart and Winston, 1979), 177–78.

CHAPTER 3

Politics and Forgiveness

Jean Bethke Elshtain

We are awash in confession these days.[1] There is the low form on daytime television talk shows and the slightly higher form in bookstores. Rectitude has given way to "contrition chic," as one wag called it, meaning a bargain-basement way to gain publicity, sympathy, and even absolution by trafficking in one's status as victim or victimizer. This confessional mode now extends to entire nations, where separating powerful and authentic acts and expressions of regret from empty gestures becomes even more difficult than it is on the level of individuals, one to another.

Given the tawdry, shameless nature of so much of our popular culture, and the way in which it traffics in, and cheapens, notions of forgiveness ("let's put this behind us," "let's achieve closure"), it would be tempting to end the matter right here and to dismiss all acts of public contrition as bogus. But that does not seem right; rather, what is required, if one aims for a more thoughtful approach, is to distinguish between instances of contrition chic and more serious acts of public or political forgiveness. What sorts of deeds warrant the solemn drama of forgiveness between nations or groups, an activity with potentially far-reaching consequences, in contrast to those easier gestures undertaken in a diluted and debased confessional mode?

When the political theorist, Hannah Arendt, called forgiveness the greatest contribution of Jesus of Nazareth to politics, she surely did not have in mind an individual figure crying: "Can you forgive me?" And, obviously, the spectacle that unfolds on daytime television in America every single day was far from her mind, a spectacle she would have denounced as vulgar and beneath contempt. Rather, she was gesturing toward a way—the only way, she claims in her great book, *The Human Condition*—for repetitive cycles of vengeance to be broken; for the often deadly playing out of horrible deeds done and equally horrible vengeance or payback sought, to be disrupted by an unexpected act that opens up space for something new to begin—that alters the horizon of expectations in some way, introducing the possibility that bloody deeds will not haunt generation upon generation, dooming sons and daughters to repeat the sins of fathers and mothers.[2]

Although individual acts of forgiveness—one human being to another—most often take place outside the full glare of publicity, there are others that are noteworthy for embodying a radical alternative to contrition chic. One thinks here of Pope John Paul II who, having barely survived an assassin's bullets, uttered his first public words from his hospital bed to his violent assailant, addressing him as "My brother, whom I have sincerely forgiven"—words that were later followed by John Paul's extraordinary visit to his brother and would-be killer in jail once he was up and about. There is a gravitas manifest in this narrative that is altogether lacking in American quasi-therapeutic, talk-showish confessions that are most often blatantly self-exculpatory rather than expressive of a demanding faith—Christianity, in this instance, the faith of which forgiveness is a constitutive dimension. Those for whom forgiveness is central and solemn engage in what theologian L. Gregory Jones calls the practice or "craft" of forgiveness.[3] Pope John Paul was practicing this craft and, in so doing, displaying to the world the ways in which forgiveness is not primarily about a singular confessional moment, but about an enactment within a particular way of life—a way of life shaped, not by a foggy sentimentalism, but by certain hard-won and difficult truths.[4]

That having been said, it still seems a bit odd to think of John Paul II's act of forgiveness as a political intervention per se, although it was an undeniably powerful moment, one seared in the memory and locked in the hearts of all who witnessed or read about it, even from afar through the medium of television and print news reports. To be sure, it might have had political consequences; the Pope's powerful words and actions might have quieted the turbulent hearts of many believers who were tempted to seek revenge for his near-murder. But I doubt that this is quite what Hannah Arendt had in mind. She was more concerned with interrupting a flow of events that seems to be on autopilot when mass murder, acts of retribution, and then more acts of killing become just the "way we do things around here," so to speak.

Within the frame of such broad-based events, often driven by desperate political purpose, individuals who are shaped by the practice of forgiveness should try to practice what they believe or preach. But only exceedingly rarely can an individual by himself or herself stem the rushing tide of violence. Are there, then, forms of authentic *political* forgiveness? Who forgives whom and for what? Remember: forgiveness is not a one-way street; it implies a relationship or some transitive dimension. Forgiveness in general is not primarily about self-exculpation in any case, *pace* pop culture distortion, but about the creation of a new relationship or order of things, the restoration of an order of things, or a relationship that has been broken or torn by violence, cruelty, or indifference.

Forgiveness is also something quite different from aloofness or detachment—just not giving a damn—which is also mistakenly presented nowadays as a form of forgiveness. What is at stake, then, is a tougher discipline by far than public acts of easy repentance, and "forgiveness" as a kind of willed amnesia proffered. It is, I want to suggest, too easy to get cynical when one contrasts the Rev. Jimmy Swaggert sobbing on television or the whole Watergate crew lapsing into multiple acts of contrition, with John Paul's forgiveness of his would-be assassin. How does one sift such matters? Political forgiveness must have a public dimension, for politics itself is public speech of a certain kind. Further, when people sincerely try to make amends it would be churlish to withhold from them any possibility that what they say or do might make any difference in the future. Perhaps one key to our discussion lies here. The public repentance of a political figure—an act related to forgiveness, certainly—cannot simply be a matter of words. Words and deeds cannot be disentangled: "by their deeds ye shall know them."[5] Again, this is far easier to conjure with and even to see on the level of individual transformation than anything like forgiveness between nation-states or warring political parties or factions. Here the sheer weight and density of history seems at times intractable: How can one "get past" a particularly horrible series of events? Doesn't one have to punish people before one can move on? Forgiveness of a strongly political or public sort presumes communities, places, and histories of a tangible, concrete sort. Real issues are involved and the stakes are often high, up to and including entire peoples who are crying to heaven against specific injustices and horrors.

When Arendt lamented the ways in which events take on a cyclical and repetitive quality, it was history or a particular version of it she surely had in her sights. People are very fond of citing Santayana's claim that those who don't know their history are doomed to repeat it. But perhaps the reverse is more likely, namely, that it is those who know their history too well who are doomed to repetition. This, then, is where the rubber hits the road. Perhaps a certain amount of "knowing forgetting" is necessary in order to elude the rut of repetition.[6] If a people's collective horizon is limited to the reencoding of past glories or horrors, the past eviscerates any possibility of future transformation. By "knowing forgetting," then, I have in mind a way to release present-day agents from the full burden of the past, in order that they not be weighed down by it utterly.[7] Forgetting, in this case, does not mean that one falls into radical present-mindedness and the delusion that the past counts for nothing; rather, one assesses and judges just what the past does count for in the present—how much it should frame, shape, and even determine present events. As Lawrence Cahoone has pointed out, too much past overwhelms the future. But too little past empties the future, or the selves we carry into the future: "Beings without memory would have no need for retribution, but no identity either."[8]

Too often these days when forgiveness is mentioned, as I have already suggested, it gets translated into a kind of bland nonjudgmentalness: "There but for the grace of God go I," translated erroneously as "I can't say anything at all about anybody else's behavior and words." But if this is the tack one takes, forgiveness is altogether unnecessary. There can never be anything to forgive if no real wrong has been suffered, no real sin committed, no evil deed perpetrated, no record of historic injustices mounted. There are certain tendencies in modern liberal culture that push us along the route of cheap grace in these matters. We are all invited to "validate" one another incessantly, but never to offer correction and reproof—on the level of individual relationships and in the wider social and political arena, alike. One thinks here, for example, of the whole "self-esteem" movement dedicated, as it is, to the principle that any criticism and any insistence upon the maintenance of certain norms or standards be rejected as a form of harsh judgmentalism. Only bland affirmations that help us to put everything negative "behind us" will do. But those practicing the craft of forgiveness recognize in such affirmations a flight from the hard work of forgiveness rather than stirring examples of it. Moreover, forgiveness in public or political life also involves the painful recognition of the limits to forgiveness, if what one seeks is full expiation, a full accounting, total justice, or a kind of annihilation of the past. There are wrongs suffered that can never be put right. Indeed, this recognition is itself a central feature of an overall structure of political forgiveness, or so I want to suggest; for it opens up space for a person or a people to partially unburden themselves from the hold the past has on them.

Here is a concrete, if hypothetical, example of what I have in mind, beginning with what might be called the individual political level and then moving to tougher cases. Suppose that a young woman first becomes aware of the history of female inequality with all the many affronts and structures of encoded inequities to which women have been subjected in the past, including the history of her own culture. A feminist consciousness dawns. How does this past weigh upon her? If the past is read as *nothing but* a story of "women's oppression," she will too easily take on the identity of a present-day victim, as if no forces have been involved in shaping her other than the concatenated effects of male dominance and perfidy. She will see the world solely through the lens of victimhood, a particular temptation in a culture that specializes in creating stock victims and in which claims to victimization carry special rhetorical resonance.[9] This invites, in turn, a politics of resentment and grievance-seeking, even retribution for past wrongs, that often gets called "justice."

But there is another possibility. Aware of these past wrongs, the young woman in question becomes a champion of fairness and equity, understanding, as she does, that politically there are things that can be done to forestall future repetition of wrongs from which women have suffered in the past. But she also refuses to read the past as a doleful tale of *nothing but*—as if no women were villains, and no men anything other than villains. The past is not forgotten but is kept alive as a tradition that must be continuously engaged. She understands that her twenty-year-old male contemporary is not responsible for bringing the previous structure of dominance and power into being. But she is also alert to the need to assess and to judge his actions from the standpoint of current standards of fairness. This imposes a burden on her, too, the burden of accountability incumbent upon all free agents. Is forgiveness involved in this latter scenario? Forgiveness of a sort is involved, in the sense that the young woman relinquishes part of the burden of the past, or a highly skewed version of that past, not allowing it to define her within the vortex of fear, loathing, resentment, and victim identity. This, then, is a form of "knowing forgetting."

There are many examples one could not turn to. How does a culture fully expiate for the Shoah? For slavery? Wrongs that cannot wholly be righted must, nonetheless, be acknowledged and part of that acknowledgment will consist in a knowing and explicit articulation of the terrible fact that full expiation is impossible.[10] This is not forgetting as a type of collective amnesia; rather, it is an acknowledgment of the full scope of a given horror and the inability of a subsequent generation or generations, not themselves directly responsible for that horror, to put things right. The events stand. Acknowledgment of these events is required both by those directly implicated and by those who merely stood by and did nothing.

Remembrance of violent deeds goes forward in all its fullness and detail. A recounting of events serves as an ongoing judgment upon those most responsible, which is tied at the same time to a tragic recognition that some wrongs cannot be righted. This must have been what Arendt had in mind, at least in part. In her controversial book, *Eichmann in Jerusalem*, she justified the hanging of Adolph Eichmann because he had perpetrated terrible crimes against humanity "on the body of the Jewish people"; but she did so in full recognition of the fact that no scale of justice had thereby been put right and that hanging every known Nazi war criminal could not do that.[11] Reversion to a strict *lex talionis* in cases of genocide, if one interprets that requirement as a strict tit-for-tat, would be hideous, implicating victims in perpetrating precisely the sorts of deeds that caused them so much suffering. Ironically, then, "knowing forgetting" as one feature of a form of political forgiveness may be most apt, not only philosophically but politically, where truly horrific abuses are concerned. Thus, Arendt knew that young Germans, infants in the Hitler years or born subsequently, could not be held accountable in any direct way for what had occurred during their lifetimes. But they were obliged to remember in order that they could be free to act in other ways. This is "knowing forgetting": recollecting the past, yes, but not being so wholly defined by it that one's only option is either to be executioner or victim (in Albert Camus' memorable phrase), rather than an accountable human agent.

Here are a few recent concrete examples of the dynamic I have in mind. They take place in the most difficult of all arenas for the dynamic of forgiveness and "knowing forgetting" to play out; namely, the realm of relations between peoples and states. But if forgiveness is to have real political weightiness as one feature of what it means to try to attain both justice and decent order and peace, it must be tested in many arenas. My first example is drawn from the bloody ground of Northern Ireland and its centuries' old troubled relationship with Great Britain. As everyone surely knows, Irish Catholics in Northern Ireland have long been a tormented people, condemned to second-class citizenship in what they perceive to be part of their land. But Irish Catholics, relatively powerless in the overall balance of what international relations thinkers call "strategic forces," have also been tormenters, as the history of IRA terrorism and death-dealing to British soldiers and to Northern Ireland Protestants attests.

It is, therefore, significant that one clear feature presaging the peace accord voted on in 1998 was the exchange of requests for forgiveness made by church leaders, Anglican and Catholic, but most famously by Cardinal Cahal Daly of Armagh, Northern Ireland. On 22 January 1995 Cardinal Daly publicly asked forgiveness from the people of Britain in a homily delivered in Canterbury Cathedral, England, the seat of the primate of the Church of England, the Archbishop of Canterbury. Cardinal Daly's words on that occasion are worth pondering, especially with an eye to the vision of a horizon of justice and decent reciprocity imbedded therein:

> We Irish are sometimes said to be obsessively concerned with memories of the past. It is salutary, however, to recall that the faults we attribute to others can be a projection of faults within ourselves which we have not had the courage to confront. . . . What is certainly true is that we all need a *healing of memories* [emphasis mine]. Healing of memories demands recognition of our own need for forgiveness; it requires repentance. The original biblical term for repentance, *metanoia*, is a strong word indicating the need for radical conversion, change of attitude, change of outlook, change of stance; and all this is costing and can be painful. The old word *contrition* expresses it well. . . . This healing, this conversion, this reciprocal giving and accepting of forgiveness are essential elements in the healing of relationships between our two islands and between our divided communities in Northern Ireland. . . . On this occasion . . . I wish to ask forgiveness from the people of this land for the wrongs and hurts inflicted by Irish people upon the people of this country on many occasions during that shared history, and particularly in the past twenty-five years. I believe that this reciprocal recognition of the need to forgive and to be forgiven is a necessary condition for

proper Christian, and human, and indeed *political relationships* [emphasis mine] between our two islands in the future.[12]

The Cardinal continued with words about starting "something new" and about how frightful it would be to "slide back into violence," an always present possibility. What he was saying and doing, Daly added, was avowedly political in the sense of drawing out of the Gospel "conclusions which are relevant to our daily living as individuals and as a society. . . ." Forgiveness was then also offered and in turn sought by the Anglican primate of Ireland.[13] A question arises here: Is this form of forgiveness, to the extent that it is accessible and enactable, available only to communicants of the Christian faith? The Cardinal suggests not, when he addresses "human" and "political" relationships more generally. For some, this is a hopelessly idealist stance, out of touch with tough realities. But the riposte would surely be that it is precisely tough realities that invite this stance; indeed, that suggest it as a necessary part of a process of negotiation, reconciliation, starting something new, and moving away from strictly retributive notions of justice to more hopeful possibilities.

Here is a second example of a delicate balancing act involving "knowing forgetting" or a relinquishment of the full burden of the past in order to envisage an altered horizon of expectation for the future: Pope John Paul II's visit to the Baltic states in September 1993.[14] The situation in Lithuania was particularly delicate for John Paul because ardent Polish nationalists had been at work stirring up memories of past mistreatment (or alleged mistreatment) of the Polish minority—some 300,000 strong—in Lithuania. Thus, according to coverage in the British journal, *The Tablet*, the Pope had to be "careful not to offend Lithuanian sensibilities," he being not only the primate of the Roman Catholic Church but, importantly, a Pole associated with Polish aspirations to self-determination. It is worth reminding the reader at this point that much of current Lithuania was once part of Poland and that the Lithuanian capital, Vilnius, is Poland's "Wilno," dear to the hearts of Poles everywhere, in part because it is the home of Adam Mickiewicz, the greatest Polish poet.

But John Paul, while acknowledging the love Poles have for that particular place, used the Lithuanian name "Vilnius" and not the Polish name "Wilno" throughout his pastoral visit, including the one time he spoke Polish—when he delivered mass in the main Polish-language church in

Vilnius. For the rest of his visit, "the Pope spoke . . . Lithuanian which he had learnt for the occasion" and "this made a tremendously positive impression on the Lithuanians." The Polish citizens of Lithuania were not so pleased "but coming from the Pope they had to accept it. The Pope exhorted the Poles to identify fully with Lithuania, and not to dwell on the past—by which he meant not to recall endlessly the time when Vilnius was part of Poland." This account shows the ways in which ethical space, stripped of irredentist and chauvinistic aspirations, can be created or expanded, making possible a more capacious form of civic identification. It is, in effect, a call to cease rubbing salt in one's own collective wound; a call for a form of remembering that does not fuel animus—for a kind of communal forgiveness.

Here is a third story. During World War II, thousands of ethnic Germans were expelled from Czechoslovakia. Their property was seized. Many were murdered. All were turned into refugees. This is the story of the famous (and infamous) Sudetenland, once home to nearly 3 million Germans, as well as 65,000 Jews and 800,000 Czechs. The German population was by far the largest. First, the Germans, when they annexed the Sudetenland, sent the Jewish population into exile. Next, according to a report in the *Wall Street Journal*, "Czechs eliminated Germans. Eduard Beneš, the pre-Communist postwar president, decreed their expulsion in 1945. At Potsdam, the Allies approved. As Germans fled toward Bavaria, Czechs took revenge: they murdered 40,000 Germans; many died at the end of a rope." This episode was long buried in the Communist deep-freeze; but since 1989, "the expulsion has become a national nettle. . . . Czechs know that every Sudeten German wasn't guilty of Hitler's crimes."[15] Although President Václav Havel condemned the expulsion, the then Prime Minister Václav Klaus (in 1994), wanted to keep the episode closed. In the meantime, Jewish and German victims of expulsion began seeking the return of their family homes on a case-by-case basis, especially those who resided in or near the belle-époque spa area of Karlovy Vary (Karlsbad). The policy agreed to by the Czechs permitted Jewish families with claims to regain their houses, but not German families. The German descendants, of course, do not understand why their troubles count for nothing; for them a primordial feature of justice was violated and has yet to be put right. One is quoted as saying, "My only crime was that for 800 years my ancestors lived in that place." German descendants want repeal of the 1945 expulsion decree, and many say they want to return to their "homeland" and to villages long emptied—ethnically cleansed—of their kind.

But this won't happen, and it isn't clear that it should happen. Why? Because recognition of a wrong does not carry along with it a clear-cut remedy and does not mean that the old wrongs can, at present, be righted to any significant extent, if what is sought is compensatory justice or restoration of the *status quo ante*. Perhaps, then, there is nothing left for the expropriated people of German descent to do but to go on with their lives, knowing that what happened to them has at long last been recognized—for President Havel admitted that they had suffered a great injustice. Under such circumstances, where retributive justice is entirely out of place and compensatory justice is prudentially impossible and philosophically murky (given the entire story of World War II), acceptance of the gesture of recognition Havel proffered becomes a form of forgiveness that makes possible other instances of soul-searching and recognition as time goes on. This is hard to take, of course, but it may be the only way to forestall the quaffing of the bitter brew of injustice suffered and recompense sought by future generations. The Havelian gesture seems right: we Czechs, although we were victims, also knew sin.

There is a follow-up to this story about the Sudetenland that details the ways in which Germany agreed to apologize for its invasion of the former Czechoslovakia, and the Czechs, in turn, expressed regret for the postwar expulsion of millions of Sudeten Germans. The Germans apologized for Nazi "policies of violence" and the Czechs expressed regret that their expulsions had "caused suffering and injustice to innocent people." But, of course, things are not thereby made right in the eyes of those who suffered most, and an organization of Sudeten Germans took strong exception to the agreement, because it provided them "with neither a claim to compensation nor a right to return to expropriated properties." As well, according to press reports, many ordinary Czechs were incensed because, given the story of the Nazi occupation, they opposed any apology to any groups of Germans anywhere for anything.[16]

One appreciates why the mutual gestures involved here are either too little or too much depending on the angle of vision from which one is viewing them. Nevertheless, these small steps, each of which acknowledges the violation of "elementary, humanitarian principles," should not be sneezed at altogether. As I have already noted, full reparation and compensation is not in the cards, either in this case or in the vast majority of similar cases. But acknowledgment and recognition of injustice is possible; and this rudimentary requirement of justice may become a constitutive feature of a larger pattern of political forgiveness. Maybe what this tells us is that there is a political version of forgiveness that must step back, most of the time, from expectations of full reconciliation and certainly from absolution. There are no sacraments, no blessings, and no benedictions in politics. Thinking politically, one might ask what sorts of deeds warrant the solemn drama of forgiveness of this sort related to, yet different from, those acts that constitute a personal redemption narrative.

Nothing I have said thus far should be taken as a permit to refrain from action where action is possible to prevent an egregious collective wrong from being committed. In life with those we love, the process of forgiveness is an enactment that is part of the very dailyness of our existence: it makes the quotidian livable. But in the affairs of what used to be called "men and states," these enactments are not and cannot be so ordinary and so direct. But that does not altogether forestall "knowing forgetting," with its complex interplay of justice and forgiveness—official recognition of mutual wrongs, some form of reparation, perhaps, and even state-level apologies. The scales may be somewhat righted. A quest for such fragile achievements within our imperfect earthly state is what the politics of forgiveness is all about.

This brings us directly to one of the most dramatic cases before our eyes over the past several years, namely the South African Truth and Reconciliation Commission (TRC). Created by an act of the postapartheid democratic parliament in 1995, the objectives of the Commission were nothing less than to help set in motion and to secure a new political culture in South Africa. The work of the Commission was divided into three distinct but related parts: a full accounting of "gross violations" of human rights (defined as the killing, abduction, torture, or severe ill treatment of any person), or any attempt, conspiracy, incitement, instigation, command, or procurement to commit an act by any person acting with a political motive; consideration of amnesty appeals; and possible reparative measures. Nearly all of these activities took place in full view of the public.

During a trip to South Africa in August 1997, I met with members of the Research Office of the TRC in Cape Town and with its director, Charles Villa-Vicencio. What I learned departed rather markedly from much of what I had gleaned about the TRC from press reports. For example, the TRC did not require that a perpetrator openly repent or apologize, although most applicants did this and such a manifestation of regret was a consideration for any amnesty request.[17] Minimally, what was demanded was that full disclosure of politically motivated crimes be proffered. The emphasis was on victims, not victimizers; for the commissioners recognized just how important truth—recounting the basic facts—is to those who have suffered wrongs under cover of darkness or, perhaps even more horribly, in the full light of day under state sponsorship.

What happened—when, where, how: we should never underestimate how important this is to survivors. I have been struck by this over and over again in my interviews with mothers of the disappeared in Argentina and with Palestinian mothers who had lost children during the Intifada.[18] Not to know is a horrible thing. And, of course, only the perpetrators have access to certain facts, since most often there are no innocent eyewitnesses to dirty deed-doing if the victims themselves do not live to tell the tale. So, the TRC was given the specific tasks of getting as "complete a picture as possible" of the "nature, causes, and extent of gross human rights violations during the period 1960–93; restoring the human and civil dignity of victims by giving them an opportunity to relate their own accounts of the violations of which they are victims; facilitating the granting of amnesty to those giving full disclosure of politically motivated crimes during this period; and making recommendations to Parliament on reparation and rehabilitation measures to be taken, including measures to prevent the future commission of human rights violations."[19]

And why undertake this? Why go down this path rather than some other? Writes Charles Villa-Vicencio, national director of research for the TRC: "It is important that we all treat one another in the best possible manner—that even if we are not fully reconciled to one another, we do not kill one another."[20] Moreover, he and others insist, truth—publicly recognized truth—is central to, indeed constitutive of, this very possibility. The process must be public; it cannot take the form of sotto voce murmurings and private mea culpas. The fact that people were murdered, maimed, and brutalized for their political views or the color of their skin must be acknowledged. Disclosure is an essential "antidote to any attempt by apartheid revisionists to portray apartheid as no more than a desirable policy that went askew." In fact, apartheid was a regime that required and legitimated violence—violence was no anomaly; it was the way things had to be done.

The purpose of this process was not, as some mistakenly or cynically suggest, to pat perpetrators on the head and send them on their way. Rather, those who violated human rights in a gross way were denied the status of martyrs to the old order. Nor will they be maintained in prison as a symbol of the past and a burden on taxpayers. Instead, they must face a very new community that has full knowledge of what they did—when, where, and how. Villa-Vicencio again: "An authentic historical record of human rights abuse" is vital because it serves "as a basis for assisting future generations to defend democracy and the rule of law in the face of any future attempt at authoritarian rule." This is a terribly complex business that takes certain theological steps toward political ends and purposes: acknowledgment, contrition, preparedness to make restitution, and the extending and receiving of forgiveness as a form of ongoing reconciliation.[21]

It is small wonder, then, that even such extraordinarily sophisticated observers as Timothy Garton Ash are capable of getting things wrong. Ash, to whom we are forever indebted for his definitive works on the 1989 European revolutions, has recently turned his attention to South Africa and to newly consolidating democratic societies more generally. I fear that, in the matter of the TRC, he is rather tone deaf. Ash sees the "reconciliation" aspect of the TRC, if "taken to extreme," as a "deeply illiberal idea. As Isaiah Berlin has taught us, liberalism means living with unresolvable conflicts of values and goals, and South Africa has those in plenty. . . . Would it not be more realistic to define a more modest goal: peaceful coexistence, cooperation, tolerance?"[22] Ash here dramatically misunderstands the meaning of reconciliation, which does not at all imply some harmonizing of interests and beliefs, or require blurring the edges of controversies. Instead, it means bringing matters into a framework within which conflicts can be adjudicated short of bloodshed. To be sure, to the extent that an Archbishop Tutu urges upon people public acts of personal reconciliation that they are not ready for, the process becomes problematic. But overall the idea is, as one South African scholar put it to me, to "make possible a future. Reconciliation is the work of many lifetimes." In other words, I take reconciliation as a political concept to mean that one no longer begins with the deadly a priori assumption that the majority or a sizeable proportion of one's fellow countrymen and women are outsiders and enemies. Rather, we are all enclosed within a single sociopolitical frame and enfolded within a common politico-ethical horizon. This is a difficult point and easily misconstrued, to be sure.

Nevertheless, many, Ash included, will continue to ask: What about justice? Here the South Africans believe they are making a contribution in challenging the most prevalent models of justice that reign among us. What they are aiming for, they insist, is *politically restorative* justice, a form of political forgiveness concerned with justice. This means it is neither cheap forgiveness nor the dominant Western mode of retributive or punitive justice. Restorative justice aims for a future that generates no new victims of the sorts of systematic misdeeds and criminality that blighted the past. Politically restorative justice, they argue, addresses the legitimate concerns of victims and survivors while seeking to reintegrate perpetrators into the community. This, they insist, is an alternative both to contrition chic with its sentimentalized gloss that masks a huge indifference, and to the horror of wrongs suffered and vengeance sought generation after generation, a *lex talionis* shorn of mercy.[23]

The TRC is quite prepared to admit that their creative view of justice is in part a compromise, but not of a sordid sort; rather, of a sort that makes politics itself possible. In a sense, certain quite legitimate demands of justice, including forms of just punishment, are foresworn in order that they might be reinstated in an order grounded in justice rather than in injustice. Ironically, the moral rehabilitation of the political world requires, at the outset, that certain features of just punishment be evacuated temporarily in the interest of a restorative project.[24] Full reparation, compensation, and just punishment are never possible when one confronts large-scale horrors; a point made to me many times over by several members of the Argentine Mothers of the Disappeared, who insisted, over and over again, that they wanted justice and not vengeance and that they knew that not all of the guilty could be punished. "That is utopian," Renée de Epelbaum told me, "and we are not utopians. We are political realists who seek justice."

With Renée de Epelbaum, the TRC commissioners are concerned with legitimating a new and fragile democratic regime, and with having sufficient time to build up a culture of human rights and constitutional guarantees. So they have come up with a political form of forgiveness as an alternative form of justice, aiming for nothing less than bestowing on future generations, in their own society and beyond, a vision of justice that challenges many of the models with which we have long been familiar. Reconstruction and restoration, they insist, is an inherent but often neglected part of judicial theory. In the words of Archbishop Tutu:

We speak about restorative rather than retributive justice. It is not the case that the perpetrators get off scot-free. They have to stand in the full glare of their city and say I did this and this and this. . . . Having to come clean has a very heavy cost. While reparation is not compensation, one of the things that has happened is that people who were treated like rubbish now have a story that the whole country acknowledges. Victims have been given an official forum where they have told their story. That is something whose value we can never compute.[25]

The cycle of violence, the TRC commissioners argue, must be broken. And they point to evidence that suggests that retributive justice, especially in a framework that simply reverses the tables of who is victimizer and who the victim, can never do this. Part of what is involved in restorative justice is a dramatic transformation in the horizon of expectations. Moreover, punitive measures when a regime falls may harden old political attitudes and keep alive morbid convictions rather than softening them. In other words, mandatory retribution can well undermine the very democratic processes on which the rule of law is based. This does not mean one takes leave of punishment entirely. It does mean that one recognizes that one must change the framework of expectation in order that future punishment can be part of an overall structure of justice; and, as well, that punishment is never an end-in-itself so much as a "last-resort" means to an end. Thus, a real challenge—and this is one confronted both by the South Africans and by anyone who enters this realm of political-ethical debate—is to determine where and when punishment and retribution might fit as part of a decent, restorative, hopeful political project. The stakes are huge for South Africa and for our fragile globe as we enter the twenty-first century. The most difficult task of all, the TRC reminds us in the most dramatic way possible, is to remember and to forget—not in the sense of collective amnesia, but in an altogether different way: as a release from the full weight and burden of the past.

Endnotes

1. My thanks to interlocutors who have commented on this paper. The challenges presented to me have been very helpful in revising it.

2. See her discussion in Hannah Arendt, *The Human Condition* (Chicago: The University of Chicago Press, 1958).

3. L. Gregory Jones, *Embodying Forgiveness: A Theological Analysis* (Grand Rapids: Eerdmans, 1995).

4. See Gerhard Forde, "On Being a Theologian of the Cross," *Christian Century*, 22 October 1997, 947–49, for a discussion of why a theology of the cross is not about sentimentalism, but rather about sin, redemption, punishment, reconciliation, God's justice, and so on. Forde worries that much contemporary language spoken from the pulpit has taken on all the coloration of the wider, sentimentalized surround—the "I'm okay, you're okay, everybody gets a pass" mentality. This turns the church into a support group "rather than the gathering of the body of Christ where the word of the cross and resurrection is proclaimed and heard."

5. Allusion to the Gospel of Matthew 7.16, 20.

6. As will become clear in the following discussion, "knowing forgetting" is also a type of remembering. I thank Lawrence Cahoone of Boston University for his emphasis on this point.

7. Patricia Cook, in her forthcoming book, *The Philosophy of Forgetting: An Inquiry through Plato's Dialogues*, notes that the Greeks conceived of forgetting in at least twelve different ways. These included passing by, disregarding, blotting out of one's mind, and not remembering. But the list also included forgiveness of a wrong, a kind of amnesty. These many different meanings are usually translated into English without differentiation as, simply, forgetting. Dietrich Bonhoeffer, in his *Letters and Papers from Prison* (New York: Macmillan, 1967), speaks of the capacity to forget as a gift of grace—again, not to be dominated by the past by musing on what-should-have-been.

8. Lawrence Cahoone, "Commentary on Jean Bethke Elshtain" (paper delivered at Boston University, 5 November 1997), 3.

9. A friend told me recently of an experiment in which a group of American teenagers was told to separate themselves according to whether they thought they were "powerless" or had some "power." The result? Everybody wanted to be "powerless." That, clearly, is the preferred identity these days; and it is a terrible problem because it blunts our ability to see real victims, when they stand before us with their concrete, not abstract or ideological, claims.

10. On this score, see the French Bishops' Declaration of Repentance issued on 30 September 1997, near a former Jewish deportation camp in a Paris suburb. The bishops declared that their predecessors in the Vichy era had been too "caught up in a loyalism and docility" toward civil authorities and had thus done far too little to spare French Jews from deportation and death. The declaration does acknowledge those who spoke out and acted courageously but concludes that there was insufficient indignation, insisting: "The time has come for the church to submit her own history, especially that of this period, to critical examination and to recognize without hesitation the sins committed by members

of the church, and to beg forgiveness." The full text of the declaration appears in *Origins* 27/18 (16 October 1997): 301–05. See also L. Gregory Jones, "True Confessions," *Christian Century*, 19–26 November 1997, 1090.

11. Hannah Arendt, *Eichmann in Jerusalem* (New York: Penguin Books, 1964).

12. Cardinal Daly's homily was not published but it did receive extensive coverage in the Irish press. (See, for example, *The Irish Times*, 23 January 1995.)

13. Cardinal Daly's homily was itself a response to a prior expression of the English need to ask for Irish forgiveness, made by George Carey, the Archbishop of Canterbury at Christ Church Cathedral, Dublin, on 18 November 1994.

14. I rely here on Anatol Lieven, "The Pope's Balancing Act," *The Tablet,* 18 September 1993, 1208–09.

15. All quotations here are from "Czech Republic Fields Demands of Germans, Jews, for Lost Homes," *The Wall Street Journal*, 15 July 1995, 1, 6.

16. All quotations here are drawn from Alan Crowell, "Germans and Czechs Agree to Part on Wartime Abuses," *The New York Times*, 12 December 1996, A12.

17. The expectation that a perpetrator would make some public apology ran high, of course. This is what made the spectacle of Winnie Madikizela-Mandela's appearance so painful, with Archbishop Desmond Tutu tearfully begging her to acknowledge her securely documented role in torture and murder; and, in the absence of such acknowledgment on her part, Tutu going on to beg the families of her victims to embrace her "in the name of reconciliation." This left a bad taste in many mouths, and it also displays what can happen when the line between a political quest for accounting as part of justice and the seeking of individual forgiveness in a more directly pastoral way get hopelessly blurred. See Carmel Rickard, "Archbishop Tutu's Confessional Box," *The Tablet*, 13 December 1997, 1592–94.

18. Conducted for a book in progress, whose working title is "Political Mothers."

19. Wilhelm Verwoerd, "Justice after Apartheid? Reflections on the South African Truth and Reconciliation Commission" (paper presented at the Fifth International Conference on Ethics and Development, Madras, India, 2–9 January 1997), 3.

20. Charles Villa-Vicencio, "Truth and Reconciliation: in Tension and Unity," Occasional Paper (Johannesburg: Truth and Reconciliation Commission, 1998), 2.

21. Ibid., 4.

22. Timothy Garton Ash, "True Confessions," *New York Review of Books*, 17 July 1997, 37.

23. The fullest elaboration of political restorative justice is to be found in Charles Villa-Vicencio, "A Different Kind of Justice: the South African Truth and Reconciliation Commission," *The Contemporary Justice Review* 2 (December 1998): 407–28.

24. For this insight, I thank Lawrence Cahoone.

25. Frank Ferrari, "Forgiving the Unforgivable: An Interview with Archbishop Desmond Tutu," *Commonweal*, 12 September 1997, 13–18.

CHAPTER 4

The Philosophy and Practice of Dealing with the Past: Some Conceptual and Normative Issues

Tuomas Forsberg

Introduction: Discourse about "Transitional Justice"

The democratization wave of the 1990s launched a new discourse on issues concerning how people deal with the past—in particular with atrocities and gross human rights violations, and those implicated in the evils of former regimes.[1] Should the perpetrators be prosecuted? If so, at what cost? But what do such prosecutions actually achieve? When are victims ready to forgive perpetrators? When is it wiser not to open up the past for debate?

These questions have always been around in one way or another; but what is new is the context of a normative democratic ethos. Not only has democratization made it possible to address such questions; the values linked to democratic culture actually make it impossible to avoid doing so. Moreover, the need to deal with the past and its injuries has become more urgent as a result of the arrival of democratization's ugly brothers: nationalism and ethnic hatred.

The new ways of coming to terms with these problems supply the grist for the mill of current discussion. Newly established truth commissions and war tribunals in various parts of the world provide us with concrete reference points. The most famous examples of such enterprises are the truth commissions in Chile, El Salvador, and South Africa; the International Criminal

Tribunals for the former Yugoslavia and Rwanda; and the adoption of the statute of the International Criminal Court. In addition to these, a wide range of other cases throughout the world have been brought under consideration. Even the debate over atrocities during World War II has revived.

In short, the present global condition is truly different from that of the Cold War. Although the Nuremberg and Tokyo trials raised international consciousness about the necessity of dealing with past atrocities, these pioneering models remained exceptions for a long time.[2] During the Cold War, political factors overwhelmingly determined how new regimes chose—and were allowed—to deal with the legacy bequeathed them by their predecessors. Moreover, dealing with human rights issues was seen as a state's internal affair. These impediments are no longer in force to the same extent. The international community is now heavily involved in directly assisting societies to democratize; and even in places like South Africa that have chosen to clear up the past on a national basis, the international community has kept close watch. It is now widely recognized that political considerations should not override the duty of acknowledging the rights of victims, and the choice of a way of dealing with the past is no longer seen as a matter falling purely within a state's domestic jurisdiction.

The acknowledgment that normative questions involved in dealing with past wrongdoings cannot be separated from objective considerations of contemporary political stability, also has its background in the cultural turn of political science. Since the concept of simple historical progress advocated by modernist liberal theory has been under assault, it has become more commonplace to assert that we cannot simply leave the past behind us but must carry the burden of history with us. If our communitarian identity is always rooted in the past, the question is not whether one should remember the past, but how.[3] Yet, the discourse about past atrocities widely rejects those postmodernist approaches that see no difference between the present and the past, the real and imagined.

This discourse has been conducted under the heading of "transitional justice." However, the very term "transitional justice" may be somewhat misleading. First, the issue of how we should deal with the past is always with us, and only in its most urgent sense does it concern transitional societies. Even stable democracies need to remember that dealing with the past should not be confined to the writing of history books. The ways in which public memory is built, official versions of the past in textbooks presented, public speeches formulated, museum exhibitions constructed, and past leaders treated are never neutral or uncontested. The concept of "justice," in turn, may focus too narrowly on one part of a complex set of issues, as we will see. Nevertheless, alternative titles are equally problematic. The German concepts of *Vergangenheitsbewältigung* (managing or mastering the past) or *Aufarbeitung der Vergangenheit* (working through the past) perhaps sound too pathetic and connote an unrealistic methodicality.[4]

The problem of finding a unifying label should not obscure the fact that a lot of progress has been made. Discourse about settling the past is now both political and academic, and mixes the roles of practitioners and theoreticians.[5] As a result, awareness of the complexity of the issues has increased. Further, learning from history and other national experiences is also now possible to an unprecedented degree. Still, the need to adapt the lessons drawn from experience into new and particular circumstances means that there is no consensus about the best way to deal with the past.[6] Indeed, academic awareness of complexity does not prevent political debates still being conducted in terms of simplistic rhetoric. A policy of forgetting is advocated by slogans such as, "Let bygones be bygones" and "We cannot change the past, so let's move forward"; whereas punishment is called for by claiming, "If we forget about the past and let the perpetrators go free, then we will be doomed to relive it" and "Offenders should always be punished." Truth commissions, too, have sometimes been justified more by rhetoric than by careful analysis. Amongst their mantras are these: "We should not forget about the past, but we can forgive," and "Truth is the way to reconciliation."

The tension between assertions of universal doctrines and particular realities is unavoidable. David Crocker has gone so far as to assert that it is neither possible nor desirable to formulate a general, crosscultural normative framework. In his view, the best that a society can do is to generate various tactics of its own for reckoning with past evil. Nevertheless, even he recognizes that a general framework might encourage each society reckoning with an atrocious past to aim at goals internationally agreed to be morally urgent.[7] While it is necessary to reject simplistic doctrines, relativism should not be embraced instead. Although it is nearly impossible to summarize the results of all the studies of "transitional justice" in an all-encompassing and neutral way, it is possible to identify the parameters upon which choices are based. For any political action, the most important of these is the conceptual framework that defines alternative strategies. Then there are its various aims and their interrelationships. Finally, there are the elements of normative assessment. These are all basic features of political action that a self-reflective analysis of transitional justice can and should examine. In what follows, therefore, I will discuss each of them, with a view to specifying some of the factors that should be taken into account in the choice of a particular strategy.

Framing the Alternative Strategies

Discourse about transitional justice rests on an obvious point, namely that there is always a choice about how to deal with the past. Although we cannot change it, we can influence the way it is remembered.[8] Because the collective memory of the past that is part of our daily life is a social construction, we can make choices between different ways of dealing with it. Whereas individuals may have only little conscious choice in their ability to remember or forget certain events or experiences, it is clearly possible for collectives to choose what is publicly remembered and what is forgotten. The representatives and institutions of a state may choose to "forget" certain events, while individuals and particular groups remember them and academics conduct animated debates over them. Similarly, the question of whether a society should forgive certain wrongdoings is distinct from the question of whether individual victims should. If a society forgives someone, he or she is taken back into the public moral community. It does not follow from this that they should also be received back into the victim's private moral community. Societal forgiveness is not a substitute for individual forgiveness. This tension between the private and the societal is well expressed by Václav Havel, who was personally inclined to let the past rest, but as president had to take society's will and need for public action into consideration.[9]

The question of remembering opens up the starkest dichotomy between alternative ways of dealing with the past. Many people seem to think that there is only one choice to be made: either remember and punish, or forget and forgive. Yet, the recent debate on transitional justice has made it clear that we face in fact two distinct choices: whether or not to remember past atrocities publicly, and whether or not to sanction the parties to the conflict. On the basis of these distinctions, we can further distinguish at least four basic strategies of dealing with the past (Table 4.1).

Table 4.1. Strategies of Dealing with the Past

		Sanction	
		Yes	No
Remember	Yes	Prosecuting	Forgiving
	No	Revenge	Forgetting

A couple of points need to be clarified here. First, "revenge" means a way of dealing with the past that aims at punishing the perpetrators without proper public examination of the past. The form of "victors' justice" that simply imposes a new version of the past over the old one, belongs to this category. Second, reparation or compensation is not a distinct strategy, because it can be linked to various ones. On the one hand, reparation can be a form of punishment; and compensation can be a bribe to the victim to keep quiet about the past. On the other hand, both can be essential parts of an apology that aspires to elicit forgiveness.

This model is only one way of representing the alternatives, but I think that it is helpful for two reasons. One of these is that it makes clear that forgiveness is not the same as forgetting, and that prosecution does not mean arbitrary witch-hunting. The model also illustrates that the main choice is not between judicial and nonjudicial means of dealing with the past, but between alternative strategies that can take both judicial and political forms. Legal institutions can execute fair and disciplined prosecution, but they can also be arenas for taking revenge in the form of show trials. Forgiving may take the form of an amnesty law; and even forgetting can find legal expression, if certain representations of history are banned. On the other hand, public examination of the past that leads to political sanctions, such as lustration, can be seen as a kind of nonjudicial prosecution.

Second, this model demonstrates the importance of the way the alternatives are framed and presented for our choosing. If the only choice were between punishing or not, it would be easy to prefer forgetting to revenge. But if one tries to defend forgetting against prosecution, various normative problems arise. Prosecution has a firm moral basis in retributive concepts of justice and in international legal practice. It is also part of our common sense thinking that they deter future violations of human rights. Moreover, forgetting can be seen as a morally weak way of dealing with the past, because of its association with moral relativism.

If, however, forgiveness is presented as a third alternative between forgetting and punishment, and not simply as a form of forgetting, our view may shift. As an alternative to prosecution, forgiveness can be seen as representing a kind of justice that is superior to retribution. The distinction between retributive and restorative justice can be formulated in terms that clearly favor the latter.[10] Here, the forgiveness that is integral to restorative justice seems to be a future-oriented and victim-centered way of dealing with the past, whereas the punishment integral to retributive justice seems backward looking and state centered.

This way of framing the alternatives may have a certain bias, insofar as positive concepts seem immediately preferable to negative ones. However, whereas the discussion of the issue of truth has focused on positive truth—the truth that emerges—it might be equally important to pay attention to "negative truth"—the cessation of lying. "Contrary to what the proponents of historicism generally believe," writes Remo Bodie, "'understanding' does not consist so much of the inclusion of external elements inside of our current horizon of intelligibility, as in their conspicuous exclusion."[11] In this way, it is, I think, possible to defend a deliberate form of forgetting over discovering the truth. Moreover, in the public sphere, the goal of "negative truth" is arguably easier to share. Similarly, it is easy to prefer "soft" restorative justice to "hard" retributive justice, provided that one ignores the deterrence function of punishment—a function compensation does not have. In practice, it may also be "cheaper" to punish a few criminals than to compensate a large number of victims.

In reality, the choice is not so much between different strategies as between different mixes of them. Forgiveness need not replace criminal prosecutions, but as in South Africa, it can offer an alternative for people who are ready to confess their wrongdoings voluntarily. Judicial and nonjudicial strategies of dealing with the past often complement each other: in societies in which judicial institutions are unable to deal with the past, the pressure for political and social sanctions typically increases.

The Hierarchy of Aims

One important conceptual issue in the discussion of transitional justice is the question of the interrelationship among various aims and objectives. In particular, the concepts of truth, justice, and reconciliation have all been central, but it is not easy to find a common understanding of how they are linked to each other. Here I will argue that the relationship between truth and justice is essential, whereas that between truth and reconciliation is contingent.

Much of the discussion of transitional justice rests on the assumption that truth is a value in itself. "What good can it do?" "It can do nothing, Baas. But a man must know about his children," answered the black gardener Gordon to his master's inquiry about why he wanted to clear up the fate of his son, in André Brink's *A Dry White Season*.[12] Uncertainty about simple facts such as whether somebody who has disappeared is dead, can be painful. Indeed, truth is a fundamental value because it is a precondition of all discourse, learning, and progress.[13] Moreover, it is a value that is widely shared.[14] Further, from the legal point of view, the case can be made that the right to know the truth has achieved the status of a norm of customary international law.[15] In this sense, it is impossible to achieve justice without truth.

Agreement on the importance of the truth, however, may well not lead anywhere, because its content and form is usually the subject of fierce dispute. It has become customary to distinguish between objective (factual), subjective (narrative), and intersubjective (shared) truth. Although objective truth has been seen as the basic form, recent discussion about transitional justice has also paid attention to the subjective and intersubjective forms. Subjective views of the past that lack clear evidence do not necessarily undermine the search for "truth." Intersubjective truth can only emerge if different accounts of the past are allowed to exist. From the point of view of the future, the acknowledgment of the facts is often more important than the simple revealing of the past. Even if factual truth is established, facts do not speak for themselves. In political life, it is the interpretation that the facts are given that is most important; and if the different interpretative frameworks do not converge, facts alone will not help to form a shared past.

Reconciliation, too, has remained a controversial and rather obscure concept.[16] For the perpetrators reconciliation means amnesty, whereas for the victims it means prosecution. In general terms, as defined by Louis Kriesberg, reconciliation is the process of developing a mutual, conciliatory accommodation between formerly antagonistic groups.[17] Yet the concept is often loaded with deeper, religious elements. It is often understood as the achievement of mutual harmony or a togetherness of souls. As Tutu's spokesman John Allen once stated, "You cannot have reconciliation without spiritual healing."[18] But reconciliation can also be stripped of such inner dimensions and refer simply to a degree of tolerance, or absence of severe disputes, between the antagonists; and it can be concretely defined in terms of behavioral criteria such as a lack of offensive conduct.

One problem with the concept of reconciliation at the societal level is that it is frequently associated with national unity. This is often very central to the whole purpose of truth commissions, as the title of the law that established South Africa's Truth and Reconciliation Commission (TRC)—The Promotion of National Unity and Reconciliation Act—clearly indicates. The process of (re)writing the truth with the help of such institutions as truth commissions promotes national unity by establishing a semiofficial narrative of the common past, "in which not history but imaginings of history are invented."[19] Yet the very aim of national unity is controversial. The idea that a people should constitute a national harmony clashes with the modern view of society, which assumes that different values do and should coexist and that conflict is thus an inevitable part of human life. As Timothy Garton Ash notes, "[T]he reconciliation of all with all is a deeply illiberal idea."[20] Similarly, Aletta Norval argues that "the idea of full reconciliation . . . comes closer to an identitarian image of apartheid than to a democratic post-apartheid society."[21] Given this, it may be legitimate to ask whether reconciliation should not be replaced with notions of more liberal civil virtues such as respect for law and human rights.

The mutual relationship between truth and reconciliation is also disputed. Truth commissions are often based on the assumption that the revelation of the truth will heal and rebuild a shattered past. In South Africa this aim was visible, not only in the very name of the TRC, but also in the slogan, "Truth is a road to reconciliation." Yet there is no certainty that truth actually will lead to such positive results. Priscilla Hayner, for example, doubts whether establishing and publicizing details about past abuses will always reduce the likelihood of future ones.[22] On the basis of recent cases to hand, the question must remain open. The result of South Africa's experience appears to lie somewhere between the extremes. The supporters of the apartheid regime and those of the liberation movement were not magically transformed into "reconciled" citizens by the power of the truth; but, notwithstanding dire warnings to the contrary, neither was the state plunged into life-threatening turmoil by the public examination of the past.

To say that the relationship between truth and reconciliation is contingent, also means that the conventional sequence of establishing truth and so achieving reconciliation can be reversed. Even if the parties to conflict are reconciled, the quest for the truth is not likely to disappear. In Finland, for example, there was a brutal and bloody civil war in 1918 between reactionary Whites and revolutionary Reds; and in the aftermath of the war the victorious Whites committed a large number of atrocities, in which tens of thousands died. Despite these traumatic events, a process of reconciliation started. It was marked by the social democratic Reds forming a democratic minority government seven years after the civil war, and it culminated in the national unity that was displayed against the common enemy, the Soviet Union, in the Winter War of 1939. This process of reconciliation was not supported by shared truth about the civil war. Until the 1960s there was no objective account of what had really happened; the official versions of history were written from the point of view of the victor. It was only gradually, and more than a generation after the war, that the truth about the atrocities emerged. Nevertheless, despite the delay, it was important to clear up the past. The emergence of the truth was considered to be healing, despite the fact that "national unity" was already achieved and no one was formally charged with criminal acts.[23]

Normative Analysis: Motivation, Process, and Success

Although the discourse on transitional justice has an essential normative dimension, the framework within which normative analysis is conducted has often been defective. I suggest that normative analysis should include three elements: the motivation and intention of the new rulers, the fairness and legitimacy of the procedure, and the results. The error has often been that only one element dominates the analysis. Furthermore, analysts have had a tendency to suppose that all the elements point in the same direction. This, however, is not always the case. On the contrary, questionable motivation and imperfect procedures have sometimes brought fairly good results; whereas respectable motivation and ideal procedures have sometimes failed to settle the conflict about the past.

The initial motivation of those who choose a strategy of dealing with the past is one important aspect of a normative assessment. If that motivation is selfish—aiming, for example, at gaining political power—then there are normative grounds for criticizing the choice of strategy. Conversely, if the initial motivation is a shared value, such as the fostering of democracy, then the chosen strategy is more acceptable. For example, truth commissions are often seen as an acceptable form of accountability, not only because power politics impede prosecution, but also because those involved in the commission share the important values of democracy and human rights.[24]

Sometimes, however, reasons other than the need to stabilize society and the search for justice lead to increased efforts to deal with the past. For example, in postcommunist Estonia the general attitude toward the former holders of power was reconciliatory. At the same time, it was considered important for the country to be culturally and politically linked with the West, and so to incorporate Western conceptions of human rights. Therefore, President Lennart Meri decided to set up an investigative committee to look at human rights violations during and after World War II, in order to show, not only that the number of atrocities was quite limited, but also that the principle of accountability still holds.[25]

Normative assessment must also consider the procedures selected for dealing with the past. For many human rights activists, judicial prosecution is seen as the ideal form of procedure, and amnesties should always be rejected.[26] Therefore deviations from judicial prosecution need to be very carefully justified. A lot of discussion on transitional justice has tried to give forgiveness such a justification. Peter Digeser, for example, suggests that political forgiveness provides a useful way for citizens to restore their relationship with a presently just government that has done them wrong in the past. It should be regarded more as a virtue than an obligation, since nobody can have the right to be forgiven.[27]

Judicial procedures should also be considered in a wider context. Even if trials are not political show-trials, they may still be seen as unjust. The Nuremberg Trials were fair in the sense that those who had committed crimes against humanity received sentences that they had deserved. Yet, they can still be regarded as a form of victors' justice, since they held only one of the warring parties accountable.[28]

For some, there is no ideal procedure, because different cases require different measures. For example, Steven Ratner and Jason Abrams suggest that while the underlying criminality of abuses can and should be measured by objective standards, there are different ways to uphold the principle of accountability.[29] However, although reminders are common that the right procedure depends on contingent factors, only a few have offered guidelines regarding the factors relevant to the choice of strategy. Tina Rosenberg, for one, has pointed out important differences between most Latin American countries and East European countries. She argues that trials are crucial for the long-term health of Latin American states that have suffered from state oppression, since the cycle of violence has continued precisely because a group of people has been able to hold themselves above the law. In contrast, most Communist repression cannot be judged in a court of law, since the sheer number of cases would overwhelm any judicial system. Rosenberg's suggestion for an alternative is a state inquiry into the mechanisms of repression, an official apology, and a purge of the chief culprits.[30]

Many recent studies have suggested that cultural factors also influence the way people deal with the past. However, what are described as cultural norms of dealing with the past can sometimes be little more than a pretext for letting perpetrators escape the demands of accountability. Is human understanding of accountability really subject to cultural variation of a radical kind? It may be true that religion and other cultural traditions affect the ways in which conflicts are resolved, but it remains questionable whether they really offer radically different readings of accountability that are morally justified.

Japan provides an interesting case in point. In her famous book, Ruth Benedict argues that Japan is based on a shame culture whereas Western countries are based on a guilt culture. In Benedict's view, typical shame cultures rely on external sanctions for good behavior, whereas typical guilt cultures depend on an internalized conviction of sin.[31] In a shame culture, public confession of wrongdoing makes no sense in the absence of demands for it. However, many analysts urge that the reason why making apologies for war crimes has been so difficult for Japan's political leadership, has to do more with the regime's continuity than with a peculiar cultural code. Indeed, Benedict's distinction does not actually deny the importance of accountability for the Japanese, since apology is a central element in their culture; it only points to a different source.[32]

Although religious elements can be helpful, societal choices should not be supported or rejected on purely religious criteria. The Christian tradition of forgiveness provided a strong cultural justification for amnesty in South Africa, but officially, the TRC referred more to the African concept of *ubuntu* (humanity) than to Christian doctrine. Moreover, the Protestant Boers felt that the idea of forgiveness had been imported from an alien, Latin

American, Catholic culture, and they therefore argued that it was wrong for the TRC to try to impose it upon them.

Yet, it is difficult for the international community to demand accountability if a society freely decides otherwise. The more democratic the country is, the more cultural ways of dealing with the past can be seen as legitimate. One should also consider how a particular country has dealt with such problems in the past. In societies where the political leadership that has committed atrocities has also pardoned its opponents, the need to prosecute may be less pressing.

The normative analysis of a strategy for dealing with the past typically focuses on the degree of success that it has enjoyed. Results, however, should not be the overriding normative concern. Actually, there is little evidence that prosecutions and forgiveness perform any better than forgetting. In history, forgetting has functioned well, if judged merely on the basis of its results. As Timothy Garton Ash has suggested, "much of postwar democracy was constructed on a foundation of forgetting."[33]

The other problem with justifying the choice of a strategy on the basis of its likely results is the lack of agreement about the standards of success. There are often strong views about the failure or success of a particular case, without any clear statement of the criteria employed. First, as we have seen, success is always relative to aims, and the aims can be many and conflicting. Second, even if some important aim is agreed—for example, that of changing a discourse—there may still be disagreement about whether or not it has been realized. For some in South Africa the TRC "changed the discourse forever," but for others it entirely "failed to transform social discourse."[34] Success is also always relative to the real alternatives, not to some ideal situation, but assessments are seldom based on any counterfactual analysis. Furthermore, as the real results of a strategy are often visible only in the longer run, most assessments can be regarded as premature. Moreover, even if a case looks like a clear failure, it may be difficult to discern whether that failure lies in the strategy itself or in its implementation. Finally, success can be measured by citizens' satisfaction with the results, instead of some kind of objective standard. But if dissatisfaction with the way the past has been managed is evenly spread among the conflicting parties, that may indicate that the process has been evenhanded and just. So, paradoxically, the fact that the South African TRC has been criticized from all sides could be taken as a sign of its moral legitimacy.

Conclusion

In this essay I have discussed the state of the art of discussion about transitional justice. This discussion has raised important and neglected themes to do with democratization and conflict resolution. In general, it has helped us achieve a better understanding of why the past matters. The importance of clearing it up and achieving a better grasp of the truth is rightly emphasized from the normative point of view. The potential dangers of attempting to do this have been shown by empirical cases to be exaggerated. The emerging conceptual framework has revealed the complexity of the aims involved, but work remains to be done in contextualizing their selection. It is widely acknowledged that it is difficult to formulate a single strategy for dealing with the past everywhere successfully; but very little systematic effort has been expended so far in developing a set of criteria by which a contingent strategy should be chosen.

In order to do this, we need to be clear about the choices available. We also need to be clear about our aims. Finally, when choosing a particular strategy at least three factors are relevant: political circumstances, the nature of the problems and knowledge about how to deal with them, and the need to identify with democratic states. Therefore, in order to strengthen human rights culture in a democratizing state, the international community can do three things: put pressure on the state in question, give advice and resources, and be exemplary in their own ways of dealing with a difficult past. The first strategy is often the most effective, but it is also the most interfering.

Finally, there are good reasons to carry on discussing transitional justice and identifying new challenges. One big challenge has to do with the international dimension. The discussion of transitional justice has relied heavily on conflict-resolution strategies that appear to work in interpersonal relations, but it has yet to venture very far into an international context. Clearly, more research on the international aspects of dealing with the past is needed. How can national experiences of processes of reconciliation be applied to relations between states or nations? It is still often supposed that a state shows weakness if it apologizes for what it has done in the past. To do so is regarded as being against its interests, because to admit past wrongs is to make oneself vulnerable to demands for reparation or compensation. Moreover, some believe that such demands would destabilize the international order. On the other hand, if honest discussion about the past can lead to reconciliation within a particular society, might it not also do so between states? If so, such a process would benefit both individual states that carry a historical burden in their international relations, and the international system as a whole, by decreasing the likelihood of future conflicts.

Endnotes

1. See Samuel Huntington, *The Third Wave: Democratization in the Late Twentieth Century* (Norman: University of Oklahoma Press, 1991).

2. See, for example, Adriaan Bos, "The International Criminal Court: a Perspective," in Roy Lee, ed., *The International Criminal Court. The Making of the Rome Statute: Issues, Negotiations, Results* (The Hague: Kluwer, 1999), 463–70; and Antonio Cassese, "On the Current Trends towards Criminal Prosecution and Punishment of Breaches of International Humanitarian Law," *European Journal of International Law* 9 (1998): 2–17.

3. Pablo de Greiff, "Trial and Punishment, Pardon and Oblivion: on Two Inadequate Policies for the Treatment of Former Human Rights Abusers," *Philosophy and Social Criticism* 22/3 (1996): 93–111; and Jürgen Habermas, "What Does Working Off the Past Mean Today?," in *A Berlin Republic: Writings on Germany* (Oxford: Polity, 1997), 17–40.

4. Helmut König, Michael Kohlstruch, and Andreas Wöll, "Einleitung," in Helmut König, Michael Kohlstruch, and Andreas Wöll, ed., *Vergangenheitsbewältigung am Ende des zwanzigsten Jahrhunderts* (Opladen: Westdeutscher Verlag, 1998), 7–14.

5. See Neil Kritz, *Transitional Justice: How Emerging Democracies Reckon with Former Regimes* (Washington, D.C.: United States Institute of Peace Press, 1995); Peter Harris and Ben Reilly, *Democracy and Deep-Rooted Conflict: Options for Negotiators* (Stockholm: International Institute for Democracy and Electoral Assistance, 1998); Michael Lund and Andreas Mehler, *Peace-Building & Conflict Prevention in Developing Countries: A Practical Guide* (Brussels: Conflict Prevention Network, 1999); and Richard Lewis Siegel, "Transitional Justice: A Decade of Debate and Experience," *Human Rights Quarterly* 20/2 (1998): 431–54.

6. Donna Pankhurst, "Issues of Justice and Reconciliation in Complex Political Emergencies: Conceptualising Reconciliation, Justice and Peace," *Third World Quarterly* 20/1 (1999): 239–56.

7. David A Crocker, "Reckoning with Past Wrongs: A Normative Framework," *Ethics and International Affairs* 13 (1999): 48–64.

8. Dominick LaCapra, *History and Memory after Auschwitz* (Ithaca: Cornell University Press, 1998), 19.

9. Adam Michnik and Václav Havel, "Justice or Revenge," *Journal of Democracy* 4/1 (1993): 20–27. Compare also Anne Sa'adah's way of distinguishing between institutional

and cultural strategies, in Anne Sa'adah, *Germany's Second Chance: Trust, Justice and Democratization* (Cambridge, Mass.: Harvard University Press, 1998), 3.

10. Howard Zehr, "Restorative Justice: The Concept," *Corrections Today* (December 1997): 68–70.

11. Remo Bodei, "Farewell to the Past: Historical Memory, Oblivion and the Collective Identity," *Philosophy and Social Criticism* 18/3 (1993): 251–65.

12. André Brink, *A Dry White Season* (London: W.H. Allen, 1979), 48.

13. For example, Habermas, "What Does Working Off the Past Mean Today," 19.

14 For an argument that truth is an overrated value, see David Nyberg, *The Varnished Truth: Truth Telling and Deceiving in Ordinary Life* (Chicago: University of Chicago Press, 1993).

15. Juan Mendez, "Accountability for Past Abuses," *Human Rights Quarterly* 19/2 (1997): 262.

16. For different definitions of reconciliation that are in use in South Africa, see Pankhurst, "Issues of Justice and Reconciliation"; Chris Spies, "A Safe Space: How Local Leaders Can Make Room for Reconciliation," *Track Two* 6/3–4 (1997): 11–15; and Brandon Hamber and Hugo van der Merwe, *What Is This Thing Called Reconciliation?* (Johannesburg: Centre for the Study of Violence and Reconciliation, 1998), available at http://sunsite.wits.ac.za/wits/csvr/artrcb&h.htm (accessed 23 June 1998).

17. Louis Kriesberg, "Reconciliation: Conceptual and Empirical Issues" (paper presented at the International Studies Association conference, Minneapolis, March 1998), 3.

18. South African Press Association, 15 April 1996.

19. André Brink, "Stories of History: Reimagining the Past in Post-Apartheid Narrative," in Sarah Nuttall and Carli Coetzee, eds., *Negotiating the Past: the Making of Memory in South Africa* (Oxford: Oxford University Press, 1998), 42.

20. Timothy Garton Ash, "True Confessions," *The New York Review of Books*, 17 July 1998, 37.

21. Alletta Norva, "Memory, Identity and the (Im)possibility of Reconciliation: The Work of the Truth and Reconciliation Commission in South Africa," in *Constellations* 5/2 (1998): 250–65.

22. Priscilla Hayner, "International Guidelines for the Creation and Operation of Truth Commissions: A Preliminary Proposal," *Law and Contemporary Problems* 59/4 (1996): 173–80.

23. Heikki Ylikangas, "Dealing with the Past in Finnish History," in *Northern Dimensions: The Yearbook of Finnish Foreign Policy 2000* (Helsinki: The Finnish Institute of International Affairs, 2000), 102–06.

24. Helmut Quaritsch, "Theorie der Vergangenheitsbewältigung," *Der Staat* 31 (1992): 519–51.

25. See, for example, Hanna Järä, "Dealing with the Past. The Case of Estonia," *UPI Working Papers*, 15 (Helsinki: The Finnish Institute of International Affairs, 1999).

26. See Aryeh Neier, *War Crime: Brutality, Genocide, Terror and the Struggle for Justice* (New York: Time Books, 1998), 106.

27. Peter Digeser, "Forgiveness and Politics: Dirty Hands and Imperfect Procedures," *Political Theory* 26/5 (October 1998): 700–24.

28. Telford Taylor, *Die Nürnberger Prozesse: Hintergründe, Analysen und Erkenntnisse aus heutiger Sicht* (München: Wilhelm Heyne, 1994), 741.

29. Steven Ratner and Jason Abrams, *Accountability for Human Rights Atrocities in International Law* (Oxford: Clarendon Press, 1997), 22–23.

30. Tina Rosenberg, *The Haunted Land: Facing Europe's Ghosts After Communism* (New York: Random House, 1995), 397–405.

31. Ruth Benedict, *The Chrysanthemum and the Sword* (Rutland: Charles Tuttle, 1996 [1946]), 222–23.

32. Ian Buruma, *Wages of Guilt: Memories of War in Germany and Japan* (London: Vintage, 1995).

33. Timothy Garton Ash, "The Truth about Dictatorship," *The New York Review of Books*, 19 February 1998, 35.

34. These conflicting assessments were presented by Yasmin Sooka and Mahmood Mamdani at the "From Truth to Transformation" conference, Johannesburg, 21–24 April 1998.

PART II

Dimensions

CHAPTER 5

❧

Innovating Responses to the Past: Human Rights Institutions[1]

Martha Minow

As a public instrument dealing with the past, law affords lessons about what produces memories for a community or a nation. Legal actors and those who influence them determine what past harms should give rise to a claim and what past violations should constitute a crime. These decisions not only express views about fairness for individuals, but also communicate narratives and values across broad audiences. Whose memories deserve the public stage of an open trial? Is the adversarial trial the only mechanism for giving public voice to past trauma? These questions deserve special attention in the context of the twentieth century, marked as it has been by mass violence, genocide, torture, and secrecy surrounding the perpetrators and planners of such violations of human dignity.

At the beginning of the twenty-first century, collective memories are constructed as often by televised trials as by libraries, museums, monuments, and history books. The constructed quality of memory arises from something deeper, though, than recent media treatments. The emerging consensus among scholars of memory in neuroscience, psychology, and other fields tells us that recollections are always constructed by combining bits of information, selected and arranged in the light of prior narratives and current expectations, needs, and beliefs.[2] Accordingly, the histories we tell and the institutions we make create the narrative and enact the expectations, needs, and beliefs of a particular time.

What can and what does this mean for the international memory of mass atrocities? International law, especially international human rights law, lacks the usual law enforcement mechanisms of state laws. Enforcement depends instead upon the more ambiguous and politicized practices of treaty adoption, media-sponsored shame, and fledgling institutions dependent upon international cooperation. The resulting tradition of institutional innovation exposes the continuing weakness in human rights enforcement and yet this very tradition is perhaps the most significant legacy of the twentieth-century human rights movement.

In the decades immediately following World War II, advocates for human rights launched three innovations. First, through the International Military Tribunal trials in Nuremberg and Tokyo, the Allies tried to model the rule of law as a method for holding human rights violators to account—even though critics charged the tribunals with selective and politicized prosecutions and retroactive punishment. Second, the United Nations replaced the failed League of Nations. It works through formal state political authority to forge international norms and practices, but it is often mired in bureaucracy and posturing. Third, nongovernmental organizations, such as Amnesty International and Human Rights Watch, grew to combine grassroots organizing and the research and lobbying activities of an elite professionalized staff. Increasingly assisted by the capacities of global high-tech communications to gather and report information and solicit grassroots support, the nongovernmental organizations are nonetheless hampered by their very independence from governments and their tendency to focus on individual victims rather than the economic and political structures that give rise to human rights violations.

More recently, this series of innovations has come to include ad hoc international tribunals, truth commissions, and the permanent International Criminal Court. As this essay will suggest, each of these three new forms, in turn, has strengths and weaknesses in forging collective memories to deal with the past and to prevent its recurrence.

Ad Hoc Tribunals

By the 1950s, the United Nations undertook efforts to codify the principles of the Nuremberg and Tokyo trials. These principles included the notion that defendants can be punished for committing a wrong condemned by the international community even in the absence of a highly specified international law, and that such wrongs include crimes against humanity. Even though contemporary critics characterized the Nuremberg and Tokyo trials as victors' travesties of justice, over time the trials received credit for helping to launch an international movement for human rights. Especially as memorialized in popular media, the trial process demanded determinations of responsibility for acts of atrocity and traced responsibility to the actions of particular individuals. The trial process could enact a drama of law-bound retribution while testing factual accounts under the adversarial form widely associated with fairness. It could also generate public occasions for telling what happened, who was responsible, and why it should be condemned.

With these kinds of aspirations, international leaders drafted proposals for a permanent international criminal court, but the intervening onset of the Cold War halted plans in this direction. The United States, in particular, proved resistant especially since observers elsewhere were making allegations of war crimes against it in Vietnam. It certainly proved difficult to locate a deterrent effect in the Nuremberg and Tokyo trials, given the ensuing mass murders in Cambodia, South Africa, Kurdistan, and elsewhere. In the meantime, some domestic trials, such as Israel's trial of Adolph Eichmann, demonstrated the continuing power of the criminal trial process to honor the memory of both victims and survivors of mass violence, and to deploy a legal framework for normative judgment.

By the end of the century, journalists and activists looked back to the Nuremberg and Tokyo trials as landmark contributions to the struggle for a just world order that also came to include the Hague and Geneva Conventions, the two Protocols of 1977, and an emerging international human rights consciousness. After the international community proved unable and unwilling to intervene militarily in the cascading violence in the former Yugoslavia, the United Nations relied on a generous interpretation of its authority to respond to threats to international peace and security and established an International Criminal Tribunal for the former Yugoslavia (ICTY) in 1992.

Antonio Cassesse, who became the president of the Appeals Chamber from the inception of the ICTY, commented that "those who set up the tribunal never intended or expected anything to happen," but the appointed judges and dedicated staff produced a body of procedural rules even in the absence of a courtroom, defendants, and a culture of legal response to impunity.[3] After a very rocky start, with few defendants in hand and little help from the North Atlantic Treaty Organization (NATO) or national governments in arresting defendants or obtaining evidence, the ICTY began to pursue prosecutions.

The claim, and the hope, is that trials held by the international tribunal will create official records of the scope of violence and the participants in it. Public acknowledgment of what happened and its utter wrongfulness could help victims and bystanders come to grips with what happened, while also locating it in the past rather than in a never-ending present. Guilty verdicts could locate individuals to blame and punish, while also clarifying that others—of the same ethnicity, religion, or background—did not commit war crimes and thus should not be swept up in a wave of group guilt. If those selected for prosecution reflect simply the happenstance of who can be arrested or who surrenders, however, then hope for fulfilling these goals must dim.

The very existence of the ICTY enabled the U.N. Security Council's creation of a second ad hoc tribunal, this time for Rwanda. Indeed, the failure to create a comparable tribunal in the face of the mass murders of 800,000 Rwandan people—largely those identified as Tutsis—during 1994 appeared to express a blatant parochial or biased concern with Europe rather than Africa. In addition, the justice system within Rwanda was so devastated that an international response seemed the only possible legal recourse. Yet the new Tutsi-led Rwandan government quickly arrested some 115,000 people in anticipation of domestic trials following the genocide. Thus, the world has been able to compare an international and a domestic trial process working on the same material.

The Rwandan domestic process proceeded apace and yet could not quickly process the enormous number of incarcerated people. With fewer than fifty lawyers in the country as the genocide ended, mustering defense counsel for the accused proved extremely difficult. Even teams of international volunteers found the job nearly insuperable. Perhaps the most dramatic moment occurred when tens of thousands of Rwandans came in April 1998 to watch the executions of twenty-two people convicted of genocide by Rwanda's courts. Included in that group was Froduald Karamira, the primary instigator of the propagandist hate broadcast that encouraged Hutus to join in mass killings of Tutsis in 1994. Crowds assembled to watch the executions. International human rights leaders objected that the underlying trials had failed to comport with international standards of justice. In particular, some defendants had had no legal representation; others had had lawyers with no time to prepare. Although domestic trials can foster a commitment to human rights and the rule of law within the nation itself, they can also seem to be, or really be, part of a continuing internal domestic vendetta elevating one group over another.

The International Criminal Tribunal for Rwanda (ICTR) has the advantage of better resources, international teams of lawyers, judges, and prosecutors. It also holds in custody many of the high-ranking figures associated with the atrocity. It assures defense counsel not only to defendants, but also to suspects at the investigatory stage.[4] The tribunal's most severe sanction is a life sentence, while the domestic courts can sentence defendants to death. None of the Rwandans executed in the domestic proceedings played as high level a role as did Jean Kambanda, the prime minister who led the nation during the genocide, pleaded guilty at the international tribunal, and received a life sentence.[5] Kambanda did promise detailed testimony about the activities of the government presiding over the massacre. The trials in the ICTR afford more care, more records, and more adversarial checks than the domestic trials.

But the international tribunal, based as it is in Arusha, Tanzania, and in the Hague, is remote from Rwanda; indeed, Rwanda ultimately provided the single vote against the tribunal's creation, once it was clear the trials would not be held within the country and thus not within easy earshot of Rwandans themselves. Who, then, is the audience for the international trials? Perhaps the United States and its mass media; perhaps the United Nations leadership. The audience problem is even more pronounced in the former Yugoslavia, where the propaganda machine excludes most reports from the tribunal, other than to characterize it as a new form of victimization of the Serbs.

Still, the international trials do demonstrate a commitment to fair trials, on a public record, with opportunities for appellate review. They have also turned the legacy of the Nuremberg and Tokyo trials into an impetus for renewing public, legal response to atrocity. Although ad hoc and temporary, the two international tribunals differed from the Nuremberg and Tokyo Military tribunal trials in several respects. They emerged from the authority of a standing institution, the United Nations, rather than the military command of victors in war. Perhaps they represented intentionally weak gestures after international failures to stop the mass violence they sought to address.

They stretched existing international law to apply to arguably domestic conflicts. They hosted the development of procedural rules and a body of precedent, administered by teams of judges assembled from around the world.

Truth Commissions

Outside the two ad hoc tribunals, however, no international process emerged for staging criminal trials. Meanwhile, nations such as Chile, Cambodia, and Uganda suffered terrifying incidents of terror and violence without the subsequent domestic political will or confidence to prosecute human rights violators. The domestic barriers have proved especially pronounced in nations where the violence is chronic and pervasive. Thus, articulation and enforcement of human rights have required creative alternatives. A notable one is the development of truth commissions: commissions of inquiry exposing and documenting torture, murders, and other human rights violations that otherwise would be denied and covered up by repressive regimes.

Although it resulted from a secret investigation led by courageous journalists and religious leaders, the Brazilian report, *Brasil: Nunca Mais*, in many ways inspired truth commission inquiries that took more public forms elsewhere. This report documented 144 political murders, 125 disappearances, and over 1,800 incidents of torture. Its summary volume became a best-seller and produced enormous public reaction, contributing largely to Brazil's early adoption of the United Nations Convention against Torture in 1985. The U.N. then itself sponsored the creation of a truth commission for El Salvador. This more public effort gathered evidence that otherwise might have been destroyed or suppressed, but it did not generate a widespread national acknowledgment of the human rights violations.

Other inquiries have collected testimony from survivors and issued public reports tracing the causes of periods of mass atrocity. The most dramatic example is South Africa's Truth and Reconciliation Commission (TRC), created by the first democratically elected parliament after the nation negotiated a peaceful transition from apartheid. Because that negotiated peace included a promise to launch a process for granting amnesty to participants in past conflicts, the TRC established a committee to receive applications from individuals seeking amnesty. It gave amnesty to only a few hundred of the over 9,000 applicants, stringently applying the statutory requirements that applicants tell the whole truth of their violations, and receive amnesty only for violations committed solely for political purposes and only using means commensurate with those purposes. The TRC also used a separate human rights committee to collect statements from survivors of violence on all sides of the preceding conflicts. Some 22,000 offered statements. Many people testified in public hearings that were broadcast around the nation.

Spawning controversy especially among opponents of the amnesty process, the TRC nonetheless provided vivid and unforgettable proof of human rights violations that had long been denied by members of the apartheid government. It also gave voice to survivors of violence at the hands of secret police, other government officials, and opposition groups. Ultimately producing a five-volume report as well as memorable national broadcasts of live testimony, the TRC most remarkably indicated the possibility of making public the names and conduct of human rights violators without unleashing vigilante revenge against them. Individual survivors received some limited solace in gaining acknowledgment from the government and the watching nation and world, and in gaining facts from exhumed mass graves, government files, and amnesty applications about who ordered what, who killed whom, what exactly was the instrument of torture, and where the loved one's bones now lie.

The TRC included sector-wide inquiries into the roles of the business community, the judiciary, the medical profession, and the mass media in the apartheid regime. The final report offered analyses of the contributions of these larger factors to the perpetuation of human rights abuses and to the maintenance of a system that dehumanized and demoralized the majority of the population. Investigations of the uses of violence by the African National Congress and other resistance groups produced condemnations of their use of force in the final report, but the report clearly treated the abuses committed by the government, in the name of the people, as the more severe wrong.

The desire for individual accountability through criminal punishment could not be satisfied by the TRC alone, however; and many in South Africa and elsewhere still hold criminal trials to be the preferred form of justice. Antiapartheid activists resisted the seeming equation of their struggles with the violations committed by the government. Apartheid sympathizers worried, in contrast, that the TRC was itself a kind of oppressive witch-hunt, lacking the protections of adversarial hearings and the presumption of innocence. Still others emphasized the possibility of a path of reconciliation rather than adversariness, and evoked both religious views and a cultural tradition of humane inclusion. Calls for truth commissions started to be heard in Bosnia, Cambodia, Argentina, and elsewhere where survivors sensed insufficient public knowledge and acknowledgment of human rights violations and continuing suffering.

A Permanent International Court

Despite slow progress, cumbersome procedures, and widespread uncertainty about their effectiveness, the ad hoc international criminal tribunals no doubt helped to generate support in many nations for reviving plans for a permanent International Criminal Court (ICC). In 1998, 120 of the world's nations—but not the United States—voted to create such a court. Designed to have jurisdiction over genocide, crimes against humanity, war crimes, and the crime of aggression, the ICC is also meant to cooperate with, and not displace, domestic justice systems.[6] The court was to take effect after sixty nations had signed and ratified the statute authorizing it; by the summer of 1999, eighty-two had signed and three had ratified.[7]

Initially, the United States was a strong supporter of such a court. Yet despite securing concessions in the Rome conference, where delegates hammered out its authorizing statute, the U.S. government decided not to endorse the ICC. Its representatives cited four chief concerns: first, U.S. military personnel could face politically motivated charges at the court; second, the U.N. Security Council retained too much control over prosecutorial decisions; third, jurisdiction remained too ambiguous, especially regarding the category of the crime against aggression; and fourth, doubts emerged about the relationship between the ICC and national courts.[8] As the sole remaining global superpower, the United States perceived itself more likely to be treated as a violator than a beneficiary of the ICC's operations. Yet it is still too soon in the life of the ICC to test this proposition or, indeed, to know how long the United States will stay out. Observers note, however, that the likely effectiveness of the ICC will itself be affected deeply by the U.S. stance.

An international criminal court could become a vehicle for generating reputable and regularized prosecutions for human rights violations. It could produce public records that cut through the myths and distortions spawned by repressive regimes. It could, of course, become subject to politicized bickering, or it could get bogged down in procedural wrangling. It could become a place of such technical expertise and debate that it has little effect on public memory. It could also so routinize the publicity and prosecution of human rights violations that it only memorializes the repetition of atrocity, perhaps with an anesthetizing effect.

A Tradition of Innovation

A rhetoric of human rights assisted and fueled those who were committed to remembering and preventing human suffering and violence in the twentieth century. People from many nations then developed that rhetoric to launch institutional innovations in response to mass torture, murders, and collective aggression. Ad hoc tribunals have conducted trials that work terrifying headlines into charges of individual responsibility, with occasion for individual defense. Commissions of inquiry afford opportunities for naming perpetrators, hearing from survivors, and reporting on larger societal patterns contributing to the degradation and terrorization of large numbers of people. Some of those commissions have prompted monetary and symbolic reparations, educational programs, memorials, and projects to strengthen democratic institutions.

The early steps for launching a permanent international criminal court hold the possibility of a more predictable and established mode of response to atrocity, and yet with the United States at least initially standing out, further alternatives will be needed. Here, the tradition of innovation itself may be a strength. Straddling the domestic and the international, courts and commissions, the governmental and nongovernmental, the punitive and preventive, the innovative human rights institutions exhibit a variety of vehicles for remembering mass violence and for giving forceful rejoinders to it.

How will these innovations help people deal with past atrocities? The scholars of memory inform us that the histories we tell and the institutions we make, create the narratives and enact the expectations, needs, and beliefs of a time. If the scholars are right, then two paradoxes emerge. Our memories are constructed, yet no one person can choose how; and our memories are not simply retrieved and yet neither are they free floating and entirely manipulable to present interests. Two truths, though, must remain bedrock. First, some versions of the past are wrong. We can create arenas for disputing or complicating accounts of the past, not in order to fabricate memory, but to enlarge which truths can be remembered. Second, failure to remember can impose unacceptable costs. Failure to remember triumphs and accomplishments collectively is a loss to the human community. Failure to remember injustice and cruelty collectively is an ethical violation. It implies no responsibility and no commitment to prevent inhumanity in the future. And even worse, failures of collective memory stoke fires of resentment and revenge.

Michael Ignatieff offered this explanation of the conflicts surrounding the former Yugoslavia:

> [T]he past continues to torment because it is not the past. These places are not living in a serial order of time but in a simultaneous one, in which the past and present are a continuous, agglutinated mass of fantasies, distortions, myths, and lies. Reporters in the Balkan wars often observed that when they were told atrocity stories they were occasionally uncertain whether these stories had occurred yesterday or in 1941, 1841, or 1441.

He concludes that this "is the dreamtime of vengeance. Crimes can never safely be fixed in the historical past; they remain locked in the eternal present, crying out for vengeance."[9] Similarly, as the saying goes, "The problem in Ireland is that the Irish will never forget and the British will never remember."

The twentieth century will not be remembered for the mass killings in the former Yugoslavia and Rwanda, Brazil and South Africa, and perhaps not even for the Holocaust, for other centuries also have been marked by enormous, human-made atrocities. But perhaps this century will be known as one that created international human rights tribunals, truth and reconciliation commissions, and public and private institutions to advance human rights. Even though "the logic of law will never make sense of the illogic of genocide,"[10] legal institutions can offer armatures for memory, and frames for the kinds of acknowledgment that prevent both forgetting and vengeance. No human institutions are perfect. Political wrangling, selective prosecution, the limits of admissible evidence, and the danger of victor's justice mar international and even domestic criminal trials for human rights violations. Truth commissions may be too tepid, too ineffectual, too nonpunitive even as they gather stories from too-often–silenced victims. A permanent international court is only as powerful as its members' commitments, and the jury is still out on that one. But each of these offers tools to help shape what we all work to recall.

Endnotes

1. Some of the material in this essay is drawn from Martha Minow, *Between Vengeance and Forgiveness: Facing History After Genocide and Mass Violence* (Boston: Beacon Press, 1998); Minow, "Instituting Universal Human Rights Law" (paper presented at "Law 2000" conference, Amherst, Mass., 3 October 1999); and Minow, "Remembering to Remember," 1999 Phi Beta Kappa Oration, Harvard College, Cambridge, Mass., 8 June 1999.

2. Steven J. Lynn and Kevin M. McConkey, eds., *Truth in Memory* (New York: Guilford Press, 1998), 23–28.

3. Interview with the author, The Hague, November 1996.

4. See Mark A. Drumbl, "Rule of Law Amid Lawlessness: Counseling the Accused in Rwanda's Domestic Genocide Trials," *Columbia Human Rights Law Review* 29/3 (1998): 545, 625.

5. Ibid., 625, n. 287; and Bernard Muma, "War Crimes Tribunals: The Record and the Prospects," *American University International Law Review* 13 (1998): 1469.

6. See Anne-Marie Slaughter, "Memorandum to the President," in Alton Frye, ed., *Toward an International Criminal Court: Three Options Presented as Presidential Speeches* (New York: Council on Foreign Relations, 1999).

7. Ibid., 7–8.

8. Ibid., 8.

9. Michael Ignatieff, "Wounded Nations, Broken Lives: Truth Commissions and War Tribunals," *Index on Censorship* 5 (1996): 110–22. [First published as "The Elusive Goal of War Trials," *Harper's* (March 1996).]

10. Lawrence Langer, *Admitting the Holocaust* (New York: Oxford University Press, 1995), 171.

CHAPTER 6

❧

National and Community Reconciliation: Competing Agendas in the South African Truth and Reconciliation Commission[1]

Hugo van der Merwe

Introduction

Societies emerging from long periods of violent conflict have to deal with the legacy of their past at various societal levels. As part of the national agenda, political institutions have to be rebuilt and political values of human rights and democracy have to be resuscitated. The needs of individual victims of the conflict must be addressed through processes of justice, reparations, and psychological healing. Another level that must be addressed through this process of reconstruction and reconciliation is that of community. National political conflicts give rise to localized conflict dynamics that can take on a life of their own and that have repercussions for the local political culture. In these situations, national political solutions and reconciliation processes are likely to have only a limited impact on local reconciliation.

In South Africa there is a general sense of confidence in the political stability at the national level. Few people fear that a deterioration in relations between national political leaders will spill into renewed violence. The problem of political violence is now mainly limited to specific regions and local communities. While a process of national reconciliation does have a very significant impact on community reconciliation, community conflict dynamics have to be addressed in their own right in order to secure sustainable peace.

The South African Truth and Reconciliation Commission (TRC) was an initiative that explicitly focused on national reconciliation, but it also engaged local communities in reconciliation processes. Initially it portrayed itself as a body dealing with all levels of reconciliation (national, community, and personal),[2] but it moved toward a narrower interpretation of its mandate as it realized the limitations of its capacity. The TRC's involvement in local communities and interaction with victims raised concerns about how community and national reconciliation are linked, and highlighted the problems with processes that override local needs in the pursuit of national goals. The context within which the TRC emerged, the legislation that guided its operation, and the meaning given to its work by the commissioners[3] imbued the TRC with a top-down notion of reconciliation in South Africa. The TRC's intervention at the community level raised various expectations among local stakeholders but resulted in disillusionment and frustration when the expectations were not met.[4]

This chapter explores the context that gave rise to the TRC legislation and strategies that focused more on national reconciliation. It then contrasts the competing perspectives of TRC staff and community stakeholders regarding the process of community reconciliation, and examines the competing reconciliation strategies preferred by different groups. The chapter also reflects on the various positive contributions of the TRC to local reconciliation processes, and then advances some ideas about the way forward.

Emergence and Operationalization of the TRC Legislation

The TRC was conceptualized and legislated at a time when there was still significant concern about cementing the transition to democracy and facilitating peaceful relations between national political parties. The parliament that oversaw the establishment of the TRC was guided by the consensus politics of the Government of National Unity in which national political leaders collaborated to find mutually acceptable solutions.[5] The TRC Act (the Promotion of National Unity and Reconciliation Act No. 34 of 1995) was an attempt to give effect to the constitutional requirement for the granting of amnesty to perpetrators of past political crimes,[6] while also providing a detailed account of these abuses and acknowledging the suffering of victims. There were significant political stakes involved in how exactly the legislation was formulated, as such a commission would determine the fate of political leaders and others responsible for past crimes and human rights abuses. The Commission was also seen as a potent political tool that could allocate moral blame and establish an official history of past events. The parliamentary debates that ensued from the draft legislation were the most extensive that the new parliament had experienced in its first two years.

The legislative process that led to the adoption of the TRC was thus one that was dominated by national political interests and power politics. While the process was remarkably open to public input, party-political negotiations and compromise shaped the outcome most significantly. The space for public input was inadequately exploited because civil society was too weak to engage effectively in national political processes where political parties had strong agendas.[7]

The legislation that created the TRC provided something for everybody. It managed to include the key demands of the various political parties and human rights advocates. This mandate was, however, excessively ambitious, and while accommodating the needs of all parties, did not guarantee significant results. The TRC's key objective, as required by the Constitution, was to grant amnesties. This was balanced to some extent by the strong efforts of the TRC to expose national patterns of past human rights abuses, and to pin responsibility on the political leaders for these abuses. While there were various places in the legislation where victims' needs and rights were recognized, these concerns guided the implementation of the Act rather than formed its basis.

To the extent that the TRC seriously engaged with reconciliation, the Act guided its attention more to the national level. At the same time, nongovernmental organizations (NGOs) and victims constantly pressured it to acknowledge the importance of local processes and to be sensitive to the needs of individual victims. The TRC was thus constantly pulled in both directions, setting up expectations that it could not ultimately fulfill. It attempted to portray itself as a bottom-up process and there are various examples of earnest victim and community engagement practices by the Commission. These examples are, however, exceptions that prove the rule—the overall structure and core functions of the TRC were driven by a top-down reconciliation agenda. The top-down versus bottom-up tension that characterized its formation and operation was particularly evident in its attempts to engage communities in human rights violations hearings.

While the TRC's mandate covered a range of responsibilities, Section 3(1) of the Act spells out its specific objectives:

> The objectives of the Commission shall be to promote national unity and reconciliation in a spirit of understanding, which transcends the conflicts, and divisions of the past by:
>
> (a) establishing as complete a picture as possible of the causes, nature and extent of the gross violations of human rights which were committed . . . , by conducting investigations and holding hearings;
>
> (b) facilitating the granting of amnesty to persons who make full disclosure of all the relevant facts relating to acts associated with a political objective and comply with the requirements of this Act;
>
> (c) establishing and making known the fate or whereabouts of victims and by restoring the human and civil dignity of such victims by granting them an opportunity to relate their own accounts of the violations of which they are the victims, and by recommending reparation measures in respect of them;
>
> (d) compiling a report providing as comprehensive an account as possible of the activities and findings of the Commission . . . , and which contains recommendations of measures to prevent the future violations of human rights.[8]

The Act does not, however, specify the exact procedure by which the TRC should go about the task of "establishing as complete a picture as possible of the causes, nature and extent of the gross violations of human rights which were committed," or by which it would grant victims "an opportunity to relate their own accounts of the violations of which they are the victims."[9] It is also not clear how the achievement of these objectives could be done in a way that would "promote national unity and reconciliation in a spirit of understanding which transcends the conflicts and divisions of the past." Nowhere in the Act is the meaning of reconciliation given any real substance.

The legislation thus provided the scope for the Commission to develop its own approach, emphasis, and parameters. While the Act provided few limitations regarding what could potentially be included in its mandate, it stipulated certain minimum results. The only absolute requirement was that relating to the granting of amnesty. The other objectives of the Act could be interpreted in a relatively flexible manner, using language such as "compiling a report providing as comprehensive an account as possible," and "establishing as complete a picture as possible." These goals of collecting information, listening to victims' accounts, and making recommendations could be done broadly and thoroughly or narrowly and hastily, depending on time and resources. Given the limited time and resources that were available, too much was probably expected from the TRC.

The TRC pursued its mandate through a range of different interventions in relation to perpetrators, victims, political parties, and state institutions. Most of these were public in nature and were subject to extensive media coverage. A central component of the TRC's strategy to engage the public in the reconciliation process was through holding community hearings at which community members publicly related their stories of victimization. These community hearings became the main focus of its initial period of operation, shaping the public image of its work and setting the scene for its subsequent amnesty hearings, investigations, and findings.

The TRC held about eighty such community hearings around the country. In preparation for the hearings, it would start by holding education meetings with various local political leaders and address public meetings regarding the goals and structure of the hearing. Statement-takers were then sent to the community to collect statements from victims at venues that were publicly advertised. Local structures, particularly the local government, were drawn into providing logistical assistance and publicity for the hearings.

After the TRC had collected a number of statements in the community they would select particular cases to be heard at the public hearings. These were selected in such a way as to represent the time frame of the TRC's mandate (1960–94), the various sides to the conflict, and the range of different forms of abuses. Particular attention was also given to "significant" cases in the history of that community.[10] Public hearings were generally held in big halls in the local township or town. Sometimes these halls were packed to capacity, but sometimes the attendance only amounted to about two hundred people.

At these hearings, victims would be called to tell their stories to the panel of commissioners. Commissioners would then ask them for clarification, for more information about what happened in the community, or about their expectations with regard to reparations and healing.

Subsequent to taking statements (and usually after the hearings), the TRC also conducted superficial investigations to corroborate the victims' stories. More detailed investigations to establish responsibility or find out more information about the incident did not happen in most cases. With over 22,000 cases brought by victims, the TRC only had the capacity to investigate the more prominent cases of assassinations, disappearances, and massacres.

The community hearings served a range of functions. In part, they were focused on victims, listening to their stories, and giving them a voice. Second, they were seen as a process that would promote understanding among different groupings in local communities, or between political parties or different races. Third, the community hearings provided a national forum where stories could be conveyed to the country as a whole. The goal was that this public outpouring would allow people from all sides of the conflict to recognize and understand the suffering caused by apartheid and the ensuing violent conflict.

Top-Down and Bottom-Up Approaches to Reconciliation

Reconciliation means different things to different people. One key dimension along which people seem to differ is that of the locus of the initiative for reconciliation. The division is between those who see reconciliation as something that is built from the bottom up, or from the top down.

The bottom-up approach is one that sees society more as the sum of its parts, or in terms of a healthy society requiring healthy individual members. On the one hand, this approach is viewed in terms of the psychological health of individuals and improved interpersonal relations among community members. Healthy (reconciled) relations are seen as arising from the restoration of the psychological health of individual members of society and a healthy network of interpersonal relations. On the other hand, the building blocks of society are seen as communities. The construction of vibrant communities is seen as the primary focus or starting point of any reconciliation process.

In contrast, the top-down approach is characterized by a perception that local dynamics lack significant autonomy. For local dynamics to change, national intervention must first take place. This will then filter down, or create the conditions (and incentives) within which local actors can pursue reconciliation processes.

The TRC's overall approach was mainly one of top-down reconciliation—viewing local reconciliation as a product of party-political interaction or national moral reorientation. This approach was at odds with the perceptions of reconciliation in many local communities, where local complexities were seen as factors that have to be addressed in their own right. While communities perceived the TRC as engaging in a valuable endeavor, its macro-narrative did not engage sufficiently with local intraparty and interpersonal dynamics to provide a solid foundation for future local reconciliation.

The TRC's Approach to Community Reconciliation

From numerous interviews and interaction with TRC staff and commissioners, it does appear that there was quite an even split within the Commission between those who supported a top-down approach and those who supported a bottom-up one. Many of the commissioners and staff came from NGO backgrounds and were very sympathetic to community concerns. They felt uncomfortable about the constraints that limited their ability to implement a more community-based approach. However, some TRC staff, for a number of reasons, favored the top-down model. A central justification or reason was the need for quick results and broad impact: "Reconciliation is not individual reconciliation. This is an ideological or religious paradigm that is not viable as a channel for major impact."[11]

One reason for the TRC's prioritization of the development of a macro-narrative that would help citizens gain a clearer understanding of the events that had shaped the national conflict, was this concern to maximize impact. Another was the lack of resources: "The TRC is not able to go into every single case and every community. It simply does not have the time and resources. We can only highlight key issues and thus throw some light on other more minor cases. Addressing these key issues will signal the way forward."[12]

Other commissioners and staff were, however, simply dismissive of a bottom-up approach. They either felt that community reconciliation was a dead

end because of the racial composition of local communities, or viewed reconciliation as a process that necessarily had to be led by national politicians with
a political perspective that transcends community membership:

> Addressing things at the community level would be to view society
> according to the old paradigm (race). It is thus a non-starter. At the
> national level we can approach things in terms of an integrative sys-
> temic form. We can develop knowledge of how past conflicts devel-
> oped, why people behaved the way they did. It could lead to greater
> acceptance. . . . National reconciliation requires national organisations
> or individuals with national standing to re-frame the political picture
> and act on it. It requires statesmanship from politicians. This can
> happen at [the] community level, but not if the dynamics are around
> race. The concept of community is closely linked to that of race. This
> makes it very problematic.[13]

A further argument for top-down approaches was that they were needed
because of the political nature of the reconciliation "mandate" and the
nature of local political dynamics:

> Local communities have . . . not been able to take an individual stand
> on the TRC. They have been guided by their political parties who have
> painted the TRC in political terms. They thus see the TRC as a game to
> give blacks the moral high ground. There was initially the hope (within
> the TRC) to get broad white participation through the NP (National
> Party) which still represents most Afrikaners.[14]

Rather than being the product simply of an analysis of the political dynamics of an individual community, the skepticism about change from below is
also reflective of a broader understanding of significant social change as
something that has to be driven at the national level.

There was also some skepticism within the Commission about the possibility of promoting reconciliation within relationships that were characterized by such severe abuses:

> The TRC cannot be expected to achieve much in terms of reconciliation
> at the interpersonal level. Attempts have been made to bring victims

and perpetrators together. These are mainly just symbolic processes. Extensive efforts go into it with very little result. It is not natural—only through great effort, and only with TRC prodding does it happen. It is not organic.[15]

Not only was this top-down approach preferred for national-level reconciliation, it was often recommended for the interaction between local leaders and their communities. The view here was that leadership has to initiate and carry a reconciliation process (often in the face of resistance from their supporters). According to a TRC staff member:

Human rights violations also have been sufficiently stigmatised at a political level to deter parties from repeating this course. At community level there is a more delicate link. It depends on skills, maturity and sophistication of community leaders, because these would determine how they handle the danger of vengeance. People can very easily take things into their own hands or mobilise community anger. It is then up to local leaders—local government, church and civic leaders to manage the situation, and to convince people to talk rather than fight.[16]

The TRC's conceptualization of community reconciliation played itself out very clearly in the way that it strategized and organized human rights violations hearings in communities. These strategic choices met with some resistance from local communities.

The TRC spread itself very thinly, trying to cover as many communities as possible. It often spent very little time in a community before holding a hearing (only four or five weeks in many cases) and often had minimal contact with the community after the hearing was completed. In the case of the East Rand in Gauteng, where thousands of people were killed in political violence, it had one follow-up workshop lasting a morning to cover a population of over one million people among whom they had convened three community hearings.

The Commission's consultations with local communities in preparation for the hearing were usually very limited. It often only consulted significantly with the local town council, who in turn were expected to communicate with other parties. Stakeholders not represented in this formal structure often felt left out. This was particularly the case with groups explicitly representing victim concerns. Victims often did not feel properly represented by political leaders. Many felt alienated from the political process and saw politicians as mainly representing the interests of perpetrators of abuses. Victims perceived politicians, for example, to be more concerned with hiding the abuses of their party members than with exposing the abuses of their opponents.

In many communities the hearings were often only one day in length, covering only ten or eleven cases of victimization. Less than ten percent of victims who made statements had the opportunity to testify in public. Many more victims wanted the opportunity to tell their stories, and felt angered that the TRC seemingly did not see their experiences as sufficiently significant. Community members felt that the hearings only scratched the surface of events in the community. They felt that the TRC should come back and hold further hearings to listen to more of their stories.

The selection of cases to be heard at the hearings was done by the TRC independently of community input. The TRC selected cases that (in its opinion) represented key events in the community's history, and cases that represented the experiences of different groupings in the community, different types of victimization, or different time periods. It was thought that this would provide a general narrative of events in that community and would allow all those present at the hearing to be able to identify with at least one of the stories told.[17]

The TRC's attempt to relate to a wide range of victims through presenting selected cases that showed a variety of abuses held little appeal to many community members. For them it was the detailed local history that held most meaning, rather than a broad picture of different forms of suffering. They still harbored suspicions about who was involved, who did what, who was informing for the police, and so on. Only hearing from a small number of victims did not satisfy this thirst for new information. At best, it was seen as a good start.

Community members were also suspicious about the selection of cases. They wondered why certain cases that they saw as particularly significant were left out. There was even speculation among some communities that this was due to secret deals between local political leaders and TRC officials aimed at covering up the involvement of party officials.

During the hearings, the TRC offered various suggestions regarding further interventions that they could make. These were generally not followed through. A commissioner at the Duduza hearing, for example, questioned a victim about his willingness to engage in a mediated dialogue with the perpetrator. The victim welcomed this suggestion, but subsequently heard nothing more. Similarly, promises of further investigations were not followed through; and while the prospect of urgent interim reparations was held out, this was only implemented in a very limited sense about two years later.

The aspects of truth that the TRC were interested in also did not always match those of the parties concerned. Some victims were more interested in identifying the local actors in their victimization. It was often of less interest to them to find out who had given the orders than to know who in the local community had assisted the police. They wanted to know whether their neighbor, whom they suspected of involvement, had in fact been working for (or manipulated by) the police. Seeing this person on the street every day without knowing whether they should greet him was, for example, something that intruded on their daily existence. The TRC's primary concern was, however, to discover involvement at the higher levels of political and security structures in order to expose broad patterns of human rights abuses at a national level.

While many TRC staff were sympathetic to bottom-up approaches to reconciliation, the TRC engagement with individuals and communities was characterized by an absence of consultation with a broad range of local stakeholders (in favor of reliance on the main political parties), a lack of sustained interaction with the community (in favor of a high-profile one-off event), a disregard for local community concerns (in favor of the use of local events to build and reinforce a national narrative of the political conflict), and a lack of services to individual victims (alongside public recognition of victims' suffering and nobility).

The TRC did, however, manage to portray itself very effectively as a community- and victim-centered process in the public mind. On the occasions when they engaged in more intensive community intervention and victim-perpetrator mediation, or where they were able to address individual victims' needs immediately, they managed to draw extensive media coverage of these successes. Respondents in the two communities studied (as well as many people in other communities and individuals involved in sectoral hearings interviewed by the author) felt that their community (or their area of work) was not given equal treatment by the TRC. From what the people saw in the media, they felt that the TRC had done much for everybody else, but that it had neglected their own community.

Community Perspectives of Reconciliation

The top-down approach outlined above stands in contrast with community perspectives that prioritize the reconstruction of local social networks and local political relationships as the basis of reconciliation. Victims, ex-combatants, and community leaders generally viewed reconciliation as a process that has to build an understanding of the specific local dynamics, renegotiate interpersonal relationships, and address concerns regarding individual local perpetrators and victims.[18]

A central element of the top-down versus bottom-up tension is the way that intergroup relations are understood. The top-down approach examines groups in abstract terms as being composed of categories of identity that derive from national political divisions (e.g., race, ethnicity, and ideology). At the local level, groups are seen more in terms of the networks of individuals who compose the group, where the group has a specific history and its goals are defined by an alliance of different interests. The individuals who are part of this group are seen as key vehicles of change, and interpersonal relations are a key basis for group cohesion.

TRC staff members within the Reparations and Rehabilitation Committee often approached reconciliation from a bottom-up perspective. Their level of focus was, however, more on the individual than the community. The attempt to be victim centered sometimes resulted in a focus that did not effectively take into consideration the context of community relations within which the victims' needs were to be addressed. Psychological healing was thus seen by some as the key component that determines or defines reconciliation. A number of TRC staff thus expressed views favoring a bottom-up approach, while expressing their regret for the many constraints that limited their ability to implement such an approach:

> The Reparations and Rehabilitation Committee views the psycho-social support as essential to the reconciliation process, but the TRC can only co-ordinate and consolidate existing initiatives. We focus on capacity-building and encouraging communities to take ownership.[19]

Psychological healing was seen by many of the TRC respondents as the key component that determines (or defines) reconciliation:

> At the intra-level there has to be reconciliation between personal and broader experience. It is the psychological equivalent of re-integration.[20]

> If we take the analogy of the wound that has to be opened up to clean out the sepsis seriously, we must ask whether this has been sufficiently dealt with. Before reconciliation there must be a pre-reconciliation phase that focuses on cleaning the wounds.[21]

Among community leaders the concern with bottom-up processes was centered on the need to address local community dynamics. The perception was that reconciliation is something that people relate to in concrete terms in relation to local conflict events and known actors:

> National reconciliation is not possible without local reconciliation. Presently they [the TRC] are attempting to build from the top down. This will not succeed. It must be dealt with first in terms of real issues where people co-operate on concrete concerns. This needs to be supported at national level, but not controlled from there.[22]

> Local leaders have a key role in peace initiatives. Provincial and national leaders are not trusted. They are not directly affected or hurt by conflict. They have to build relationships at the level where they operate.[23]

The violence of the past is highly personalized in people's memories. Despite high levels of political awareness and a general understanding of the broader political dynamics of the past, people approach reconciliation in personal terms. They hold individuals accountable. They want these individuals to explain their actions and express remorse, rather than representatives of a group apologizing on behalf of others. Issues such as the relationship between the community and the police, for example, still revolve around individual members of the police service. Their continued presence was seen as casting a shadow over broader transformation initiatives by the police:

The TRC has a role in exposing those elements involved in past abuses. People in the community should stand up and point them out. I don't know of any [local police] who have applied for amnesty. The police will no longer close ranks to protect each other. There is now a feeling of each one for himself. People have identified individuals, but this must be done publicly. By identifying those responsible we will help clear the name of other police. There should not be just a blanket blame of all police for what happened.[24]

Community members perceived the TRC as not showing sufficient interest in local dynamics. They saw it as being concerned mainly with the national conflict dynamics rather than being interested in local experiences:

The reconciliation process must be regional or local. A process that is national creates problems: There is a lack of sufficient interest in the local events. Local people do not think their stories are seen as relevant.[25]

Among leaders in Duduza who were concerned that internal divisions were a serious issue in their political party and the community, there was a feeling that the TRC was not concerned with this dimension of reconciliation:

Reconciliation in Duduza has nothing to do with race. The conflict only directly involved blacks, but the TRC is not interested in this. They would rather spend their resources investigating the role of whites and the NP [National Party].[26]

The TRC was also seen as not giving local people enough time, information, feedback, or space to make an input:

The TRC failed to reach real victims. Reconciliation is not about important individuals, but the common people need to reconcile. Prominent people were approached to make statements. Thousands of people who still have birdshot pellets lodged in their skin abound in Duduza. Maybe I do not understand the workings of the TRC.

Until such time when someone comes to Duduza and impartially, without discrimination, interviews victims and survivors of apartheid ills independently of biased learned input from local politicians, people themselves will come out with the solution. People themselves will prescribe the formula for their own reconciliation.[27]

Victims felt strongly that they were not properly consulted about the hearings, and that the TRC should have spent a lot more time educating them about the process of the hearings and about its work more generally, facilitating statement collecting, keeping them updated about developments in their cases, and ultimately addressing their individual concerns regarding reparations and truth. NGO staff who worked with victims also echoed these concerns:

The TRC's approach to reconciliation is very vague. It does not have a coherent vision of where it is taking people. It lacks an organised strategy to reach out to communities and involve them. Victims do not know what to expect and they are absent from any participation in the policy process. The TRC has a very poor communication strategy. It only involves NGOs immediately before a hearing and then there is no follow-up. There is no clear engagement strategy of linking with organisations to provide assistance.[28]

In observing the failure of the TRC to bring the various parties on board in the process, some community leaders also held the view that there is more flexibility among local politicians than at the national level. This space allows greater maneuverability around promoting reconciliation:

If the TRC does not come back, a public hearing can be held by other organisations. Such a local initiative could get support from both sides. People are ready to tell their stories. The local IFP [Inkatha Freedom Party] may well be supportive—they are not in concert with the national IFP who called for the disbandment of the TRC.[29]

National leaders have different agendas from the local leaders. Local leaders would have been willing to participate more than national leaders in the TRC. Particular local circumstances create particular opportunities.[30]

The TRC as Foundation Catalyst for Community Reconciliation

Despite various efforts by the TRC to engage in an internal and external debate about the meaning of reconciliation and what processes are required for its promotion, it ultimately (when time started running out) fell back on the most explicit requirements of its mandate, and handed back responsibility for the logic of its actions to the legislators.

Some commissioners gradually realized this shortcoming and re-presented their goal as that of establishing a foundation for building reconciliation. If the success of the TRC is judged on this basis, there may be some grounds for optimism. If we recognize reconciliation as a long-term process that requires ongoing efforts of empowerment, confrontation, pain, dialogue, exchange, experimentation, risk-taking, the building of common values, and identity transformation, then the TRC's work might be evaluated more favorably.

The TRC did help certain groups articulate their views. It engaged people in a renewed debate about options for the future—how to deepen the experience of community at various social levels. However, this process generated conflict. Rather than leading to greater unity, disagreements about what reconciliation means and what an appropriate process would be, have led to greater visibility of differences and increased tension. It was a lot easier for institutions to deal with the demands of individual victims than with more outspoken collective voices. The sacrifices needed from all sides in the conflict have been more clearly spelled out, and the journey toward reconciliation is recognized as one that will not be achieved through a miracle or act of grace.

The TRC has clearly provided victims with a channel for expressing their pain, anger, needs, and demands. In some communities this was a once-off experience. The TRC's intervention elicited wide and enthusiastic interest, victims became organized and vocalized their concerns, and to some extent challenged the power structures that they saw as becoming complacent. The disappointment that followed the TRC's exit from the community—the lack of investigations of perpetrators, the lack of follow-up on the concerns of victims, and a perception of having been used—induced cynicism and left little enthusiasm for further pursuit of reconciliatory goals.

In other communities the victims and other groupings have managed to sustain an organized voice. Other initiatives emerged that did not rely purely on the TRC to address these concerns. The latter provided one input that spurred mobilization or facilitated clearer articulation of needs and ideas. It also provided legitimacy for certain voices, goals, strategies, and values. People subsequently looked at other initiatives to take this process along similar trajectories but with greater sensitivity for local particularities.

The decision by political parties in South Africa to establish the TRC rather than provide a blanket amnesty or set up a war crimes tribunal appears to have been widely supported. It created, however, the illusion that people were united on what this approach was about—its basic conception, goals, and implementation. Rather than demonstrating a certain unanimity amongst different sectors, it may have been an indication of how different actors managed to read their own interpretation of reconciliation into the legislation.

Instead of resolving the conflict around issues of justice, perhaps the TRC mainly just succeeded in containing the most explosive disputes through the legislative institutionalization of a framework to regulate the settlement of disputes relating to human rights abuses of the past. As part of its process of regulation, it also allowed space (and incentives) for different groups (political parties, victims, etc.) to engage with the underlying issues related to reconciliation. It thus almost acted as a lightning rod by attracting controversy, and in this process provided a forum for the articulation of different views about the basis of the new social and moral order that is envisioned by these groups.[31] In terms of viewing the TRC as a reconciliation process, it may thus be most constructive to regard it as a starting point, a vehicle that has managed to bring out the various viewpoints, values, needs, and interests and put them on the table. The actual decisions made by the TRC (granting amnesty, declaring particular individuals to be human rights victims, writing an account of past abuses) are a very small component of a long-term reconciliation process in a country that has undergone much violent conflict, and which still experiences so many divisions, structural inequalities, and severe underdevelopment.

If reconciliation is seen as not simply resolving particular ruptures in relationships that need repair, but rather as a process of building a society's capacity to reconstruct relationships in an ongoing way, the TRC may be seen as a starting point in the creation of a new culture of storytelling, and articulation of values and needs by groups at all levels of society.

This cultural transformation is, however, far from secure. Some of its benefits have been demonstrated, and certain groups in society have engaged with it. It is not necessarily a process that has been accepted as something with general application to other arenas of conflict or division. The mechanisms for implementing such cultural practices are also not in place.

Because of all the controversy around the operation of the TRC, the lessons (both positive and negative) that have come out of it need to be clearly articulated in the public mind so that the TRC model is not simply copied or rejected when looking at further reconciliation initiatives. The basic principles of story-telling and restorative justice have been part of NGO practice in South Africa for some time. The TRC appears to have given such processes greater legitimacy and public recognition.

Much of the burden for future reconciliation initiatives now rests on NGOs and church structures. Most have been involved in this kind of work for many years. The TRC has changed the playing field in subtle ways, introducing both new opportunities and new obstacles. One thing, however, that many of these facilitators of reconciliation complain about is that the TRC did not engage them sufficiently in its work. The TRC, in its attempts to be evenhanded, distanced itself from civil society organizations that had been aligned with the antiapartheid movement. The fear is now that it will be difficult to pick up where the TRC left off because of the lack of coordination between these role players.

Conclusion: A Few Lessons about Community Reconciliation

Victims are individuals with unique experiences and needs. Each victim has to go through a personal journey of dealing with the past. Similarly each community has a unique history of conflict. There were common dimensions that existed all over the country, but the particular shape and intracommunity dynamics took on many different forms. A reconciliation process needs to address these individual and community-specific histories.

A single uniform national process is only capable of sketching a skeletal picture of community histories in broad terms. If left at that, it is in danger of minimizing the importance of dealing with particular issues when trying to squeeze the history of the community into standard categories of meaning. A national process can draw attention to some of the dynamics and pressures that impact on a local community, but it does not "explain" the local history.

The violence experienced in these communities contained many dimensions, and inflicted deep damage on numerous social relations. While the main dimension of the conflict may have been between the oppressed black population and the state, this conflict was fought in various covert ways that undermined and coopted sections of the population and created internal divisions that require dedicated remedial attention. Different forms of suffering were given different levels of recognition and priority by the TRC. People were victimized in different ways and thus have different needs in terms of reparations and social and physical reconstruction. These different interests often compete with one another and can lead to new conflicts within the community.

While the TRC focused largely on black-white divisions, community members felt that this was not a central issue when looking at gross human rights violations. Most of the violence experienced by members of black communities was at the hands of other blacks. Whites featured only indirectly in some stories as the ones giving the instructions for abuses. Community members were generally more focused on local perpetrators in their community. They were very aware of the need to address racial divisions in society, but saw these more in the light of socioeconomic divisions (rather than gross human rights violations as defined by the TRC). While the TRC was distressed by the lack of white attendance at the hearings, for the communities concerned this was not a serious setback, as the stories about gross human rights violations were about intracommunal divisions. Reconciliation initiatives aimed at bridging the racial divide experienced in local communities would thus have to examine different forms of victimization, and not simply focus on past violence.

A significant division has emerged between the population and the political structures. Victims in particular seem to feel alienated from the political system. They do not feel that their needs are taken seriously by any of the political leaders. In extreme cases, victims see the political structures as "perpetrator structures" representing the interests of ex-combatants and potential amnesty applicants within their ranks. Thus, when the TRC consulted with the community via the political structures, it meant, from a victim's perspective, that they were consulting with the perpetrators rather than the victims.

A longer-term reconciliation initiative would thus need to take the consultation process two steps further. It needs to engage with less developed community structures or networks that do not have a formal voice. Particularly in communities with a history of intense conflict, certain interest groups may not have organized and mobilized because of fear and/or because of lack of resources. Unless these interests are helped to acquire a voice, the process will not reach all sectors of the community. Victims need to be empowered to continue to speak out. Their voices are often seen as threatening by established power structures, and they will thus not be heard effectively unless a process is designed that specifically ensures their participation. In addition, the agenda for reconciliation should be open ended, not circumscribed by a specific interpretation of the conflict such as the racial divisions under apartheid, or by a focus on only narrowly defined gross human rights violations.

Local processes also need to give greater scope for the complexity of victim and perpetrator identities. Many of those who approached the TRC as amnesty applicants were also victims of human rights abuses. Similarly many of those who testified as victims had also played an active role in the conflict, and were at times perceived by other groups to be the perpetrators of abuses. By categorizing people as victim or perpetrator, and then allocating separate procedures for their participation in a reconciliation process, the complexity of the situation is denied, and a simplistic, distorted understanding of the past is perpetuated.

Communities need to be engaged in creating their own agenda for reconciliation, and designing processes that allow local stakeholders to drive the process. The example of the TRC can help provide a general model to communities in South Africa regarding how the issue of past human rights abuses can be pursued in much greater depth. Local processes that engage with specific local concerns are needed in taking the process forward. National support for such local processes is essential. A serious commitment at the national political level to transparency, victim support, and a commitment to prosecution of perpetrators of human rights violations would be key elements in supporting local reconciliation initiatives. Top-down and bottom-up processes are both essential for a more sustainable long-term reconciliation process. They should, however, be pursued in a complementary fashion rather than at the expense of one another.

Endnotes

1. This chapter relies largely on research conducted during 1997 in Duduza and Katorus, two communities on the East Rand. It also draws extensively from ongoing research and intervention work by the Centre for the Study of Violence and Reconciliation (CSVR) in numerous communities throughout South Africa over the last four years. The research was made possible partially through funding provided by the United States Institute of Peace for the author's Ph.D. dissertation (Hugo van der Merwe, "The Truth and Reconciliation Commission and Community Reconciliation: An Analysis of Competing Conceptualizations and Strategies" [George Mason University, Virginia, 1999]).

2. See, for example, the discussion of different levels of reconciliation in the *Truth and Reconciliation Commission of South Africa Report*, vol. 1 (Cape Town, Juta, 1998), chapter 5, 107.

3. The TRC was run by seventeen commissioners appointed by President Nelson Mandela. Under the chairmanship of Bishop Desmond Tutu, they were the main decision-making authority. They were each appointed to one of three committees that comprised the Commission: the Amnesty Committee, the Human Rights Violations Committee, and the Rehabilitation and Reparations Committee.

4. While I am very critical of the TRC's role at community level, its positive role in many other regards must be acknowledged. While it did make an important contribution to national reconciliation, this chapter argues that this might sometimes have been done at the expense of progress at the local level.

5. Interview with Willie Hofmeyr, chair of the Parliamentary Portfolio Committee on Justice, 3 March 1998.

6. The guarantee of amnesty was included in the Constitution on the insistence of the National Party. Without this concession, it seems, they would not have relinquished power to a democratically elected government.

7. See also Hugo van der Merwe, Polly Dewhirst, and Brandon Hamber, "Non Governmental Organisations and the Truth and Reconciliation Commission: An Impact Assessment," *Politikon* 26/1 (May 1999): 55–79.

8. The Promotion of National Unity and Reconciliation Act No 34 (1995), Section 3(1).

9. While not arguing that the legislation should have been completely prescriptive, what needs to be noted is that the Act provided extensive leeway for the Commission to take on an enormously broad range of tasks. It thus made the process vulnerable to extensive internal disagreements and conflicts among the public regarding what people could legitimately expect from the TRC.

10. The question of what is considered significant was itself controversial, as is explained later in this chapter.

11. Interview with TRC commissioner A, June 1997.

12. Interview with TRC commissioner B, June 1997.

13. Interview with TRC commissioner A, June 1997.

14. Ibid.

15. Ibid.

16. Interview with TRC staff member A, May 1997.

17. Interviews with TRC commissioner C, June and July 1997.

18. Some community leaders interviewed, particularly those from the Inkatha Freedom Party, did support top-down approaches to reconciliation. These are discussed in more detail in Van der Merwe, "The TRC and Community Reconciliation."

19. Interview with TRC staff member B, August 1997.

20. Interview with TRC staff member C, May 1997.

21. Interview with TRC staff member B, August 1997.

22. Interview with community leader in Duduza, June 1997.

23. Interview with community leader A in Katorus, September 1997.

24. Interview with community leader B in Katorus, September 1997.

25. Interview with ex-combatant in Katorus, September 1997.

26. Interview with victim in Duduza, April 1997.

27. Interview with community leader in Duduza, October 1997.

28. Interview with NGO staff member, June 1997.

29. Interview with community leader B in Katorus, September 1997.

30. Interview with ex-combatant in Katorus, September 1997.

31. A survey conducted in 1998, for example, found that most South Africans felt that the TRC had contributed to racial tension ("Most believe truth body harmed race relations, survey finds," *Business Day*, 27 July 1988).

CHAPTER 7

❧

Putting the Past in Its Place: Issues of Victimhood and Reconciliation in Northern Ireland's Peace Process

Marie Smyth

Since the late 1960s, out of a population of one and a half million in Northern Ireland, three and a half thousand have been killed in the political upheavals locally referred to as "the Troubles." Official records show that over forty thousand people have been injured in the same period, and by March 1995, the British government had paid £814,219,000 in personal injuries compensation, with a further £300,516,000 paid for damages to property.[1] In comparison to other conflicts, Northern Ireland's Troubles are described as "low intensity" with an overall death rate of 2.25 per thousand population, comparable with the Middle East or South Africa, and worse than Turkey (0.57) and Argentina (0.32). On the other hand, El Salvador (20.25) had almost ten times the death rate, and Cambodia (237.02), where about a quarter of the population died, had a death rate almost a hundred times greater than that of Northern Ireland.[2] Yet, as Frankl points out:

[S]uffering completely fills the human soul and conscious mind, no matter whether the suffering is great or little. Therefore the "size" of human suffering is absolutely relative.[3]

It is to this "filling of the human soul and conscious mind" and to the other aspects of its past that Northern Ireland, now, poised as it is on the edge of peace, struggles to address itself. This chapter will delineate some of the issues surrounding victimhood as a result of the conflict in Northern Ireland, particularly issues of definition and contested views of victimhood.[4] These will be discussed in the context of assessing the prospects for the emergence of strategies to manage the past and for the development of a reconciled account of that past.

Definitions of Victimhood

In one sense, all residents of Northern Ireland—and many beyond—have been affected by the cumulative effects of three decades of violence. Many people who have lived through Northern Ireland's Troubles do indeed have some sense of themselves being harmed by the events of the last thirty years, and many harbor a festering anger at various political players or institutions. Many fear a return to violence, and do not yet trust that political difference can be managed in a nonviolent manner. Many have a strong sense of the harm done to others who were bereaved, injured, or suffered human rights violations. Such harm, done to a member of one or other community, takes on a wider significance in violently divided societies such as Northern Ireland. It is perceived as a harm to every member of that community. Anger, fear, and grievance are public and communal, while perhaps only long-term grief and most forms of remorse are relegated to the private sphere.

The negotiation of this terrain is rendered even more difficult, since within the politics of Northern Ireland the cultures of contemporary loyalism and republicanism are cultures of victimhood.[5] Both loyalist and republican paramilitaries have referred to their status as victims in order to justify their recourse to armed conflict. Loyalists invoke their victimization at the hands of the IRA, whereas republicans invoke their victimization by British imperialism and loyalist sectarianism. The status of victim renders the victim deserving of sympathy, support, outside help, and intervention by others in order to vanquish the victimizer. Victims, by definition, are vulnerable, and any violence on their part can be construed as the consequences of the victimization process and the responsibility of the victimizer. It is a phenomenon observable elsewhere, that those who have participated in the violence of the past, particularly those who have killed and injured others, themselves lay claim to victimhood. Without such a status, their violence becomes too naked, politically inexplicable, and morally indefensible. The acquisition of the status of victim becomes an institutionalized way of escaping guilt, shame, or responsibility.

Political violence has pervasive effects, not merely on those that are injured or killed. Social and political institutions in Northern Ireland have been shaped by the divisions within the society and have adjusted themselves in response to ongoing violent conflict. The cultures of denial and silence that prevailed within such institutions during the years of conflict remain.[6] In that sense these institutions, too, can be regarded as "victims" of the conflict.

In 1997 the British government appointed a Victims Commissioner, Sir Kenneth Bloomfield, to report on the situation of victims and eventually set up a unit (the Victims Liaison Unit) in the Northern Ireland Office to coordinate their affairs. Bloomfield, reporting on the human costs of the Troubles, found "some substance in the argument that no one living in Northern Ireland through this most unhappy period will have escaped some degree of damage."[7] Whilst the experience of grievance may be widespread, definitions of victimhood such as those used by Bloomfield do not facilitate the targeting of humanitarian resources at those worst affected, nor the development of social policy to address the suffering caused by the violence of the past. Such practical concerns have moved to the foreground as political agreement has been achieved, and the Bloomfield Report refers to the need of the Victims Commission "to aim its effort at a coherent and manageable target group."[8] Issues of definition have become central: overinclusive definitions equate the enormous suffering of some with the lesser suffering of others, thereby creating further grievance.

The Contested Nature of Victimhood

From early in the Northern Ireland peace process, the contested nature of victimhood emerged. To begin with, inclusive definitions, relying on human suffering as the qualification for victim status, were used, notably by Bloomfield. This inclusivity posed challenges to those who had to countenance the inclusion of those from the community that had harmed them in the same "victim" category as themselves. Tentative, and eventually more confident, alliances that crossed the sectarian divide were formed between those who had suffered.[9] Yet it was not sectarian division that, in the end, posed the most difficulty for unity among those bereaved and injured in the Troubles. The main fault line was to form, not along the politico-religious divide, but between those who supported and those who opposed the Good Friday Agreement. Attempts to draw distinctions between categories of victims became more marked following the intensification of the activities of the anti-Agreement lobby. The terms "innocent" and "real" were used by some groups as a means to exclude others from the category of genuine victimhood.

A growing number of new voluntary groups—for example, FAIR (Families Acting for Innocent Relatives) and HURT (Homes United by Republican Terror, later changed to Homes United by Recurring Terror)—began to be formed from mid-1998 onward. Many of these groups sprang up in the border regions, where deaths in local security forces had been highest. Many of these groups adopted "exclusive" approaches, claiming to represent "victims of terrorism," "innocent victims," or "victims of Nationalist terror." Their activities mainly consisted of meeting politicians and voicing opposition to prisoner releases. By November 1998, FAIR had been invited to join the Touchstone Group, a group established at Bloomfield's recommendation to advise the government on victim issues; but in the end, they did not take up their seats. From another quarter, pressure was applied to the government's Victims Liaison Unit to include prisoners in their remit; but, thanks to lobbying by the new victim groups, this has become increasingly unlikely.

Toward a Common View of the Past

It is unavoidable that priorities must be defined, and resources allocated to those who have suffered most. But since there are competing claims for priority, the requisite decision making must be informed by some universally agreed understanding of the different effects of the Troubles on different sections of population of Northern Ireland and beyond. An indiscriminate definition of victims conceals the way in which damage and loss has been concentrated in certain locations and communities. Since no one can rely on his or her necessarily subjective assessment of the damage done, it is necessary to find a way of achieving an approximate consensus that discriminates in terms of age, location, gender, and so on.

The distribution of deaths caused by the Northern Ireland conflict has been used as an indicator of the impact of the Troubles. This is a relatively unequivocal measure, and although it raises some definitional issues,[10] it does appear to be the least problematic concept. It also serves as a reasonably good surrogate for other effects of the Troubles, such as injury[11]; and the death rate of specific geographical locations is correlated with other conflict-related factors, such as reported exposure to Troubles-related violence and its psychosocial consequences.[12] The number of deaths per annum shows a correlation coefficient of .93 when compared with the annual number of injuries associated with the Troubles. Deaths and injuries can be seen as the primary human cost of the Troubles, and although injuries outnumber deaths by approximately ten to one, they follow the same patterns of distribution in the population. Therefore, the distribution of deaths can be used as an indicator for targeting intervention and associated resources.

An Overview of the Troubles

This overview is drawn from a comprehensive database of deaths due to the Troubles between 1969 and 1998. The database was constructed as part of The Cost of the Troubles Study, and its construction and analysis is described in greater detail elsewhere.[13]

Deaths over Time

The early 1970s saw the highest death rates of any of the thirty years of the Troubles. In 1972, a total of 497 people died, making it the year of the largest number of fatalities. Just over half of all deaths in the Troubles occurred in the period 1971–76. In terms of the intensity of the conflict, these five years stand out over the entire three decades. After 1976, the number of deaths in any one year never again reached the same level (125) and in only seven years was it greater than 100. Data on injuries follows a similar pattern, with almost a third of all injuries suffered between 1972 and 1977. Alterations in security policies and changes in military and paramilitary strategies meant that, by the late 1990s, the Troubles had settled into what became known as "an acceptable level of violence."

There are several implications of this distribution of deaths over time. First, those generations of the population that experienced the conflict of the 1970s have an experience of intense conflict that subsequent generations lack. When these older generations assess the level of conflict, the spectrum of intensity used by them is broader than that available to younger people.

Secondly, those generations who lived through the earlier phases of the conflict have a greater cumulative experience of the Troubles; in terms of dealing with the past, they have not only more past but also more extreme experiences of it to deal with.

Time and the Perception of Threat

Time, and therefore age, are also factors in forming perceptions about which of the various armed groups are most responsible for deaths in the Troubles. Forty percent of the deaths (452) perpetrated by loyalist paramilitaries occurred between 1974 and 1976; and 47 percent of all the deaths caused by republican paramilitaries occurred between 1971 and 1976. The years 1971–73 saw the most proactive security activity by the British Army, indicated by the number and share of the total deaths due to them in the last five months in 1971 and all of 1972 and 1973. Just over half of all deaths caused by the British Army (163 or 51.6 percent) occurred between 1971 and 1973 compared to 15.3 percent (7 deaths) attributable to the Royal Ulster Constabulary (RUC). Republican and loyalist paramilitaries were responsible for even larger numbers of deaths during this period (502 and 216, respectively), although the peaks of paramilitary activity came later.

Again, perceptions of the relative roles of the various armed groups are likely to be shaped according to experience, which varies over time. For example, those who experienced the early 1970s are more likely to perceive the security forces as the greater threat to life than subsequent generations.

Cause of Death

Overall, firearms accounted for approximately 60 percent of all deaths, followed by explosion, which accounted for approximately 30 percent. Deaths caused by explosions were concentrated in the 1970s, whereas those by shooting were fairly evenly distributed across the entire period. The predominance of death by firearms in the Troubles casts some light on the pressure during the peace process for the decommissioning of weapons, and of firearms especially. The concentration of deaths due to explosions in the early 1970s again points to variations between generations of the kinds of injuries sustained.

Status of Persons Killed

In common with contemporary conflict in other parts of the world, it has been civilians, rather than any of the armed groups (including the security forces), that make up the largest category of deaths. Civilians account for over half of those killed. Overall, deaths among the security forces make up an additional 30 percent of all deaths, and those among members of paramilitary organizations make up 16 percent. The pattern is similar for injuries, with the proportion of the total injured who are security force personnel standing at around 30 percent.

These proportions vary according to geographical location, so that in some areas in Northern Ireland, local experience does not follow the overall Northern Ireland pattern. For example, in Dungannon, whilst 42 percent of victims were civilian, a larger share (46 percent) had an association with the security forces; and 20.4 percent of these were members of the Ulster Defence Regiment. The security forces thus contributed the largest single percentage of those who died in the Dungannon area. Members of republican paramilitaries make up the rest of the Dungannon victims, whilst there does not appear to be a single member of a loyalist paramilitary among them. This pattern is unique to the Dungannon area. Yet local experience, even though it belies the overall Northern Ireland pattern, is likely to be the most powerful in shaping perceptions of the Troubles.

Overall in Northern Ireland, the percentage of civilian deaths varied not only geographically, but over time, falling in the period 1972–73 during the postinternment violence, and rising again in 1974–76 with an increase in the number of bombings and sectarian attacks. The share of civilian deaths increased again in the 1990s, although this was partly due to the drop in levels of security forces casualties. Again, different generations and those in different locations will have formed different perceptions about which category—civilian, security forces, or paramilitary—has been most at risk.

Gender

Those killed in the Troubles have been overwhelmingly male (91.1 percent). Gender aspects of the conflict are highly significant, since Northern Ireland is a society highly segregated by gender. The world of formal politics and paramilitarism is predominantly male, particularly on the unionist/loyalist side, whilst the job of supporting prisoners, rearing children alone, grieving the dead, and working in the community is female. Men and women, therefore, have radically different experiences of the Troubles, and although they report similar stress levels,[14] the consequences of the Troubles have been differentiated by gender.

Age

Disproportionate numbers of younger people of both genders have died in the Troubles. More than a third of those killed were in their twenties, with over half in their twenties or thirties, and one in six victims age 19 or less. The death risk to the 20-to-24 age group was more than twice as high as that to any group over 40. Just under a quarter of all victims was age 21 or less and another half was age 22 to 39. Almost three-fourths of those who died were under the age of 40. This is perhaps one of the few areas where perceptions throughout Northern Ireland are consistent: young people have been generally perceived as being at greater risk. This may explain differences in younger and older people's estimations of the risks involved in crossing the sectarian divide.

Religion or Ethnopolitical Differences

Each community uses the religious (or ethnopolitical) breakdown of deaths in the Troubles (Table 7.1) to support its own claim to greater suffering and to undermine the other's. As a result, this is one of the most sensitive breakdowns of data on Troubles-related deaths. In the original data, religion was not recorded for victims from outside Northern Ireland, who are shown in Table 7.1 as "Non-Northern Ireland" (NNI). Nor did the data identify the religious affiliation of a large proportion of those killed among Northern Ireland's security forces, which explains the bulk of the "not known" category.

Table 7.1. Distribution of Deaths by Religion

Religion	Frequency	Valid %
Unknown	333	9.2
Protestant	1065	29.6
Catholic	1548	43.0
Non-Northern Ireland (NNI)	655	18.2
Total	3601	100.0

More Catholics than Protestants have died in the Troubles. Furthermore, given the smaller proportion of Catholics in the general population, Catholics have a higher death rate than Protestants. The significance of this will be explored later.

The local security forces—the Royal Ulster Constabulary and the former Ulster Defence Regiment (now the Royal Irish Rangers)—are known to be 92 percent Protestant. Their deaths were recorded in the "not known" category. Security forces' deaths in the "not known" category can therefore be redistributed between the two religious groups. Furthermore, death rates can be calculated per thousand of the population, giving a more accurate reading of the impact of deaths on each community. Death rates can take into account changes in the relative size of the Catholic and Protestant populations of Northern Ireland by calculating the rate from the base of either the 1991 Census of Population, or from an average of the 1971, 1981, and 1991 censuses. These results are shown in Table 7.2.

Columns 2 and 3 of Table 7.2 show the death rates for Protestants and Catholics calculated from the base of the 1991 census only. Columns 4 and 5 show the rate if it is calculated using a base of the average of the population figures in the three censuses, since the deaths occurred over a period in which there were changes in the religious balance of the population in Northern Ireland.

In the body of Table 7.2, the Civilians row shows death rates for Catholic and Protestant civilians only. Using the 1991 census figures alone, the rate is 2.48 per thousand for Catholics compared with 1.46 per thousand for Protestants. Using the average of the three censuses, the rate is 3.01 per thousand for Catholics compared with 1.26 per thousand for Protestants.

However, to exclude security forces' deaths is to omit a cohort of deaths that is largely Protestant, as discussed above. Since the religious affiliation of

Table 7.2. Death Rates by Religion (per 1,000 Population)

	1991 Census		Average 1971, 1981, and 1991 censuses	
	Catholic	Protestant	Catholic	Protestant
Civilians	2.48	1.46	3.01	1.26
Civilians plus security	2.5	1.9	3.1	1.6
Excluding "own" deaths	1.9	1.6	2.3	1.4

substantial numbers of these deceased had not been recorded, the death rates by religion have been recalculated, attributing "Protestant" identity to a proportion of cases in accordance with the known religious composition of the security forces. The Civilians plus security row in Table 7.2 shows that, using the 1991 census figures alone, the rate then becomes 2.5 per thousand for Catholics compared with 1.9 per thousand for Protestants. Using the average of the three censuses, the rate becomes 3.1 per thousand for Catholics compared with 1.6 per thousand for Protestants.

In the last row, all deaths that were attributable to perpetrators within the same community as the victim—all Catholics killed by republican paramilitaries and all Protestants killed by loyalist paramilitaries—were removed. The new figures show only deaths due to the "other" community, and gives a new rate, using the 1991 census figures alone—1.9 per thousand for Catholics compared with 1.6 per thousand for Protestants. Using the average of the three censuses, the rate becomes 2.3 per thousand for Catholics compared with 1.4 per thousand for Protestants.

The risk for the two groups varied substantially over time. Between 1969 and 1976 (using 1971 census figures) the Catholic death risk was more than twice that of Protestants, whereas this was reversed between 1977 and 1986. In the final period of the Troubles, the risk for Catholics was about 50 percent greater. Again, this has implications for perceptions of the Troubles; for example, Catholics with experience of the early period will be more inclined to overstate the overall risk to Catholics than younger Catholics.

That there have been more deaths (in both relative and absolute terms) in the Catholic community than in the Protestant one, does not necessarily accord with the subjective assessments of many observers of the Troubles. Why this is so becomes apparent when the issue of responsibility for killings is examined.

Responsibility for Deaths

Paramilitary organizations were responsible for the largest share—eighty percent—of all deaths, as Table 7.3 shows. Furthermore, republican paramilitaries were responsible for over half of all deaths. The categories of "republican" and "loyalist" paramilitaries each cover a number of different organizations. Within the republican grouping, the IRA (formerly the Provisional IRA) was responsible for the largest number of deaths (1,684 or

Table 7.3. Organizations Responsible for Deaths

Organization responsible	Frequency	Valid percentage
Republican paramilitaries	2001	55.7
Loyalist paramilitaries	983	27.4
British Army	318	8.9
UDR	11	0.3
RUC	53	1.5
Civilian	11	0.3
Other	216	6.0
Total	3593	100.0

eighty-five percent of all deaths attributed to republican paramilitaries). Other republican organizations killed substantially fewer people; for instance, the factions associated with the Irish National Liberation Army (INLA) killed 127 people. It was not possible to attribute accurately all the deaths due to loyalist paramilitaries to the particular loyalist organizations, so 449 deaths were simply attributed overall to loyalist organizations. Of these, 254 were attributable to the Ulster Volunteer Force (UVF) and 177 to the Ulster Freedom Fighters (UFF).

In terms of the ratio of those killed within an organization to those killed by them, republican paramilitaries killed five and a half other individuals for each of their members who died, whereas loyalist paramilitaries killed eight and a half. The equivalent statistic for the British army was just over half a person, and for the Royal Ulster Constabulary just less than a sixth of a person.

It emerges, therefore, that although Catholic deaths account for a greater share of deaths than Protestant ones, and the Catholic death rate is higher, republican paramilitaries carry responsibility for the majority of deaths. This suggests that not all killings were sectarian (since many of those killed by republicans were Catholics), and that the picture is more complex than the stereotypical view of Catholics and Protestants killing each other. Perceptions about who poses the greatest threat to a community are explored in the light of Table 7.4, which shows deaths by religion according to organization responsible.

The largest share of Protestant deaths has been caused by republican organizations, which are responsible for seventy percent of the total. If the "Unknown" category is treated as before (i.e., if ninety-two percent

Table 7.4. Deaths by Religion by Organization Responsible

Organization reponsible	Unknown	%	Protestant	%	Catholic	%	Non-Northern Ireland (NNI)	%
Republican paramilitaries	278	83.5	745	70.0	381	24.7	597	91.4
Loyalist paramilitaries	25	7.5	207	19.5	735	47.6	16	2.5
British Army	4	1.2	32	3.0	266	17.2	16	2.5
UDR			4	0.4	7	0.5		
RUC	1	0.3	7	0.7	43	2.8	2	0.3
Civilian			9	0.8	2	0.1		
Other	25	7.5	60	5.6	109	7.1	22	3.4
Total	333	100.0	1064	100.0	1543	100.0	653	100.0

are regarded as Protestant), then republican paramilitaries have been responsible for over eighty percent of all Protestant deaths in the Troubles. Conversely, almost half of Catholic deaths are attributable to loyalist paramilitary activity, with over one-fifth of Catholic deaths caused by security force activity, in which the British army played the most significant role. Thus, Table 7.4 tends to support the perceptions of each of the two communities that paramilitaries on the other side constitute the greatest threat to them.

However, the next largest threat to each community comes from paramilitaries on their own side. The size of this threat is shown in Table 7.4. Almost one-fifth of all Protestant deaths are the responsibility of loyalist paramilitaries, while over one-fourth of all Catholic deaths were due to the activities of republican paramilitaries. This last figure is partially explained by the republican bombing campaign, in which city center bombs killed random civilians, many of whom happened to be Catholic. Republican paramilitaries have been the most frequent cause of the deaths of other republicans, on account of feuds and the practice of executing informers. The British Army has been responsible for only slightly more than thirty percent of deaths of republican paramilitaries, whereas, in contrast, republican paramilitaries themselves have been responsible for almost all of the deaths among the security forces. Every armed organization responsible for deaths in the Troubles has killed more civilians than any other category of victim, whilst the paramilitaries who claim to defend their own community have in fact been a significant source of deaths within them. Once again, we can see here major divergences between common perception and empirical reality.

Localization of Deaths and Fatal Incidents

When analyzing the data about deaths according to location, two measures have been used: first, the number of deaths occurring within an area; and second, the ratio of deaths to the number of residents of the area. In both cases, the rate was calculated per thousand population. There is wide variation in the rate of fatal incidents, between, for example, Belfast (4.69 per thousand) and Ards (0.12 per thousand). This wide regional variation illustrates how experience of the Troubles has been concentrated in particular locations, whilst others have remained relatively untouched. The overall death rate for Northern Ireland is 2.2 per thousand. Belfast, Newry and Mourne, Derry, Armagh, Dungannon, and Craigavon have been the most affected in terms of absolute numbers of fatal incidents. In both absolute and relative terms the greatest intensity of Troubles-related deaths has been experienced in Belfast, where the rate per thousand population is almost twice as high as the next highest district, Armagh.

Elsewhere death rates calculated for postal districts show how particular parts of Belfast (particularly North and West Belfast), Derry/Londonderry, South Armagh, and "Mid Ulster" have experienced high intensities of violence.[15]

In summary, according to this empirical picture of the Troubles, suffering has not been evenly distributed geographically, nor indeed according to gender, religion, status, or age. For this reason it is not possible to generalize from a particular experience to that of other localities, other groups, or Northern Ireland as a whole. Perhaps one of the most problematic features of the Northern Ireland conflict is precisely this tendency to generalize from local experiences, especially local experiences of loss. Appreciation of the diversity of experiences of the Troubles is still in its infancy.

The Contribution of Empirical Data

Different perceptions of the suffering caused by the Troubles would agree that it has not been evenly distributed. However, these perceptions may well be at variance with the conclusions drawn from the empirical data as to where the ill effects have been concentrated. Attention to this divergence, and an attempt to reach an agreed communal assessment of the damage done by the Troubles, would be an important first step toward a common strategy for dealing with the legacy of the past. In this way, the achievement of a reconciliation of perceptions could be of practical use in forming policy for addressing the needs of those affected by the conflict.

Our argument is that empirical data are useful in identifying the actual areas of greatest damage, thus informing public policy priorities for humanitarian intervention in a manner that transcends sectarian perceptions. Empirical data often challenge biased perceptions of Northern Ireland's Troubles; and this is a useful service to the development of a new negotiated account of our collective past.

The Role of Victims in Reconciliation

Those who have endured great suffering, such as Holocaust survivors, are popularly cast in a role that is described by Lawrence Thomas as that of potential or actual "moral beacons" for a wider constituency.[16] This is because of what Thomas calls "the principle of Job"; namely, the widespread assumption that "great suffering carries in its wake deep moral knowledge."[17]

Such persons are often held up, implicitly or explicitly, as instances of a higher state or examples of a feat of self-transformation. If they can forgive the great injuries inflicted on them, then those who have suffered less have little justification for persistent grievance. In Northern Ireland, Gordon Wilson, whose daughter was killed by the IRA bomb at Enniskillen, was a recent example of such a moral beacon. He was forgiving of his daughter's killers and conciliatory in his political attitudes. Globally, Nelson Mandela has been cast in this role, through a focus on his victimization by imprisonment under apartheid and his subsequent political magnanimity.

Yet, not every victim is eligible for the role of moral beacon, according to Thomas. In the United States, African Americans, although qualified to be beacons by virtue of their suffering of slavery, tend not to be regarded as such, whilst Jews, particularly Holocaust survivors, are regarded in this light. Suffering per se is not a sufficient qualification.

This tendency to elect some and not others is manifest in Northern Ireland's Troubles. The widow of an alleged informer, the victim of punishment beatings, or the wife of a prisoner are unlikely to qualify as moral beacons, in spite of their suffering. One of the criteria of qualification seems to be that the suffering must be "undeserved" (according to dominant values). In societies divided by racism, sectarianism, or ethnic conflict, ambivalent attitudes toward the suffering of certain categories of people, and even blaming victims for their misfortunes are commonplace. One party to the conflict does not necessarily regard the suffering of the other party as problematic; for their suffering can be a sign of one's own triumph. The moral beacon, therefore, must reflect the dominant political values. This has been manifest in Northern Ireland in the attempt to qualify some victimhood as "innocent" or "real," in order to discount the suffering of certain bereaved or injured—an attempt that has gathered momentum through the enhanced political role of certain victims' groups.

Thomas's "principle of Job" is, of course, a popular assumption open to question. Is it safe to assume that suffering necessarily results in accelerated moral development, and therefore increases the sufferer's suitability for roles of moral leadership? Victor Frankl's observation of life in the death camps of World War II records how some prisoners collaborated, jeopardized others' lives, and cooperated with the regime in order to save themselves.[18] Suffering and oppression, it seems, can diminish as well as increase moral integrity. Elsewhere, experience of great suffering is also commonly used to explain subsequent violent behavior. C. Crawford, for example, found that thirty percent of loyalist prisoners he interviewed had had "members of their family" killed by the IRA or republicans[19]—although he does not specify the closeness of relationship assumed by his definition of "family." These prisoners' experience of bereavement, by implication, is taken to explain their subsequent taking up of arms.

Media representations of those bereaved and injured in Northern Ireland's Troubles have often encouraged the creation of "moral beacons." In interviews with the recently bereaved, journalists have been wont to ask immediate family members if they forgive the perpetrator—often within hours or days of the death. The bereaved person's response has then been presented as a moral benchmark by which viewers can gauge the degree of their own entitlement to revenge. Those closest to the loss, who are perceived to be most entitled to blame and seek revenge, thus become moral leaders of a sort.

Some politicians in Northern Ireland have sought to exploit this function of victims from time to time. Unassailable moral authority for a political cause can be acquired by reference to or by association with them. An example of this was the campaign for "Protestant civil rights," launched in the form of a "Long March" in 1999. The campaign incorporated many of the newly formed victims groups, who came together under an umbrella organization, Northern Ireland Terrorist Victims Together (NITVT). NITVT's campaign was for a range of demands, including a declaration by the IRA that the war is over; decommissioning, including the ballistic testing of weapons; the destruction of paramilitary weapons; the disbanding of terrorist groups; and an international tribunal to investigate the role of the Irish government in the development of the Provisional IRA. Politicians who opposed the Good Friday Agreement from the Democratic Unionist Party (DUP) and part of the Ulster Unionist Party (UUP) marched alongside members of these victim groups.

The mainstream UUP, too, at a point when members were balking at the prospect of going into government with Sinn Féin, used a similar strategy. The UUP supported Michelle Williamson, whose parents had been killed in the Shankill Road bomb in 1993, in going to court to obtain a judicial review of the secretary of state's ruling that the IRA cease-fire was being maintained. David Trimble (the UUP's leader) accompanied her to court. Had the ruling been overturned, Sinn Féin would have been excluded from the political process.

On the other hand, by the end of September 1999, Fraser Agnew, United Unionist Assembly Party member, resigned from the Long March campaign, saying, "I believe innocent victims are being manipulated and exploited for political ends. It's almost like emotional blackmail."

One further event concentrated focus on the issue of victims. On 20 August 1998, a massive explosion in the Omagh town center killed twenty-eight people; a twenty-ninth was to die later, as were two unborn children. The bomb had been planted by the self-styled Real IRA. Shock and revulsion overwhelmed the political process, and Omagh served to focus attention on the issue of victims for a considerable period. Ministerial visits to the town were followed by announcements of various public investments in the locality over subsequent months. The Omagh Fund was established, and fund-raising for it became widespread. The devastation caused by the bomb provided, for once, a clear focus for concern about victims. Furthermore, because politicians across the board were united in condemning the bombing, this concern was universal. It seemed reasonably clear what was needed in this case, and government and other public figures could do something positive about the so-called "victims' issue." The scale and immediacy of the suffering of people here served temporarily to sideline all other victims' concerns. It was as if caring for the victims of Omagh was somehow caring by proxy for the thousands of others who had suffered in isolation and without support.

As the political profile of the "victims issue" increased, attention was deflected from other parts of the humanitarian agenda. That, overall, it is the poorest people who have suffered most in the Troubles, that they live in communities blighted by militarism and deprivation, and that the overall amount of humanitarian assistance given to them has been paltry, was no longer a central matter of public concern. Omagh, then, provided a clearly defined opportunity for an outpouring of humanitarian aid, expressing universal concern about a group of people that could unequivocally be regarded as "innocent" and "real" victims.

Continuing attempts by politicians to hijack the victims issue have meant that progress on this matter, as with progress on many other issues in Northern Ireland, is at the mercy of politics. The chasm that originally yawned between unionists and nationalists, and that now increasingly yawns between those who support the Good Friday Agreement and those who do not, will determine the kind of attention that victims receive under the new Northern Ireland Assembly's government.

Unlike South Africa, Northern Ireland cannot anticipate a radical change in political dispensation in the near future. The situation is now, to use South African terms, as if the transitional Government of National Unity had become permanent. In Northern Ireland, the nature of the Agreement ensures bilateral decision making on a permanent basis. The nature of this arrangement, where no one "side" can take unilateral decisions on behalf of the entire government, has implications for the management of the past, issues of victimhood, and the process of reconciliation in Northern Ireland.

The widespread sense of suffering and grievance within Northern Irish society presents a range of practical and moral challenges to the prospect of peace building. The management of this aspect of the peace process has been conducted in various ways by different bodies. The voluntary sector has seen a sudden proliferation of interest in the provision of services to victims and their families. The media have begun to present various reviews of the suffering of the last thirty years. Some have called for a South African-style truth commission; others, for public inquiries into various deaths, especially when collusion between paramilitaries and security forces has been alleged or where the bodies of the disappeared have yet to be recovered. Unfinished business of different sorts, all the legacy of the last thirty years, has begun to be aired and sifted through again, this time with a heightened expectation of resolution. Now that the Troubles appear to be over, people want these things sorted out. Before moving on to a new chapter in history, the loose ends of the past require tying up. Justice, truth, healing, and closure are the desires expressed in much public discussion. Issues of reconciliation and forgiveness have been raised by outsiders and professional observers (but rarely, if ever, by local grassroots bodies).

Conferences about "managing the past" or "burying the past" have been staged, as if the difficulties and suffering caused by the Troubles were now mainly in the past. By thus conceptualizing the divisions between people, it has been possible to come together, albeit tentatively at first, to discuss them. Yet the bereaved relatives, the maimed bodies, the chronic pain of physical disablement, and the lost livelihoods—all the consequences of the past—continue in the present and will persist into the future.

In George Orwell's *1984*, the Party slogan was: "Who controls the past . . . controls the future; who controls the present controls the past."[20] The nature of the settlement in Northern Ireland means that no one agreed version of the past may ever emerge. In South Africa, the version that has emerged through the work of the Truth and Reconciliation Commission has been the version compatible with the overall orientation of the ruling African National Congress. In Northern Ireland, no one party or side will hold the power to determine the process of managing the past or unveiling the truth. Yet the Northern Ireland Assembly must manage the impact of the past on the present and thereby on the future. How should it do so? What methods, principles, and understandings should inform its management? And how will the appetite for truth, justice, closure, and healing be satisfied? The nature of its new government suggests that Northern Ireland will witness a less clear-cut, more self-contradictory, and more inconclusive process than has occurred in South Africa. The contents of that process have yet to be determined.

The Question of a Truth Commission

That contemporary loyalism and republicanism in Northern Ireland are cultures of victimhood has already been asserted. Throughout the peace process, calls for a truth commission have come from those who feel aggrieved at various armed groups. However, there is nothing to suggest that any of the armed parties to the conflict would participate in such a process, or that incentives are available that could persuade them to do so. The prospects for a truth commission in Northern Ireland are marred by a supply and demand problem: the demand for truth far outstrips supply. The successful institution of any truth commission process in Northern Ireland would depend, among other things, on a change in political culture—on a moving beyond competing claims to victimhood, and the creation of an atmosphere of political responsibility. It would also depend on the ability to provide incentives such as the prospect of amnesty to encourage the participation of the armed parties. Given the political furor amongst anti-Agreement politicians—unionists in particular—over the provision for the early release of prisoners, it is difficult to imagine unionists risking the further fracturing of their camp by supporting an offer of amnesty. Inquiries into particular incidents, such as "Bloody Sunday,"[21] are politically feasible (though fraught). Although some continue to advocate a truth commission for Northern Ireland, such a wholesale process does not yet seem possible.

Justice and Closure

The sense of injustice felt by different groups and individuals in Northern Ireland may, in the long run, prove the most serious obstacle to the achievement of peace. This sense of injustice springs from various sources. Some of it has been exacerbated by aspects of the peace process itself, such as the early release of paramilitary prisoners. From early on in the process, since both republican and loyalist parties had constantly voiced demands for the release of prisoners, it was clear that concessions to paramilitary prisoners would have to form part of any agreement. Prisoners themselves were crucial to the peace process, and their views were regularly sought—the secretary of state, Mo Mowlam, met with prisoners in January 1998, in order to encourage their support for the cease-fires and the peace process. The government anticipated that the sensitivities of the bereaved and injured would hinder the acceptability of the early release of prisoners. Consequently, in the early days of implementation many apologies were made to victims, invoking the larger goal of peace as justification. Yet some of the bereaved and injured were still unwilling to sacrifice what they considered to be justice—that prisoners should serve the full term of their sentences. The early release of prisoners, therefore, exacerbated these victims' sense of injustice.

Others' sense of injustice sprang from the lack of legal pursuit of the paramilitary perpetrators of injuries, or the lack of prosecutions. Meanwhile, those who had suffered at the hands of the security forces felt doubly denied justice, first in the original act and then in the lack of redress.

It is in the nature of political agreements that considerations of justice are sometimes placed lower in the list of priorities than the need to compromise. Where such decisions have been made, justice in individual cases may never be achieved, and some of those who have been made to relinquish their particular claims to justice have not done so willingly. Some advances have been made, such as in reopening certain controversial legal cases and in instituting public inquiries. It remains to be seen whether justice will thereby be achieved to the satisfaction of the victims or their families.

What is clear is that the goal of achieving justice and that of achieving closure or peace of mind can often be at odds with one another. For many, the reexposure of the wrongs of the past through public inquiry or other legal or public processes represents the reopening of old wounds, and the restimulation of traumatic and painful memories. Many have chosen to forgo their claim to justice in the interests of avoiding the pain of this process and achieving a different kind of closure, whilst others have found themselves unable to contemplate the prospect of any kind of peace without justice. While notorious cases such as that of Bloody Sunday, which have an iconic significance for one community, may be reopened in order to achieve a symbolic political solution as much as personal satisfaction, other lesser-known cases that do not hold such politically symbolic significance will undoubtedly be left unresolved. This has been so even in South Africa, where the Truth and Reconciliation Commission has been forced to operate representatively rather than comprehensively.

Healing

Finally, since the cease-fires there has been an upsurge in interest in attending to the damage done by the violence of the past. One tendency has been to pathologize this damage and see it exclusively in mental health terms, with counseling as the solution. The evidence is very clear that most of those who have suffered in the Troubles have had their main and most effective support from their immediate families, neighbors, and communities.[22] Where professionals are consulted it is likely to be the family doctor, who, particularly in the past, often offered medication as a means of coping. The demands on families and communities that have been the most affected by the Troubles have been heavy indeed, with some communities bearing a disproportionate burden of grief and loss over several decades. The issue of healing, therefore, is not just an individual or indeed a family issue. It is a community issue, with an individual and family aspect to it. In the past—and even in the post–cease-fire situation—support services have not been equipped to deal with the loss and grief caused by the Troubles. The culture of silence and denial that was once a "coping mechanism" for many continues to operate, rendering much potential support impotent. It is generally agreed that the retraining of many professionals is required, although it remains to be seen whether the resources to do so will be forthcoming. It is also clear that the proper resourcing of interventions is required, since most of those communities worst affected are also the poorest and most marginalized in the United Kingdom. Poverty compromises health in general terms, and healing from the wounds of the past requires an environment in which safety, respect, and willing and sympathetic listeners are available. This environment is beginning to be available to the few bereaved and injured who are able to avail themselves of the small number of services available in the voluntary sector. However, since May 1998, the government has spent only £5.25 million in this field, and has not announced any further funding. The galvanizing of political will is a prerequisite to further achievement here.

Conclusion

The widespread preoccupation with the past in Northern Ireland, due to an equally widespread sense of grievance and hurt, underpins the importance of understanding the insight articulated by Santayana: "Progress, far from consisting in change, depends on retentiveness. . . . Those who cannot remember the past are condemned to repeat it."[23] The past is often experienced as unmanageable. Individual and collective memories surface unbidden. A desire to suppress the past can be motivated not only by the desire to avoid pain, or to achieve reconciliation or accommodation with former enemies, but also by a desire to avoid responsibility, shame, and guilt. Whatever the motivation, burying the past in the sense of suppressing it is not a reliable strategy, as many elderly war criminals have discovered late in life. Things that lie buried do not necessarily decompose. Some take root and grow, only to resurface or be unearthed by former enemies, often when least expected.

In the light of such a widespread sense of victimhood, can reconciliation be achieved? Is reconciliation even necessary in order to achieve a long-lasting peace? Can people forgive even if they can't forget? Is it fair to ask people to forgive when regret and remorse have not always been expressed? And, in the long run, will a failure to attend to some of these issues in the present store up problems for the future? No one in Northern Ireland is yet in a position to answer these questions. The lessons from other societies, although often not easy to draw, are available to learn from. On the former Yugoslavia, Dubrevka Ugresic comments:

> In the fragmented country both real and psychological wars were waged simultaneously. Mortar shells, psychological and real, wiped out people, houses, cities, children, bridges, memory. In the name of the present, a war was waged for the past; in the name of the future, a war against the present. In the name of a new future, the war devoured the future. Warriors, the masters of oblivion, the destroyers of the old state and builders of new ones, used every possible strategic method to impose a collective amnesia. The self-proclaimed masters of life and death set up the co-ordinates of right and wrong, black and white, true and false.[24]

The majority of people in Northern Ireland have peered over the brink of full-scale civil war, and have sought to turn back. In that sense, the past and its losses are remembered painfully and with profit. For the present, perhaps respect for the diverse versions of the past is the best that can be achieved. Reconciliation, like forgiveness, is a gift, a miracle. Perhaps such grand miracles will be granted the people of Northern Ireland in the future. For now, most are content with the modest miracles of devolved government and power sharing.

Endnotes

1. K. Bloomfield, "We Will Remember Them: The Report of the Northern Ireland Victims Commissioner, Sir Kenneth Bloomfield" (Belfast: HMSO, 1998), 4.

2. See M.T. Fay, M. Morrissey, and M. Smyth, *Mapping Troubles-Related Deaths in*

Northern Ireland 1969–1999 (Derry/Londonderry: INCORE/United Nations University/University of Ulster, 1998), 44.

3. Viktor Frankl, "Experiences in a Concentration Camp," in *Man's Search for Meaning* (New York: Washington Square Press/Pocket Books, 1959), 64.

4. See also M. Smyth, "The Human Consequences of Armed Conflict: Constructing 'Victimhood' in the context of Northern Ireland's Troubles," in M. Cox and A. Guelke, *A Farewell to Arms? From War to Peace in Northern Ireland* (Manchester: Manchester University Press, 2000).

5. M. Smyth, "Remembering in Northern Ireland: Victims, Perpetrators and Hierarchies of Pain and Responsibility," in B. Hamber, ed., *Past Imperfect: Dealing with the Past in Northern Ireland and Societies in Transition* (Derry/Londonderry: INCORE, 1998).

6. See, for example, A. Healey, "Systemic Therapy in a Culture of Conflict: Developing a Therapeutic Conversation," *Child Care Practice* 3/1 (1996): 68–86.

7. Bloomfield, "We Will Remember Them," 14 (paragraph 2.13).

8. Ibid.

9. The Cost of the Troubles Study was organized by the author and involved members of both of the two main traditions in Northern Ireland who had been injured or bereaved by loyalist or republican paramilitaries or by the security forces. WAVE, the largest voluntary organization offering services to those affected by the Troubles, also operates on an explicitly cross-community basis.

10. See M. T. Fay, M. Morrissey, and M. Smyth, *Northern Ireland's Troubles: The Human Costs* (London: Pluto, 1999), 126–32.

11. Ibid., 136.

12. See M. T. Fay, M. Morrissey, M. Smyth, and T. Wong, *Report on the Northern Ireland Survey: The Experience and Impact of the Troubles,* The Cost of the Troubles Study (Derry/Londonderry: INCORE/United Nations University/University of Ulster, 1999), 67–79.

13. See Fay et al., *Northern Ireland's Troubles.*

14. See Fay et al., *Report on the Northern Ireland Survey*, 74.

15. See Fay et al., *Mapping Troubles-Related Deaths*, 74.

16. L. M. Thomas, "Suffering as a Moral Beacon: Blacks and Jews," in H. Flanzbaum, ed., *The Americanization of the Holocaust* (Baltimore: Johns Hopkins, 1999), 198–210.

17. Ibid., 204.

18. Frankl, *Man's Search for Meaning.*

19. C. Crawford, *Defenders of Criminals? Loyalist Prisoners and Criminalisation* (Belfast: Blackstaff, 1999), 132.

20. G. Orwell, *1984* (London: Secker & Warburg, 1949), Part 2, chapter 9.

21. The events referred to as "Bloody Sunday" occurred on 27 January 1972, when British Paratroopers fired live rounds into an illegal but otherwise peaceful civil rights march in Derry, killing thirteen people instantly, and wounding a fourteenth who died

later. Seventeen other people were injured. The Tribunal of Inquiry set up after these events under Lord Widgery exonerated the soldiers, and was regarded in the Catholic community as a "whitewash." More recent calls for a fresh inquiry, together with the publication by the Irish government of "Bloody Sunday and the Report of the Widgery Tribunal: The Irish Government's assessment of the new material, presented to the British Government in June 1997" (Dublin: Government Information Services, 1997), led to the establishment of a full-scale judicial inquiry later in 1998.

22. See Fay et al., *Report on the Northern Ireland Survey*, 82.

23. George Santayana, *Life of Reason or The Phases of Human Progress*, 5 vols., 2nd ed. (New York: Charles Scribner's Sons, 1936), 1: 284.

24. Dubravka Ugresic, *The Culture of Lies* (London: Phoenix, 1998), 6.

CHAPTER 8

❧

Does the Truth Heal? A Psychological Perspective on Political Strategies for Dealing with the Legacy of Political Violence[1]

Brandon Hamber

Throughout the 1900s wars not only moved from being conflicts between nations to being conflicts between ethnic groups, they also systematically began to result in more and more ordinary civilian casualties. During World War I five percent of all casualties were civilian; by World War II the figure had risen to fifty percent.[2] In current conflicts, for every soldier killed there are eight civilian casualties.[3] Some authors claim that as many as ninety percent of all casualties are civilian, and add that these people are generally from the poorer sectors of society.[4] War and civil strife no longer affect only the combatants. Entire societies are victimized, civil institutions are destroyed, and the social fabric severely undermined.

Dealing with the aftermath of such conflict therefore demands strategies of social transformation aimed at rebuilding the shattered political, economic, and social relationships characteristic of prolonged strife. Recently, processes such as truth commissions have been identified as helping in this task by exposing the full magnitude of the destruction and breaking the silences of oppression and repression. Patricia Hayner is of the opinion that such institutions can promote reconciliation, outline necessary reforms, allow victims to air their pain, provide acknowledgment of a long-suppressed past, and hopefully keep abuses from being repeated.[5]

Despite there having been over fifteen truth commissions in the last two decades,[6] it is the South African Truth and Reconciliation Commission (TRC) that has commanded the most international attention. This has been one of the most extensive to date. Enormous resources were put into publicizing its work and popularizing its mission, both domestically and internationally. It has been heralded as a unique and significant advance in the field of reconciliation and transitional justice, on account of its exposure of the truth through a combination of victims' testimonies and the granting of amnesty on condition of full disclosure of the crimes committed. Not only has this opened up new possibilities within the field of transitional justice; it has also provoked debate about whether truth commissions really can contribute to healing and reconciliation in societies struggling to come to terms with a history of human rights abuse.

This chapter will address the issue of healing and the role of victims[7] in the context of political transition. It will show that a linear progression, and a set of uniform traumatic responses to violence, are not typical of the psychological healing process following political conflict. This has implications for the role of truth commissions in dealing with the aftermath of large-scale political violence. Simplistic discourses about the causal relationship between full disclosure (truth) and healing (reconciliation) adopted by the South African TRC will be explored, and the social, individual, and political consequences of this outlined. The gap between individual processes necessary to bury the past, or at least come to terms with it to some extent, and the collective or national process will be highlighted. Finally, this chapter will make some comparative remarks about the current context in South Africa, and point out the challenges of dealing with a legacy of violence that is in a constant state of change and development.

Impact of the Past

It is easier to imagine the death of one person than those of a hundred or a thousand. . . . [W]hen multiplied suffering becomes abstract. It is not easy to be moved by abstract things.[8]

The nature and extent of political violence in apartheid South Africa is relatively well documented. The brutal impact of decades of systematic segregation, social and economic degradation, and more specifically the direct impact of a plethora of gross violations of human rights are eloquently captured in the report of the South African TRC. Although specific psychological effects upon, and exact responses of, particular individuals are unique and difficult to assess, psychologists and mental health workers increasingly claim to have begun to identify a range of common psychological symptoms.

It is not the purpose of this chapter to outline these in detail. The psychological and physical impact of past conflicts at the individual, community, and to some degree broader societal levels, is highlighted throughout the TRC's report. In essence, this argues that "South Africans have had to deal with a psychological stress which has arisen as a result of deprivation and dire socioeconomic conditions, coupled with the cumulative trauma arising from violent state repression and intra-community conflicts."[9]

But can the impact of a violent past on individuals and society be captured in words? One way of doing so is by means of the concept of "extreme traumatization," which was developed by mental health workers in the Chilean context. Extreme traumatization is characterized by an individual and collective process occurring in a specific social context;[10] namely, when authorities have the power to violate human rights regularly, causing successive and cumulative injuries.[11]

Consistent to some degree with this notion of extreme traumatization, the TRC's report gives paramount importance to the socioeconomic and political context of victims, when considering the psychological impact on them of human rights violations. It points out, for example, the fact that poor living conditions caused additional emotional difficulties that intensified other traumas, "resulting in a complicated traumatic cocktail that demanded more than a mere therapeutic or healing intervention."[12] It explicitly states that "the mental health of a person could not be seen or understood in isolation from socioeconomic realities."[13] The report thus supports the views of a host of mental health professionals who are increasingly moving away from the medical model toward recognizing the importance of social context for mental health.

Truth Commissions and Healing

When people face what nothing in their past has prepared them for, they grope for words to name the unknown, even when they can neither define nor understand it.[14]

Despite little research and empirical evidence, the ability of processes of recovering the truth to contribute to healing and reconciliation with the past has been ubiquitously asserted.[15] In its report, the TRC affirmed the "healing potential of storytelling, of revealing the truth before a respectful audience and to an official body."[16] Elsewhere I have argued that truth commissions have a healing psychological potential.[17] Psychologically speaking, sleeping dogs do not lie; past traumas do not simply pass or disappear with the passage of time.[18] The past will not let itself be ignored and past traumas can always be expected to have emotional consequences for an individual and society at some later stage.[19] Psychological restoration and healing can only occur through providing space for survivors of violence to be heard, and for every detail of the traumatic event to be reexperienced in a safe environment. Such space a truth commission could furnish.

The importance of having wrongdoing acknowledged and of uncovering the truth is also commonly affirmed as healing for survivors. Mary Burton, one of the TRC's Commissioners, believes that it has contributed to a greater exposure of the truth[20] and that some answers have been given to survivors about who was responsible and why certain atrocities happened.[21] These detailed accounts have built a historical record that will contribute to the prevention of similar atrocities in the future. By removing the fear of repetition from the lives of survivors and the families of victims, more psychic space is created for healing.

Victims react to extreme trauma in accordance with what it means to them. It is meaning that counts and not diagnosis.[22] Therapy aims to uncover the meaning that individuals have given to their trauma; thus, it is important to put fragments of traumatic memory into personal historic perspective.[23] An officially authorized truth commission, albeit significantly more limited than an individual therapy context, can provide a framework in which victims can begin to understand, integrate, and create new meanings for themselves. By recovering the truth and creating a realistic perspective on past human rights abuses, truth commissions may be able to assist this process.

Official acknowledgments and reparations can also be instrumental in healing.[24] They can serve as symbolic markers defining spaces for grieving and for addressing trauma. They can also help to remove responsibility from victims and alleviate their feelings of guilt, which are common in such cases. A process of "social reparation" is also desirable for the individual and for society. Ideally this involves the revelation and condemnation of past human rights violations, the formal doing of justice, an individualized and collective healing process, and structures to prevent future violations.[25] Truth commissions, depending on their mandate, can, to lesser and greater degrees, further this process. In South Africa formal justice has been the most obvious missing ingredient.

Truth commissions can also break the silence characterized by extreme and severe traumatization. Burton believes that breaking the silences of the past and creating a vivid and unforgettable record of the atrocities committed under apartheid has been one of the greatest successes of the TRC;[26] and some twenty-five non-government organizations across South Africa concur.[27]

Survivors who testified before the TRC affirmed the usefulness of its publicizing of the plight of victims, and the resultant increase in awareness among certain sectors of the population of the extent of past atrocities.[28] Victims' own testimonies speak volumes in this regard. Mr. Sikwepere, who came to the TRC to tell of being blinded after he was shot in the face, said: "I feel that what has been making me sick all the time is the fact that I couldn't tell my story. But now it feels like I got my sight back by coming here and telling you the story."[29]

Nonetheless, the long-term ability of a once-off statement or public testimony to address the full psychological impact of the past is questionable. Some survivors and families of victims only began to experience a range of psychological problems months after their testimony.[30] While Burton believes that giving public testimony has been healing for some survivors—"The right to be heard and acknowledged, with respect and empathy, did contribute to a process of healing in many cases"[31]—she acknowledges the real difficulties of attempting to come to terms with the past. In South Africa the revealing of the truth and the reopening of wounds have been extremely painful. Some survivors still remain angry about amnesty for perpetrators, and some perpetrators and beneficiaries of the system still deny their responsibility.[32]

The TRC has undoubtedly begun a healing a process for many, and for a fortuitous few it may have spurred on a complete recovery. However, despite these successes, it would be an error to exaggerate the ability of truth commissions or public testimony to address en masse the needs of individuals struggling with a personal and social history of human rights abuses.

Revealing Is Healing

Cut a chrysalis open, and you will find a rotting caterpillar. What you will never find is the mythical creature, half caterpillar, half butterfly, a fit emblem for the human soul, for those whose cast of mind leads them to seek such emblems. No, the process of transformation consists almost entirely of decay.[33]

Some of the strongest advocates of truth commissions often espouse an oversimplistic view of what it takes to address the impact of human rights violations, whether due to a lack of appreciation of the complexity of victimization or simply to a sincere desire to address and bury past traumas quickly. It should not be assumed too easily, as the banners displayed by the TRC did, that "Revealing is Healing." Hayes writes: "Just revealing is not just healing. It depends on how we reveal, the context of the revealing, and what it is that we are revealing."[34] All the public revelation of truth in the world will not guarantee immediate psychological restoration. Telling the story is only one component of the victim's typically lengthy and painful healing process. A truth commission may be a necessary first step, but in itself is insufficient to meet the myriad psychological needs of individuals. As the TRC's own report acknowledges, in many cases the experience of testifying or making a statement "initiated more than it closed."[35]

Any strategy for dealing with the needs of victims after political conflict must acknowledge their social and cultural context. To some degree the TRC did this in its report, but it was only late in its public proceedings that its rhetoric consistently acknowledged the long road that victims would have to travel toward healing. In interviews with twenty-five nongovernmental organizations in South Africa, the TRC was often praised for opening the door for more reconciliation work, and for popularizing the need for psychological support. At the same time the TRC was criticized for creating the impression that healing is simply a linear process or something that is easily brought about.[36]

Issues of context—social, political, and cultural—are primary, not secondary factors in the psychological process of a victim's response to violence suffered.[37] Responses such as self-blame, vivid reexperiencing of the event, fear, nightmares, feelings of helplessness, depression, relationship difficulties, feelings of social disconnectedness, anxiety, and even difficulties arising from substance abuse are not dysfunctional symptoms of a traumatic disorder, but normal responses to being placed in an extremely abnormal social environment.

This process is complicated further by the highly individual and culturally specific nature of the impact of violence on individuals and of how people choose to deal with it. Certainly, common or collective wisdom that it is better to "cough it out" (as they say frequently in South African townships) than to keep pain festering inside, can be identified in many societies. Furthermore, much of the discipline of (psychoanalytic) psychology is dedicated to dealing with repressed pain and willing the truth out. Nonetheless, when it comes to models such as truth commissions, there is little research that measures the exact psychological impact of uncovering the past on individuals, and even less on how it affects society.

Individual and collective processes of healing are also often collapsed into one another in the field of transitional justice, but the healing of an individual and the healing of a nation are not the same thing.[38] Michael Ignatieff challenges the notion of speaking about nations as if their psyches are the same as those of individuals (e.g., as in the assertion that by truth telling the nation will be healed). He feels that it is problematic enough to vest an individual with a single identity, let alone to talk of the healing of a fissured national identity as if it was an individual with a conscience, identity, and memory.[39] Leslie Swartz, reflecting on the South African TRC, makes a similar point:

> Individuals who . . . are given the role of speaking for the nation's pain, are not necessarily "healed" or helped by this process, and may in fact find the experience unhelpful and distressing. The sensitivity of the TRC to this issue is praiseworthy, but it is easy for us to get lost in the confusion between psychoanalytic views on how individuals can best be healed, and what is essentially the political need for a country like South Africa to find a way to meet the challenges of the future.[40]

Thus, social processes aiming to acknowledge pain and provide space for victims to speak out can be necessary starting points, but progress thereafter can be haphazard and slow. The political process is fundamentally different from the personal healing process; a country and its politicians may be ready to move on before victims have come to terms with the magnitude of their personal pain. So, when it comes to dealing with victims the challenge is to "work with a spirit of humility about what we can offer and an acceptance that there is no quick fix or magic bullet that will rid people everywhere of the suffering brought about by violence."[41] Healing is an inescapably prolonged and enigmatic process. There are often no clear starting points, and fairly often no clear signs that the psychological impact of the past has been completely ameliorated. Personal healing is distinctive, and it often stands at odds with social demands to bury the past.

Bridging Past and Present

"I told you the truth," I say yet again. "Memory's truth, because memory has its own special kind. It selects, eliminates, alters, exaggerates, minimizes, glorifies, and vilifies also; but in the end it creates its own reality, its heterogeneous but usually coherent versions of events; and no sane human being ever trusts someone else's version more than his own."[42]

Truth commissions are caught between the internal needs of victims (and their ambivalence over holding onto or letting go of the past) and society's external political exigencies, including the need for stability. This implies that dealing with the past is a matter of undergoing a process, and not crossing a magic boundary. Strategies for dealing with the past such as truth commissions can ease this process, provide a framework for dealing with conflict, and may even approximate victims' personal needs and society's political needs over time. This has occurred in some cases in South Africa. However, despite the integral link between their own internal states and their social context, victims can never override the internal psychological journey they have to make as they struggle to make sense of their loss.

All of South African society has been traumatized to some degree. This requires the type of social and political rehabilitation policy that the TRC has partly championed. The need for ongoing medical and psychological support services to thousands of individual victims of past violence must remain a national priority. In addition, where societal functioning and cohesion have been damaged, or where there is abject poverty, repairing community and cultural bonds and structures may be as important as offering psychological assistance to individuals.

Reparations are integral to this process, but here the new South African government has faltered significantly. A year after the TRC published its recommendations about long-term reparations, the government had still not discussed the issue substantially in parliament. Survivors are becoming increasingly disillusioned with the process as their hopes of receiving adequate reparation are steadily undermined by government claims that they cannot afford to compensate survivors satisfactorily.[43]

Furthermore, despite many scholars and commentators lauding the uniqueness of the South African attempt to trade truth for justice, the legacy of a culture of violence and continuing unease with impunity have received limited attention to date. Exchanging truth for amnesty may result in more information being made public, but public information alone does not guarantee nonrepetition. The impact of a truth for justice trade-off needs to be measured, not only by its ability to achieve political stability, but also by the degree to which the lessons of the past are absorbed into the present.

Despite the TRC and its revelations of police misdoings, a significant number of gross human rights violations continue to be perpetrated by the police service in postapartheid South Africa. In the eighteen months between April 1997 and September 1998, the Independent Complaints Directorate reported that 1,081 people had died in police custody or as a result of police action. The torture of criminal suspects by the police continues. The Directorate received seventy-three complaints about police torture over the same period, a figure suspected of underrepresenting the abuses taking place.

South Africa, similar to countries such as Brazil, Argentina, and Chile,[44] is suffering from ongoing authoritarianism and resultant human rights violations by the police (although the political nature of these violations has decreased significantly). This is happening in spite of the instatement of democratic governance and the TRC's investigations into past misdeeds. There is little evidence, at least at this stage, that the TRC's exposure of the past is profoundly influencing the current practice of the police service. If anything, the new climate of high rates of crime and increasing public demands for tougher policing paradoxically give the police a freer hand to commit violations. A recent survey revealed that 70 percent of South African respondents of all races either "agreed" or "strongly agreed" with the statement that "criminals have too many rights."[45] In addition, thirty-one percent of all South Africans feel the police have the right to use force to extract information from criminal suspects.[46] Thus, not only does a legacy of authoritarianism still exist within the South African police, but the brutality of apartheid has left remnants deep within the core of every South African. An entrenched culture of human rights has not been, perhaps predictably, the immediate byproduct of the TRC process.

Despite the TRC's efforts to highlight ongoing police abuses in its report,[47] it appears that the general public considers the violations committed by the police under the apartheid system to be fundamentally different from those taking place today. Political and criminal violence have been artificially severed in the process of transition; a distinction, which, in most cases, is impossible to sustain. Ironically, then, one could argue that the better the work done by bodies such as truth commissions, the more they create the impression that political violence and criminal violence are fundamentally unrelated.

Against these arguments, Archbishop Desmond Tutu, chairperson of the TRC, believes that its amnesty provisions have not encouraged impunity in South Africa, because amnesty was only granted to those who pleaded guilty and accepted responsibility for what they had done.[48] However, the exact impact of amnesty on ongoing levels of impunity and the public's anti-human rights sentiment in South Africa, is not yet fully understood. Amnesty always implies some level of social acceptance of the violation, or at least some justification of it.

The granting of amnesty is also generally at odds with the feelings of most survivors of violence. Ideally, these want truth from the perpetrators, but they also want them prosecuted. Justice through the courts is the preferred way of dealing with perpetrators among victims.[49] Contrary to Article 2.2 of the Universal Declaration of Human Rights, which states that no exceptional circumstances *whatsoever* may be invoked as a justification for torture, several torturers from both the apartheid state and the liberation forces have been granted amnesty. In light of the current attitudes to human rights in South Africa, and ongoing police abuse, it is difficult not to conclude that a subtle, but stubbornly residual air of impunity still lingers in South African society.

Further, when considering how best to deal with the past after civil conflict it is useful to make a distinction between what can broadly be termed "horizontal" and "vertical" types of violence. Vertical violence refers to the violence committed by the state against its citizens, and citizens' violence against the state. This is the kind of violence that truth commissions typically investigate and deal with. Horizontal violence refers to that between fellow citizens, and is sometimes called "community violence" or "intra/interorganizational violence." This kind typically occurs in the latter phases of states committing extensive forms of vertical violence.

The violence in South Africa during the period of negotiation from February 1990 to April 1994, typified by conflict between the African National Congress and the Inkatha Freedom Party (some of which was covertly sponsored by the state and its agents), is a good example of horizontal violence. This period in South African history accounted for the greatest number of fatalities. The South African Institute of Race Relations reported 14,807 deaths during the negotiation period, a time when South Africa was supposedly normalizing. This is in stark comparison to the previous five years, when the Institute reported only 5,387 deaths from political violence.[50]

It is obviously important that institutions such as truth commissions come to terms with vertical violence; and this has been the main focus of the South African TRC. Nevertheless, in the long term it is often the micro-effects that ripple through communities destroying the social fabric, and these require equal, and generally more extensive, attention.[51]

Relatively speaking, the horizontal violence that took place within South African communities was sorely neglected by the TRC. The Commission itself admits that it "failed to make significant breakthroughs in relation to violence in the 1990s."[52] It further notes that:

> While Commission figures for reported violations in the earlier part of its mandate period are under-represented in part because of the passage of time, they are under-reported in this later period because the abuses are still fresh in people's memories and closely linked into current distribution of power incidents.[53]

It is vitally important to acknowledge that apartheid has left a legacy of violence and mistrust within communities themselves, and not merely between the state and its citizens. Many communities in South Africa remain internally subject to division and conflict. Reconciliation at the community level remains vital to long-term stability and development;[54] for it is within communities and at local levels that future violence is likely to manifest itself.

More than likely it will erupt in power struggles for support of the poorer sections of the society who make up a sizeable percentage of the entire population. In this context, disaffected individuals whose structural conditions remain unchanged, and those who feel that their rights to justice were sacrificed for minimal return by the amnesty laws and other negotiated compromises, will become easy recruits of opportunistic politicians ready to exploit past resentments.

It is therefore very important indeed that steps are taken to deal with horizontal violence and rebuild the social fabric of communities. These steps need to be culturally specific, sustainable, and developed at a community level. A truth and reconciliation commission may help create the conditions for appropriate measures, but it is civil society and local bodies that are best placed to take them. Truth commissions are severely limited in their ability to provide ongoing programs to repair the long-term impact of deep-rooted social conflict.

Individual interventions, characterized by culturally specific counseling or psychosocial support, are also necessary.[55] Those affected by political violence need, above all else, to feel part of their community again and to share their grief and suffering with others in it.[56] Public testimony and truth commissions can be useful in breaking down some of the previous barriers and silences, but future individual interventions will need to be considerably more profound.

Learning from Hapless Heroes

God does have a sense of humour. Who in their right mind would have ever imagined South Africa to be an example of anything but awfulness. . . . We South Africans were the unlikeliest lot and that is precisely why God has chosen us. We cannot really claim much credit ourselves for what we have achieved. . . . We were destined for perdition and were plucked out of total annihilation. We were a hopeless case if there ever was one.[57]

The first step in dealing adequately with the past is to open debates about truth, justice, reparation, memory, and forgetting. South Africa has thrown the doors wide open and as a result has moved somewhat down the road. Much has been accomplished but the process of reconciliation is still far from complete. South Africa has provided human rights practitioners and strife-torn countries the world over with a glimmer of optimism as they struggle for reconciliation. Through a flawed Commission, South Africa has provided a beacon of hope and an exemplary means of dealing with certain dimensions of situations of conflict, violence, turmoil, and sectional strife.[58]

However, this optimism has encouraged the drawing of simplistic conclusions about trauma and its treatment. The past's wide-ranging impact on victims is being conveniently bundled directly into a ready-made concept of trauma; and, in turn, the healing of victims is being portrayed as a linear task requiring only particular interventions such as counseling and public testimony to ensure resolution.

The stark reality, from a psychological perspective, is that a more nuanced and composite understanding of trauma is needed if we are to adequately integrate a process of addressing the needs of victims into strategies for dealing with the past. Such strategies must recognize the importance of dealing with the individual and its environment over a long period of time. Governments operating during times of transition may find themselves at odds with victims and some communities, since the desire to move on at a political level normally comes faster than at the individual level. Individual recovery over time is intrinsically linked to the reconstruction of social and economic networks, and of cultural identity.[59] Some go as far as to say that war victims will not develop psychiatric symptoms if their social status is officially supported.[60]

When considering the needs of survivors in countries struggling to deal with the past, trauma counseling and support for victims should not be considered the only pivot on which the healing of the individual hinges. Support services are, of course, necessary and any structure set up to deal with the past should not neglect them. However, an overemphasis on the need for such services can deflect attention from the other needs of survivors. For many victims, it is unlikely that they will divorce questions of truth, justice, the attribution of responsibility for violations, compensation, and official acknowledgement from the healing process.

Northern Ireland after the Good Friday Agreement provides a rich example of this. There, an official truth recovery process, although not impossible, seems unlikely in the immediate aftermath of the change of government.[61] During transition, the balance of power between the opposing forces generally determines government policy.[62] In Northern Ireland, at this stage, the opponents are quite equally weighted and are opting to keep the embarrassing truths hidden, preferring not to take responsibility for their actions. This is mostly due to fear that such acknowledgment, public or otherwise, would make vulnerable their political position as parties vying for power in the new dispensation. At the formal governmental level the time is not right to begin the difficult quest of uncovering the past, although the truths that remain buried will have to surface at some point.

To deal with some of the violence of the past, the British government and the European Union have made enormous resources available for trauma-related projects and victim support. Although these are certainly needed, their provision is one of the easiest options to consider (besides doing nothing at all) in responding to the complexity of the legacy of violence. The funding of trauma services is much less politically charged than funding a wide-ranging truth recovery process or a tribunal. It is therefore unlikely that funds will be made available to set up a truth commission to focus comprehensively on the involvement of the British forces, the police, and paramilitaries in the violence of the past.

In Northern Ireland, at the moment, it is only safe to talk about victims of past atrocities in a relatively descriptive way. The process is too fragile to start dealing with the complexities of political violence and its many shades of complicity. However, until the complicated and fraught issues of truth, justice, and the official acknowledgment of wrongdoing by all sides are dealt with, it is doubtful that victims will feel the past is completely behind them. In all societies in transition, direct individual psychological support for victims needs to be complemented by economic transformation and social reparation if the project of healing is to be significantly advanced.

For survivors of human rights atrocities, healing is directly related to the interdependent concepts of truth, justice, and reparation.[63] Truth complements justice; justice can reveal the truth. Reparation is a right, integral to reestablishing the rule of law and the survivor's belief in a just future. Reparation and punishment are the symbolic markers telling the survivor that justice has been done. Simply put, social justice is both reparation and an essential component of the victim's healing process.

Endnotes

1. My thanks to Sophie Kevany for her editorial assistance.
2. UNICEF, *Children in Situations of Armed Conflict* (New York: UNICEF, 1986),

cited in D. Summerfield, "Addressing Human Responses to War and Atrocity: Major Challenges in Research Practices and the Limitations of Western Psychiatric Models," in R.J. Kelber, C.R. Figley, and B.P.R. Gersons, eds., *Beyond Trauma: Cultural and Societal Dynamics* (New York: Plenum Press, 1995), 17.

3. R. Goldstone, "A Court that Needs a Fair Trail: the International War Crimes Court," *Time Magazine* (3 August 1998), 69–70.

4. D. Summerfield, "Addressing Human Responses to War and Atrocity," 17.

5. P.B. Hayner, "Commissioning the Truth: Further Research Questions," *Third World Quarterly* 17/1 (1996): 19–29.

6. P.B. Hayner, "Fifteen Truth Commissions, 1974 to 1994: a Comparative Study," *Human Rights Quarterly* 16 (1994): 597–655.

7. The terms "victim" and "survivor" are used here interchangeably. On the one hand, The Promotion of National Unity and Reconciliation Act that established the South African TRC speaks of victims; and it defines them as all those who have suffered physical or mental injury, emotional suffering, or a substantial impairment of human rights because of gross violation of human rights in the course of the political conflicts of the past. The Act includes both direct and indirect survivors in its definition of victims. In addition, many of the survivors with whom we have had contact over the years describe themselves as victims. On the other hand, many who have suffered human rights violations use the word "survivor" because of its more positive connotations—although some consider this to be characteristic of Western mental health workers trying to be politically correct.

8. Mario Vargas Llosa, *The War of the End of the World* (London: Faber and Faber, 1998), 384.

9. *Truth and Reconciliation Commission of South Africa Report*, vol. 5 (Cape Town: Juta, 1998), chapter 4.10, 127.

10. D. Becker, "The Deficiency of the Concept of Post-Traumatic Stress Disorder when Dealing with Victims of Human Rights Violations," in R.J. Kelber et al., *Beyond Trauma*, 107.

11. E. Lira Kornfeld, "The Development of Treatment Approaches for Victims of Human Rights Violations," in R.J. Kelber et al., *Beyond Trauma*, 122.

12. *TRC Report*, vol. 1, chapter 11(g).5, 365.

13. Ibid.

14. Eric Hobsbawn, *The Age of Extremes: The Short Twentieth Century, 1914–1991* (London: Abacus, 1998), 287.

15. K. Asmal, L. Asmal, and R. S. Roberts, *Reconciliation Through Truth: A Reckoning of Apartheid's Criminal Governance* (Cape Town: David Philip Publishers, 1994); A. Boraine, A. J. Levy, and R. Scheffer, eds., "Dealing with the Past: Truth and Reconciliation in South Africa" (Cape Town: IDASA, 1994); G. Simpson and P. van Zyl, *South Africa's Truth and Reconciliation Commission*, Occasional Paper (Johannesburg: Centre

for the Study of Violence and Reconciliation, 1995); and J. Zalaquett, "Introduction," *The Report of the Chilean National Commission on Truth and Reconciliation* (London and Notre Dame: University of Notre Dame Press, 1993), vol. 1.

16. *TRC Report*, vol. 5, chapter 9.6, 351.

17. B. Hamber, *Do Sleeping Dogs Lie? The Psychological Implications of the Truth and Reconciliation Commission in South Africa*, Occasional Paper (Johannesburg: The Centre for the Study of Violence and Reconciliation, 1995).

18. B. Hamber, "Remembering to Forget: Issues to Consider when Establishing Structures for Dealing with the Past," in B. Hamber, ed., *Past Imperfect: Dealing with the Past in Northern Ireland and Societies in Transition* (Derry/Londonderry: INCORE /University of Ulster, 1998), 57.

19. B. Hamber, "The Burdens of Truth: An Evaluation of the Psychological Support Services and Initiatives undertaken by the South African Truth and Reconciliation Commission," *American Imago* 55/1 (Spring 1998): 9–28.

20. However, some would argue that the TRC only uncovered a small amount of the truth in South Africa. In parts of the country very little new information emerged. For example, in the Vaal region outside Johannesburg, a site of extensive political violence including a number of massacres, only three South African policemen applied for amnesty (Piers Pigou, former TRC investigator, in a communication to the author, 1999).

21. M. Burton, "The South African Truth and Reconciliation Commission: Looking Back, Moving Forward—Revisiting Conflicts, Striving for Peace," in B. Hamber, *Past Imperfect*, 13–24.

22. Summerfield, "Addressing Human Responses to War and Atrocity," 20.

23. Lira Kornfeld, "The Development of Treatment Approaches for Victims of Human Rights Abuses," 125.

24. B. Hamber, "Repairing the Irreparable: Dealing with Double-Binds of Making Reparations for Crimes of the Past," *Ethnicity and Health* 5/3 (2000).

25. I. Agger and S.B. Jensen, *Trauma and Healing under State Terrorism* (London: Zed Books, 1996), 202.

26. Burton, "The South African Truth and Reconciliation Commission," 13–24.

27. H. van der Merwe, P. Dewhirst, and B. Hamber, "Non-Governmental Organisations and the Truth and Reconciliation Commission: An Impact Assessment," *Politikon* 26/1 (1999): 55–79.

28. B. Hamber, D. Nageng, and G. O'Malley, "Telling It Like It Is: Survivors' Perceptions of the Truth and Reconciliation Commissions," *Psychology in Society* 26 (2000): 18–42.

29. *TRC Report*, vol. 5, chapter 9.9, 352.

30. Interview of T. de Ridder of the Trauma Centre for Victims of Violence and Torture in Cape Town, by author, June 1997.

31. Burton, "The South African Truth and Reconciliation Commission," 20.

32. Ibid., 13–24.

33. Pat Barker, *Regeneration* (London: Penguin Books, 1992), 184.

34. G. Hayes, "We Suffer Our Memories: Thinking about the Past, Healing and Reconciliation," *American Imago* 55/1 (Spring 1998): 43.

35. *TRC Report*, vol. 1, chapter 11(g).16, 367.

36. Van der Merwe et al., "Non-governmental organisations," 55–79.

37. P. J. Bracken, "Hidden Agendas: Deconstructing Post-Traumatic Stress Disorder," in P. J. Bracken and C. Petty, eds., *Rethinking the Trauma of War* (London: Free Association Books, 1998), 55.

38. B. Hamber and R. Wilson, "Symbolic Closure through Memory, Reparation and Revenge in Post-Conflict Societies" (paper presented at the "Traumatic Stress in South Africa" conference, Johannesburg, 27–29 January 1999).

39. M. Ignatieff, *The Warrior's Honor: Ethnic War and the Modern Conscience* (London: Chatto and Windus, 1998), 169.

40. L. Swartz, *Culture and Mental Health: A Southern African View* (Cape Town: Oxford University Press, 1998), 184.

41. Bracken, "Hidden Agendas," 58.

42. Salman Rushdie, *Midnight's Children* (Vintage, 1995), 211.

43. Hamber et al., "Telling It Like It Is."

44. B. Hamber, "Living with the Legacy of Impunity: Lessons for South Africa about Truth, Justice and Crime in Brazil," *Unisa Latin American Report* 13/2 (July–December 1997): 4–16; and P.S. Pinheiro, "Democracies without Citizenship," *North American Congress on Latin America [NACLA]: Report on the Americas* 30/2 (September/October 1996): 7–42.

45. "Reality Check Survey of the Attitudes of South Africans," *The South African Sunday Independent*, 28 April 1999.

46. See P. Pigou, N. Valji, and R. Greenstein, *Assessing Levels of Human Rights Knowledge amongst the General Population and Selected Target Groups* (Johannesburg: Community Agency for Social Enquiry, November 1998).

47. See *TRC Report*, vol. 5, chapter 8.68, 330.

48. D. Tutu, *No Future without Forgiveness* (London: Rider, 1999), 51.

49. Centre for the Study of Violence and Reconciliation and Khulumani Victim Support Group, "Survivors' Perceptions of the Truth and Reconciliation Commission and Suggestions for the Final Report" (unpublished submission to the Truth and Reconciliation Commission, 1998); and Hamber et al., "Telling It Like It Is."

50. It should be noted that the division between what is called political violence versus criminal violence in South Africa has always been blurred, resulting in some discrepancies between different agencies' statistics on fatalities during this period. Further, statistics cheapen the life of each individual killed and also obscure other forms of repression. Looking only at the number of deaths that took place in the 1980s does not tell the whole

story. For example, between 1984 and 1986 the South African police shot dead 300 children—but they also wounded 1,000, detained 11,000 without trial, arrested 18,000 on charges relating to political protest, and held a further 173,000 in police cells awaiting trial (*South Africa: Breaking New Ground* [London: Catholic Institute for International Relations, 1996]).

51. B. Hamber, "Have No Doubt It Is Fear in the Land: An Exploration of the Continuing Cycles of Violence in South Africa," *Zeitschrift für Politische Psychologie* 7/1–2 (1999): 113–28.

52. *TRC Report*, vol. 5, chapter 6.53, 206.

53. Of 9,043 statements received on killings, over half of these (5,695) occurred during the 1990–94 period. These figures give an indication of violations recorded by the Commission during the negotiations process. See the *TRC Report*, vol. 2, chapter 7.7, 584.

54. H. van der Merwe, *The South African Truth and Reconciliation Commission and Community Reconciliation: A Case Study of Duduza*, Occasional Paper (Johannesburg: Centre for the Study of Violence and Reconciliation, 1998).

55. Cultural specificity here does not mean that the cultural dynamics of those affected by violence need attention in order to discover their universal core, but rather that these dynamics determine that the experience of violence is thoroughly cultural. See P. J. Bracken and C. Petty, "Conclusion," in Bracken and Petty, *Rethinking the Trauma of War*, 187.

56. Ibid., 188.

57. Desmond Tutu, *No Future without Forgiveness*, 229.

58. Ibid.

59. Summerfield, *Addressing Human Responses to War and Atrocity*, 25.

60. L. Weisaeth, "Psychiatric Problems in War," in L.T. Arcel, ed., *War Violence, Trauma and the Coping Process: Armed Conflict in Europe and Survivor Responses* (Denmark: International Rehabilitation Council for Torture Survivors, 1998), 31.

61. For a full discussion of the prospects of a truth commission in Northern Ireland, see Hamber, *Past Imperfect*.

62. Jamal Benomar, "Confronting the Past: Justice in Transition," *Journal of Democracy* 4/1 (1993): 13.

63. Hamber et al., "Telling It Like It Is," 42.

PART III

Cases

CHAPTER 9

Passion, Constraint, Law, and Fortuna: The Human Rights Challenge to Chilean Democracy

Alexandra Barahona de Brito[1]

Introduction

The way that Chileans have dealt with past human rights violations committed by the regime of Augusto Pinochet Ugarte (1973–90) since the transition to democracy has been characterized by a combination of passion and constraint. There has been a refusal simply to bury the past—a moral commitment that avoids the simple and convenient route adopted by other countries. At the same time, action has been limited by constraints, self-imposed as well as external, by a political and constitutional setting that poses challenges to wider action, and by the caution that arises from the fear of challenging the balance of power.[2] The framing of the ideas of "reconciliation" and "democratization" by the political elite in Chile has meant that one has ironically stood in the way of the other, rather than being mutually reinforcing. However, law[3] and *fortuna*[4]—one a rigid and codified factor, the other an unpredictable and uncontrollable phenomenon—have challenged so-called "reconciliation" and the forces of constraint. In doing so, they have opened—and continue to open—the door to a wider truth and justice, as well as to generate a new impetus toward "democratization."

This has been especially apparent in what can be seen as the "second" phase of the search for truth and justice. The first phase, during the first successor civilian government under President Patricio Aylwin Azócar (March 1990–March 1994), can be seen largely as a "political phase" and was dominated by the executive. It largely determined what should or should not be done about the past, as part of the political measures undertaken to mark a break with the past, and to mark the ethical and political territory of the new democracy. It was a process essentially dominated by the elite, which aimed at retaining control of policy to avoid challenging a new accommodation between the military and the right, on the one hand, and the democratic forces on the other. Although other bodies—the legislature, the courts, and civil society organizations—intervened, they did so as clearly subordinate actors. At the end of the Aylwin administration "closure" was officially announced, with the declaration that the transition was over and the legacies of the past dealt with.

Since then, the struggle for truth and justice has entered a predominantly "judicial phase," with initiative shifting away from the executive. In this phase, which corresponds loosely with the government of Eduardo Frei Ruíz-Tagle (March 1994–March 2000), the executive became largely reactive, responding to events generated by the courts. Here, the continued search for justice has taken on a dynamic, rhythm, and life of its own, working itself out according to "rules of the game" that are peculiar to the judiciary. The latter has its own institutional logic, which the executive does not control and cannot easily hinder. At the same time, the issue has transcended national boundaries, acquiring an international political-judicial dynamic that the Chilean executive can neither control nor ignore. The impact of the work of informal ad hoc transnational coalitions of human rights organizations (HROs), political party activists, victims, and victims' relatives would have been of little importance, however, had it not been for *fortuna*, which made a key contribution to widening the horizon for retrospective accountability. It has also challenged the limited scope of an oft-cited "reconciliation" and, in so doing, of an equally limited democratization process. And it may bring about a new "political phase" in the struggle for human rights. This chapter tells the story of how the continuing battle over the past has evolved in Chile.

The Transition and the Aylwin Administration: Truth with "Reconciliation"

In his inaugural speech of 12 March 1990, newly elected President Aylwin announced that dealing with past abuses and promoting national reconciliation would be the main aims of his government. The government of the Alliance of Parties for Democracy (Concertación de Partidos por la Democracia, CPPD), a coalition between the Socialist Party and the Party for Democracy (Partido Socialista, PS-PPD) on the one hand, and the Christian Democratic Party (Partido Democrata Cristiano, PDC) on the other, adopted a four-pronged strategy to deal with the past: strong executive commitment to disclosing the truth and making compensation, and to the doing of justice and implementation of wider institutional reform "as far as possible."

The strongest thrust of the government's policy was to uncover the truth about past violations. To that end, it established the Truth and Reconciliation Commission (Comisión de la Verdad y la Reconciliación, CNVR) by Decree 355 on 24 April 1990. Nine commissioners were charged with analyzing the system of repression under military rule, focusing on the most serious human rights violations resulting in death and disappearance, finding the information to discover the whereabouts of the victims, and recommending reparations and measures to prevent such violations from taking place again. The Commission worked for nine months from 9 May 1990 to 9 February 1991, and the government published its report (named after the Commission's president, Rettig) in March. The results were announced nationwide on television by a tearful president, who apologized on behalf of the state for the human rights violations committed by the Pinochet regime. The Rettig Report became an immediate best-seller, and was published both as a book and serialized by a national newspaper.[5]

In order to promote the continuation of the search for truth, the government established the National Reparation and Reconciliation Corporation (Corporación Nacional de Reparación y Reconciliación, CNRR) on 8 February 1992, which legally established the "inalienable right" of relatives to find the "disappeared." By 1996 the CNRR had managed to investigate another 850 cases that the CNVR had not had time to consider.[6] It was also the instrument by which compensation for the victims and their families was arranged.

In January 1992, in compliance with the recommendations of the Commission's report, the government passed a Reparations Law to benefit about 7,000 individuals. It gave a monthly "salary" of US$380 to each family affected by disappearances or deaths resulting from human rights crimes, and offered them various health and education benefits, as well as exemption from military service. By September 1992 nearly eighty percent of eligible families were receiving benefits. As of June 1999, US$95 million had been paid out to the families (3,986) and direct victims (2,800).[7] In addition, the government established a Return Office (Oficina de Retorno) in August 1993 to assist returning exiles. Furthermore, following negotiations with the Association of the Exonerated (Comando de Exonerados) and within the legislature, a law was passed extending provisional benefits to 58,000 public sector employees discharged between 1973 and 1990.

The other two prongs of the CPPD policy focused on justice for violations and on wider institutional reforms of the constitution, the legal system, and the military. Neither of these two policies fared as well as the previous two. In the wake of the release of the CNVR report, the government proposed the reform of the judiciary, which had come under fire for failing to safeguard human rights. On 11 March 1990, the so-called Cumplido laws (named after the then-minister of justice) were sent to the legislature. They proposed the reform of the Arms Control Law, the State Security Law, the Code of Military Justice, and the Penal Code, and thus the reduction of strong "authoritarian enclaves" within the legal system. The bills also dealt with the plight of political prisoners through a series of transitory provisions to ensure a review of their cases, retrial, and/or release. These reform measures essentially failed. To this day, military tribunals retain jurisdiction over crimes committed by members of the armed forces on active duty. Civilian judges still do not have authority to investigate military premises, three of the five members of the military appeals courts (Cortes Marciales) are still on active service, and the Army General Auditor, a ranking general, still sits in the Supreme Court. At the same time, the release of the prisoners took almost five years due to right-wing opposition within the legislature.[8]

As far as prosecutions are concerned, Aylwin famously advocated justice "as far as possible." The government did not plan to promote prosecutions, as the Alfonsín government had done in Argentina (1983–89), with a "Trial of the Century" against the leaders of the military juntas. Nor did it abolish the Amnesty Law that the Pinochet regime had passed in 1978, which covered all violations committed between 11 September 1973 and 10 March 1978. Instead, according to what became known as the Aylwin Doctrine, the president argued that while the law precluded prosecutions, it should not preclude investigation of the facts with a view to locating the disappeared. By June 1993 relatives and victims had taken about 200 cases of violations to court, but the great majority had not reached a satisfactory conclusion.

The limited outcome of these attempts at institutional reform and justice was the product of two contradictory forces. Two sets of constraints, one self-imposed and the other externally imposed, counterbalanced the commitment to do something positive to deal with the past: the overwhelming desire for accommodation in the name of "reconciliation," and the balance of power in favor of the old repressors and their allies. In addition, law and *fortuna* initially worked against the search for retrospective accountability.

Of all the transitions in Latin America, Chile's was arguably the most restricted, because it was there that the military retained the highest degree of power and legitimacy. The Constitution of 1980 protected the military. The Pinochet dictatorship had succeeded uniquely in institutionalizing and legitimating itself through the Constitution, radically transforming the juridical and ideological foundations of the political system, and finally ensuring a step-by-step passage to a "protected democracy." General Pinochet was eventually defeated in a plebiscite on 5 October 1988, when a majority of voters opposed his staying in power for another eight years. But he had been defeated only by a narrow majority of 54.71 percent, and he retained a degree of power and legitimacy higher than any other outgoing dictator in the region.

Between October 1988 and December 1989, negotiations had taken place between the regime and the opposition and resulted in constitutional reforms that were approved in a plebiscite in July 1989.[9] However, although the reforms loosened the old regime's stranglehold on the political system somewhat, they fell far short of full democratization. Between the electoral campaign of December 1989 and March 1990, more so-called "tie-up" laws (*leyes de amarre*) were passed, which further restricted the nascent democracy.[10] Laws were passed granting security of tenure to civil servants, ensuring that a sweeping change of personnel would not occur. Nine appointed senatorial positions were created and filled by supporters of the regime.[11] The Constitutional Tribunal was so composed as to place obstacles in the way of future reform initiatives. On 26 January 1990 a new Organic Constitutional Law of Congress was passed, forbidding Congress from investigating the Pinochet government or from bringing constitutional charges against acts of corruption and treason committed prior to March 1990.

Continued military autonomy and the "Pinochet Factor"—the popularity of the general and his continued position as commander-in-chief of the Armed Forces—represented real as well as psychological obstacles to action on the human rights front. The CPPD was unable either to curtail military institutional autonomy significantly or get Pinochet to resign. The general restructured the high command, placing loyal followers in top positions. He rejected a proposed new law for the Armed Forces put forward by the coalition in 1989 and presented another law, which came into force on 27 February 1990. This gave the military full control over its own education, health, salaries, pensions, retirements, and promotions. It allowed the president and the Defense Ministry to choose from only a small number of generals nominated by the high command. The military remained as voting members of the Security Council (Consejo de Seguridad Nacional, CSN). This gave them the power to present their views to the president, whenever they feel national security or stability is at stake, effectively constituting an institutionalized means for the application of military pressure to the civilian government. Each branch of the military was allowed to designate one of the appointed senators. The law also set minimum levels for the military budget and automatically entitled the military to ten percent of the gross sales revenue of the state-run copper company, the Copper Corporation (Corporación del Cobre, CODELCO). In addition, just before the CPPD took power, the secret police, the National Central Intelligence Agency (Central Nacional de Inteligencia, CNI), was dissolved with no civilian oversight and an estimated 19,000 people incorporated into the Army intelligence unit, the Dirección de Inteligencia Nacional del Ejército (DINE, National Intelligence Directorate).[12]

Another constraint suffered by the government was the overrepresentation of the right in the legislature, which was assured by a biased binominal voting system established by Pinochet. Because of this and the appointed senators, the right-wing parties, the National Renovation (Renovación Nacional, RN) and the Independent Democratic Union (Unión Democrática Independiente, UDI), had secured 49 of 120 seats in Congress and 16 of the 38 elected seats in the Senate. Because any significant reforms or human rights policies required constitutional reforms, and because these, in turn, required a two-thirds majority vote in the Senate, the support of the right for the legal framework inherited from Pinochet blocked many initiatives from the outset. The abolition of the 1978 Amnesty Law, initially part of the CPPD electoral platform in 1989, became unthinkable, and attempts to reform the Armed Forces law and the judiciary foundered.[13]

In addition to these externally imposed constraints, self-constraint prevented greater action to ensure justice. It is only fair to say, however, that this self-constraint was coupled with a passion for the cause of human rights, which has been amply documented. Chile is the country that developed the strongest, most durable and largest human rights movement in the Americas. This had profound links with the CPPD parties, legal associations, think tanks, and international HROs. Under the protective umbrella of the Catholic Church, a long-term organic relationship had evolved between party activists and human rights workers. The solidarity between the parties and the movement ensured that the government would not drop the issue once it came to power. The unification of the left and center (through successive alliances since the antiregime protests of the mid-1980s) in a coalition committed to human rights, also ensured loyalty to the rights cause; as did the coalition's inclusion of one of the main groups representing the victims, the Socialists. In conjunction with the HROs, the CPPD began to elaborate a high profile and well-defined human rights agenda in preparation for government from 1988 onward, and the issue of accountability for past rights violations was prominent during the electoral campaign in 1989. In Chile, therefore, the passion for "truth" and "justice" was particularly strong and politically difficult to sidestep.[14]

This passion, however, coexisted with extreme caution. The way that reconciliation was conceived of, the way that *convivencia* (peaceful coexistence or accommodation) was emphasized so insistently, meant a de facto acceptance of coexistence with authoritarian enclaves within the political system. In 1994 President Aylwin declared that the transition to democracy was over, even though the Constitution remained unreformed and such enclaves abounded. Reconciliation and *convivencia* were thus prized over a deepening of democracy, which was seen as a threat to stability. Edgardo Boeniger, the strategist of the CPPD and minister of the presidency under Aylwin, writes that the government's action was not just limited by external constraints: "[T]he essential responsibility of the government was to rebuild national coexistence, a concept that excluded efforts to impose the laws of the democratic victors, even if they had had the parliamentary majority and willingness to do it."[15] From the outset then, a limited drive for truth and justice was part of a willingness to live with a curtailed democratization process.

Finally, under Aylwin, law and *fortuna* did not aid the human rights cause. Misfortune made its presence felt dramatically after the launching of the Rettig Report. Not long after it had been made public, the Manuel Rodríguez Patriotic Front (Frente Patriótico Manuel Rodríguez, FPMR) assassinated Jaime Guzmán, the intellectual star and political leader of the right and former advisor to General Pinochet.[16] This event served to obscure the launching of the report and gave credence to right-wing claims that the regime had been correct to combat "subversion." Overall, continued terrorist action by the FPMR and another terrorist group, the United Popular Action Movement (Movimiento de Acción Popular Unido, MAPU-Lautaro), did not favor those seeking to punish human rights violations, as it helped to legitimize the antisubversive activities of the military. *Fortuna* did sometimes work in favor of human rights, however, as with the discovery of mass graves in Colina in March 1990, only two weeks after Aylwin took power; and in June 1990, in Pisagua, where nineteen bodies were found, some still wearing blindfolds.[17] This had the opposite effect of left-wing terrorism; it proved that state terrorism was the key problem to be addressed.

But it was the law that least favored the search for justice. The legal establishment was, with notable exceptions, resistant to truth and justice. The Supreme Court had cooperated extensively with the Pinochet regime, helping to legitimate it and ignoring human rights claims. The authoritarian tendencies of the court had been reinforced by the Rosende Law of June 1989, which increased the number of sitting justices favorable to the outgoing regime. The Supreme Court opposed Aylwin's interpretation of the Amnesty Law after the transition. On 24 August 1990 it unanimously upheld the constitutionality of that law. Between 1990 and 1993 the Court sent the great majority of cases to the military courts, where they were closed by means of a "preventive" application of the amnesty law. Three examples suffice to show the general inclination of this court: on 26 January 1990 it suspended Judge Carlos Cerda without pay for two months for not applying the law in a case involving thirteen disappeared persons; in June 1991 it closed the investigation of the execution and clandestine burial of twenty-six individuals that had taken place in the Calama desert in 1973, upholding a military court's decision to apply the amnesty law; and in September 1993, in what was considered a landmark case, for the first time the court held that a DINA agent, Maria Joui, was directly responsible for the disappearance of at least one person; but it nonetheless applied the amnesty law here, too.

However, this was not so for a major case resolved under the Aylwin administration, which set off the first civil-military crisis since the transition. Due to U.S. pressure, the 1978 amnesty had not covered the assassination in 1976 of Allende's foreign minister, Orlando Letelier, and Ronnie Moffit, his secretary, in Washington, D.C., by agents of the first and most bloody secret police of the dictatorship, the DINA. The investigating judge, Adolfo Bañados, established a direct link between the Embassy Row bombing and the DINA, indicting the former head of the secret police, retired General Manuel Contreras, and his aide, Brigadier General Pedro Espinoza. This event led to a severe reaction by the military.[18] On 28 May 1993 soldiers of the Army Special Forces, the Black Berets, surrounded the presidential palace, La Moneda, in an action that became known as El Boinazo (because of the berets—boinas—worn by the troops). This event was widely interpreted as a warning to the government not to pursue human rights trials and further investigations of the so-called "Pinocheques" case.[19]

The government's reaction was not long in coming. It responded to the pressures by attempting to pass legislation to limit possible future judicial proceedings; thus, convivencia dictated the limits of justice. But equally, the passion for justice limited the sacrifices to be made for convivencia. The so-called Aylwin Law proposed that informants who offered the courts information leading to the location of the disappeared should remain anonymous and be guaranteed impunity; that up to fifteen Appeals Court judges should investigate the cases full-time; that trials should take place in total secrecy; that the amnesty law should be applied automatically after disclosure; and that those convicted of post-1978 crimes should be held in special facilities. By September 1993 the proposal had failed due to opposition from the right (which wanted no reinterpretation of the amnesty) and the Socialists, and a general outcry by HROs. Two months later, Judge Bañados found Contreras and Espinoza guilty of the murder of Letelier, sentencing them to seven and six years of imprisonment, respectively.

But El Boinazo had had its desired effect. For a while, at least, the human rights issue disappeared from the political agenda. The Supreme Court became even more assiduous in closing cases. On 23 September 1993 it applied the amnesty law in the Pisagua case, the investigation of the execution of nineteen persons whose bodies had been found in a clandestine cemetery discovered on 2 June 1990.[20] In October of that year, the Court refused to heed a government request and appoint a special prosecutor to investigate the assassination in 1974 of former commander-in-chief of the Army, General Carlos Prats, and his wife, Sofía Cuthbert, in Buenos Aires by DINA agents. Following El Boinazo, the military courts closed fourteen cases in which the Supreme Court had upheld the application of the amnesty law. Soon, Chileans were preoccupied with the electoral campaign of 1993 to elect a new government in March 1994.

Despite a growing silence around the human rights issue, the Aylwin administration came to a close without any measures passed to halt judicial proceedings. Thus, the issue of justice was set to reappear on the political agenda under Frei. At the same time, the stage was set for a shift in the influence of the law upon it. Although the amnesty law did not permit the prosecution of crimes committed before 1978, it did not protect perpetrators of abuses committed after that date. In addition, it was only the pro-regime loyalties of the judges then sitting in the Supreme Court that stood in the way of more progressive interpretations of the amnesty law. Their longevity was not indefinite; eventually the CPPD government could appoint new judges, increasing the probability of a court more friendly to the cause of the victims.

The Frei Administration: Unraveling "Reconciliation" and Broadening Justice

On 11 December 1993 President Frei was elected with fifty-eight percent of the vote. As he took office in March 1994, the twice victorious CPPD faced the same constraints that it had experienced under Aylwin's rule. It retained seventy seats in the Chamber while the right-wing coalition, the Union for Progress (Unión por el Progreso, UPP) gained fifty. In the Senate, it held twenty against the eighteen held by the right because of the existence of the appointed senators. However, although this president lacked the same moral and political commitment to truth—the same "passion"—that Aylwin had demonstrated, the courts were dealing with cases that would produce renewed civil-military tensions.

In March 1994, fifteen members of the intelligence communications directorate of the Carabineros police (Dirección de Comunicación de Carabineros, DICOMCAR) were convicted of the 1985 murder of three militants of the Communist Party (Partido Comunista de Chile, PCCh). As a major human rights organization reported at the time, this verdict "breached a wall of impunity which held intact for more than 20 years," as a court at last had issued a sentence "commensurate with the gravity of a human rights crime."[21] One of the men indicted was General Rodolfo Stange, director of the Carabineros at the time. President Frei called for his resignation, which led to a backlash from the military and the right. Stange refused to comply; the then-minister of the interior, Germán Correa, was forced to step down; and a military court later dismissed the case.

Despite this defeat, other cases continued to work their way through the courts. On 30 May 1995 the Supreme Court confirmed the sentence against Contreras and Espinoza. Military reactions were initially negative; the Army protected Contreras from arrest for five months. However, both men were finally imprisoned and are now serving their sentences. On 13 August 1995 the Appeals Court of La Serena ordered the state to pay US$263,000 in damages to the family of a truck driver and member of the PDC, Mario Fernández López, who had been tortured to death on 17 October 1984. This was the first case ever of damages being awarded for human rights violations.[22]

Following the Supreme Court decision on the Contreras case, the government again came under pressure from the right and the military, and tried to pass legislation to limit prosecutions. In May 1995 the president presented a bill to Congress to allow the courts to suspend all trials in which penal liability had either been proscribed or extinguished by previous legislation. This initiative failed for the same reasons that had prevented Aylwin from passing any laws to put a stop to prosecutions. In September 1995 the administration proposed a package of three laws, linking the human rights issue with various institutional reforms. This proposal failed as well. The right also rejected Frei's proposal that all human rights cases remain open until the fate of the disappeared had been established. It presented an alternative bill, which proposed that special judges be appointed to resolve all remaining cases, that these be empowered to close definitively all cases for which no new information was forthcoming, and that all cases already in the military courts remain there. The bill was never passed, thanks to the opposition of the PS-PPD and the UDI. This was the last attempt made to put a legal end to prosecution. At this time, there were in the courts an estimated six hundred suits concerning one thousand military officers.

The government had hoped to limit the scope of justice. But it had done so to limit conflict and not because it was opposed to justice. Indeed, while it did not actively pursue justice, it supported the search for the disappeared and the work of the courts. In November 1997, for example, President Frei vetoed the promotion of Brigadier Jaime Lepe, a close associate of Pinochet in the DINA, because of his involvement in the disappearance of Spanish citizen and U.N. official, Carmelo Soria, who was assassinated in 1976 by a DINA agent. In March 1998 the government announced the creation of a DNA databank to identify the disappeared. The government is also acting as co-plaintiff in the trial by an Argentine court of Enrique Arancibia Clavel, a former intelligence agent involved in the Prats assassination. It has adopted the same position in two other major cases.[23]

But it was not the goodwill of the executive that shifted the balance in favor of justice; it was law and *fortuna*. About two years after the government had tried to limit justice, the law began to shift in favor of the human rights cause.[24] From 1997 onward, the jurisprudence of the Supreme Court began to show the first signs of cracking in favor of human rights. Already in 1995 divisions had become apparent within the court: a reform had revealed that its judges were divided on amnesty cases, with a minority regularly voting against decisions not to apply the Aylwin doctrine.[25] A later reform of the structure of the court and the appointment of new judges in 1998, who took office in 1999, shifted the balance further in favor of the human rights cause. A number of rulings illustrate this shift.

On 8 August 1997 the Supreme Court voted to expand the investigation into the former Colonia Dignidad, a colony of German immigrants with Nazi associations implicated in various human rights cases, to include 112 cases of disappearance between 1975 and 1977. On 19 November 1997 it reversed an amnesty ruling for the first time, rejecting the decision of a military court to close the case of the arrest and disappearance of two members of the PS, Rodolfo Espejo and Gregorio López. On 12 March 1998 the court ruled against closure in the case of the illegal detention and disappearance of twenty-four peasants in Paine in 1973, and thus against application of the amnesty. On 2 April it decided unanimously to reject the closure by a civil court of the case of the kidnapping and disappearance of six PCCh militants in September 1987. On 6 May it deviated from previous jurisprudence and determined that handing lists of names of violators to the civil courts did not represent a threat to national security in the case of three disappearances. On 15 May it voted not to apply the amnesty law in the case of eight people detained and made to disappear by the DINA in Valparaíso between 17 and 27 January 1975. On 24 June the president of the court, Roberto Dávila, stated that he favored a law interpreting the amnesty in such a way as to avoid continued conflicts over the human rights issue, provoking angry reactions on the right. On 21 August the court applied the amnesty law to the case of the disappearance of two members of the Revolutionary Left Movement (Movimiento de Izquierda Revolucionaria, MIR).[26] However, the vote was divided three to three, and the law was only applied because of the principle that any court decision must favor the accused. On 3 September it ruled that the military courts in Concepción should initiate proceedings against two CNI agents accused of the murder of five members of the MIR on 23 August 1984. The court had previously voted against closure of the case.

On 10 September in a particularly significant case, the Supreme Court applied the Geneva Convention for the first time since 1973 in the July 1974 case of the kidnapping and disappearance of a member of the MIR, Pedro Poblete Córdoba, by the DINA.[27] This gave primacy to international law over the amnesty law for the first time, opening the path for future challenges to the legitimacy and sanctity of this legal mechanism for impunity.

The picture, however, was not altogether bright. Positive Supreme Court rulings were counterbalanced by negative ones. On 10 October 1997, for example, following a request by the military public prosecutor, the court recommended that the lower courts apply the amnesty law to over one hundred cases then in the courts.

For many, it seemed that the human rights issue was no longer alive by the beginning of 1998. Indeed, what some saw as an "unnatural" silence prevailed, with an externally or self-imposed censorship ensuring little coverage of the past and an absence of a critical opposition press. As one report indicates, "even anti-Pinochet jokes, traditionally a rich vein of humor during the military government, were exiled to cyberspace."[28] At the same time, Chilean law prevents open coverage of ongoing court cases. Thus, in contrast with Argentina, where an active left-wing press reported on the progress made in an ongoing case, silence reigns in Chile until a verdict is reached, diminishing the social impact of evolving investigations. Censorship is still strong. Books about the past or touching on topics bearing on the perceived interest of the old regime have been censored since 1990.[29] In accordance with the 1958 State Security Law, expressions of criticism of Pinochet and others associated with his rule have continued to meet with fines or jail sentences. Since 1990, an estimated fifteen journalists and eight politicians have been charged under Article 6 (b) of this law.[30]

It was to take an unpredictable injection of *fortuna* to truly shake up the political system, shift the balance between passion and constraint, and infuse the law with a new energy in favor of human rights. In May 1998, two months after the failure of a constitutional accusation motion leveled against Pinochet by the left in Congress to prevent him from taking up his lifetime senatorial position, a new criminal suit was brought to the Spanish courts accusing the general and others of the disappearance of two hundred people during Operation Condor.[31] On 3 October the French government denied Pinochet the right to enter the country due to accusations of human rights violations pending against him. Days later, on 16 October 1998, the general was arrested in London, after investigating Judge Baltazar Garzón of the National Audience (Audiencia Nacional, AN), the highest court in Spain, issued an arrest warrant for him.[32]

On 5 November the AN unanimously confirmed Spain's right to judge the general, and on 10 December 1998 Pinochet was indicted for genocide, terrorism, and torture by Judge Garzón. Meanwhile, in the United Kingdom, the House of Lords ruled on two occasions, on 25 November 1998 and 24 March 1999, that Pinochet could be extradited, even though the second decision limited the crimes for which he was extraditable. In January 2000, the British government finally announced that it would release the general for humanitarian reasons, allowing him to return to Chile because of his age and ill health.[33]

The Pinochet Arrest: Reconciliation versus Democratization

The Pinochet arrest has led to the reemergence, with a vengeance, of the issue of past violations in Chile. Latent social divisions and political animosities have been reawakened and, as at the outset of the transition to democracy, the debate about the trade-off between justice and political stability is back on the political agenda. Since 1990 reconciliation has been an end and good prized as highly as truth, and more highly than justice. Indeed, as in other cases of negotiated transitions, the most important debate in the Chilean case has been about the compatibility of peace with justice. Can justice be pursued without a breakdown of the new democracy due to a military backlash? Or can democracy survive if the principle of equality before the law, one of its ethical foundations, is not clearly established and lived up to?

During the transitional period, this debate was conducted famously between José Zalaquett, one of the members of the truth commission, and Aryeh Neier, then president of the New York-based HRO, Human Rights Watch. In the early 1990s, both were often to be found at international conferences, talking about general principles or about the Chilean "way" and its applicability to other cases of transitional justice in Eastern Europe or South Africa. While Zalaquett counterpoised the ethics of conviction with the ethics of responsibility and emphasized political context and constraints, Neier talked about the duty to punish such crimes.[34] Those writing specifically about the Chilean case have also been divided. Some have argued that the government has not gone far enough, that it imposed constraints upon itself *avant la lettre*;[35] others, that it has been too committed to accommodation and has held a limited vision of citizenship rights;[36] and still others, that it framed the question too narrowly and has thus failed to accompany retrospective policies with forward-looking, wide-ranging institutional reforms that would have given accountability (and democratization) a better chance.[37] On the other hand, others have argued that, however limited, the government's policies have gone as far as could have been hoped for in existing conditions.[38] Comparative studies that set the case of Chile alongside other actual cases, rather than judge it by an ideal standard, tend to be more favorable in their evaluation. In this light, it is undeniable that Chile has indeed gone further in limiting impunity than any other country.[39]

Neither the peace versus justice debate, nor the more specific discussion about the Chilean case, has been entirely resolved. Each side's argument has some justification and yet neither is completely convincing. First, it is difficult to ascertain to what degree constraints are real or self-inflicted. Boeniger may claim that more was not done because it did not figure in the Aylwin government's plans, but this may be a politician's attempt to deny that weakness was the driving force of the government in which he participated. Still, close observation of the Chilean political process does not reveal an abundance of missed opportunities. Room for political maneuver has been in short supply. Counterfactual exercises would be necessary to "prove" that more could have been done, but such exercises rarely prove anything, as there are too many intervening variables to account for. Second, it is not clear how trials and the disclosure of the truth actually contribute to democracy, as the "duty to punish" school argues. Yet, there is also evidence that a "burying" of the past—in the sense of a letting-be—can be damaging to democracy in the long run, because it tends to involve leaving authoritarian enclaves unchallenged.

Without claiming to resolve this dilemma, I would suggest that Pinochet's arrest may have opened up a key opportunity to further the democratization process, precisely because it has upset the myth of "reconciliation" and *convivencia* among Chileans. Some have tried to argue the opposite—that attempts to do further justice, especially in cases that involve the former dictator, will prove disastrous for democracy. In keeping with the principle of accepting the "inevitable" limits in place since 1990, the Chilean government has always argued that Pinochet's arrest posed a threat to Chilean democracy. There were some initial indications that they could be right. The arrest unified the right for the first time since the transition, enabling it to mobilize and leading to the first street demonstrations by the right since the downfall of Allende, many of them violent. It brought out the "uncivil" right: members of Congress and others received death threats, there were bomb threats, and rumors proliferated of the reemergence of the Anti-Revolutionary Forces of Fatherland and Liberty (Fuerzas Anti-Revolucionarias Patria y Libertad, FA-PL) and Omega-7, two ultra–right-wing groups that had operated during the Allende regime. The arrest also threatened to split the governing coalition, which is still the most democratic force in Chilean politics, whatever its limitations. While the PDC tended to support the return of the general to Chile, the PS-PPD were more ambiguous. Within the Cabinet, Socialist ministers Jorge Arrate and Jaime Tohá, among others, took a stance against the government's position, while Undersecretary for Human Rights, Carmen Hertz, resigned over the treatment of the arrest. Within the lower ranks of the PS-PPD there were many who wish to see Pinochet judged. The decision of PS-PPD deputies to go to London, together with the victims of repression, shows that there is greater identification with the victims of repression than with any putative attack on the country's sovereignty. For many Socialists, reconciliation has never taken place in Chile. For them, feelings of injustice have merely been suppressed and the current crisis has served to reveal "the real Chile." Indeed, many argue that the transition was never completed and that by accommodating Pinochet and his allies, the coalition has abdicated from any serious commitment to push forward the process of democratization. In addition, the campaign for the January 2000 elections became heated. The only hope of the right—having never gained more than thirty-five percent of the vote—was to exacerbate the differences within the coalition. It also began to focus on stirring up old fears of a return to the chaos of the Allende years and the radicalization of the left.

Pinochet's detention also renewed civil-military tensions. General Izurieta has tried to depoliticize the military since becoming commander-in-chief, lowering the profile of the Army, modernizing and depersonalizing its command, and purging it of officers associated with past repression. He issued an internal circular prohibiting—on pain of sanctions—all public participation in acts related to the arrest. His slow reforms and his moderate position, however, have been threatened by the arrest. Much as the distance between the more moderate right and the radical right narrowed, the arrest has brought together "institutionalists" and Pinochetistas, narrowing the space for reform.[40] In the Senate the four appointed senators who are former military officers went so far as to call for the suspension of all business, including the discussion of the 1999 budget, until the release of Pinochet.

These initial worries, however, have been amply counterbalanced by more positive effects that are beneficial for democracy and justice. First, the general is no longer sacred. He is no longer the untouchable and almost venerated father figure that he was only a month before his arrest. The arrogant invincibility conveyed in an interview with *The New Yorker* only a month before his arrest, has been demolished and his image irremediably damaged.[41] It is unlikely that he will remain an appointed senator, and there is even a vague possibility that he will be summoned to a national court. On 12 January 1998 a court of appeals judge, Juan Guzmán Tapia, accepted a criminal complaint of genocide against Pinochet by Gladys Marín of the PCCh. This was the first time that a court in Chile had accepted direct charges against the general. As of November 1999 there were fifty-five such cases in the courts; and although almost two years have passed since charges were filed without any charge being made against the general, this contrasts sharply with the past. Only three years earlier, on 19 July 1995, Pinochet had successfully sued Arturo

Barrios, the president of the Socialist Youth, just for saying that criminal charges should be brought against him for human rights violations. The Supreme Court had sustained the suit, and Barrios was jailed. A suit has also been filed against other former members of the regime.[42]

Many Chileans have begun to face the truth for the first time since 1990, something many had managed to avoid when the Rettig Report was published. For the first time since the early years of the Aylwin administration, there has been open and lively debate in the press, even the conservative press, about violations and the meaning of the past for Chilean democracy. The political right has begun to admit openly that the disappearances were part of deliberate government policy under the military. No one has questioned the right of relatives to know the whereabouts of the disappeared, which is considered a top priority for Chilean democracy. Even the military has begun to make gestures of accepting the need for further work on the past, even if it is still far from accepting responsibility. Navy commander-in-chief, Admiral Jorge Arancibia, has made statements in favor of a national accounting of events; and the Air Force has taken the unprecedented step of declining to contest jurisdiction over a trial involving some of its former officers.

Many cases that had languished in the courts for years were finally resolved after the arrest. In addition, this new impetus toward justice was further promoted by the subsequent taking of office of a new slate of judges in January 1999. This pro-human rights shift led to the emergence of the so-called "post-Aylwin doctrine." This is based on the idea that disappearance is a continuous crime and as such cannot be amnestied until death is ascertained. Although, as described above, a positive trend was already evident, Pinochet's arrest does seem to have reinforced it, encouraging and galvanizing the courts into action. Two important postamnesty cases, the murder of trade union leader Tucapel Jiménez on 25 February 1982, and of twelve members of the FPMR in Operation Albania on 15–16 June 1987, were concluded after years of stalling.[43]

On 14 September 1999 General Humberto Gordon, a member of the military junta (1986–88) and former director of the CNI, and Brigadier Jaime Schmied Zanzi, who headed the metropolitan division of the CNI, were charged and detained for the Tucapel murder.[44] A total of fourteen men have been indicted and arrested in connection with this case. The Albania case was ordered to be reopened on 30 March 1999. Twelve suspects were arrested, including the former head of the DINE, General Rámsez Álvarez y Herrera Jiménez, and a new judge was appointed on 10 April. Finally, in October 1999, seven officers, including former CNI director, retired General Humberto Leiva, retired Brigadier General Marcos Derpich, and Álvaro Corvalán, the former chief of operations of the CNI, were sentenced for kidnapping and homicide in the case.[45]

Important jurisprudential shifts have occurred within the Supreme Court that may widen the scope for future prosecution of crimes covered by the amnesty. Only days after the Pinochet arrest, on 28 October, the court voted to reopen the investigation of the disappearance of a member of the Communist Youth, Carlos Humberto Contreras Maluje, who had been detained on 3 November 1976. For the first time, it cited as a reason the fact that a disappearance is an ongoing case as long as the death of the person is not definitively confirmed. As with the decision invoking the Geneva Convention, this sets a precedent that challenges the sanctity of the amnesty law. In the case of the disappearance of Enrique Poblete Córdova in July 1974, the Sala Penal also cited the Geneva Convention, reversing earlier jurisprudence that had accepted the military's declaration of a state of war during that period. On 7 January 1999 the court ordered a military court to reopen the case of the arrest and disappearance of twenty-six people in Parral, in southern Chile, in 1973–74. In this ruling, it again held that disappearance is an ongoing crime that is understood to have been committed after the amnesty law, since the missing persons had not been found. Again, on 2 July 1999, the court unanimously rejected a habeas corpus appeal on behalf of General Arrellano Stark and four other officers arrested and charged with kidnapping during the "Caravan of Death" of October 1973.[46] In this decision the Supreme Court again ruled that the amnesty could not apply, because death could not be legally certified and therefore the persons involved must be presumed missing and the crime ongoing.[47] On 26 August the Santiago Appeals Court rejected the appeal by the defendants, and ordered that another DINA agent, Fernando Larios, should be indicted, bringing to six those charged for the crime.[48]

In the wake of the Caravan of Death decision, an increasingly worried military protested against what they saw as a change in the rules of the game, with the amnesty law no longer serving to protect them. Army generals met for three days to discuss the verdict and the commander of the three forces met with Defense Minister Edmundo Pérez Yoma on 23 July 1999 to protest the "parade" of officers taken through the courts. In 1997, an estimated 150 soldiers appeared before the courts; in the first six months of 1999, 120.[49] The Army also protested against the Tucapel case arrests, but no action was taken to prevent the course of justice. Indeed, in both the Tucapel and Albania cases, the Army gave investigating judges access to DINE records that were crucial to the indictments and arrests. At the same time, the first cracks in military solidarity began to appear. In April 1999 the army major serving time in jail for the murder of PDC truck driver, Mario Fernández, made a public apology for what he did; and in the same year, the first officers confessed to knowledge of "dirty war" deeds, including throwing people into the sea. The pact of silence was weakened for the first time.[50]

To its credit, the Frei government stated that it could not submit to pressure to interfere with judicial proceedings. But it was galvanized into seeking yet another "political solution" to the human rights problem. Tripartite discussions were held among General Izurieta, the minister of the interior (Raúl Troncoso), and the archbishop of Santiago (Francisco Javier Errázuriz) in 1998–99. Further confidential meetings were held among human rights experts, the UDI, RN, Church leaders, military officers and representatives of the victims. This finally led to the establishment of a Dialogue Forum (Mesa de Diálogo). At the time of this writing, the Forum has convened twice, the first session being held on 31 August 1999. It brought members of the armed forces and representatives of the victims' relatives face to face for the first time.[51]

At the same time, proposals were tabled to allow civilian judges to investigate military premises and to place human rights cases under civilian jurisdiction, although neither has gone beyond the Lower House at the time of writing. Indeed, constitutional reform returned to the agenda. It was announced as an objective in May 1999 by the president, and a proposal was put forward in June 1999. Significantly, in May 1999 "the insufficiencies of our democracy" were finally admitted to by President Frei in his state of the nation address. Given its links with wider issues of reform, the struggle for justice has become part of the struggle to define the nature of democracy itself.

Pinochet's detention may also contribute on a more immediate level to counteracting the weight of fear and concomitant immobility of the political system. In Chile conflict had become synonymous with chaos; and the strengthening of belief that Chilean society can sustain some level of conflict without degenerating into chaos, would strike the single strongest political blow against the right, which constantly argues the opposite. There is now evidence that the right's argument is more rhetoric than reality. A MORI poll of 2 December 1998 showed that seventy-one percent of Chileans felt unaffected by the Pinochet arrest and that 66 percent did not believe democracy was in danger. The courts have prosecuted individuals and jailed them without a return to dictatorship. Two years ago it would have been unthinkable that anyone should touch Pinochet. Yet he was arrested and Chilean democracy has been sustained. It is natural that the military should rattle their sabers and that the right should defend the interests of their allies, but no one has called for an end to democracy. Thus, the search for truth and justice is challenging a narrow vision of democracy based on an imposed consensus about the necessity of subordinating any drive toward deepening citizenship to the need for stability and accommodation with undemocratic institutions and groups.

Conclusion

Chileans still have a long way to go in their search for truth and justice. In the military arena, unlike the Argentine top brass, the Chilean armed forces are still unapologetic. The commander-in-chief has insisted that the armed forces have no information regarding the whereabouts of the disappeared. Thus, forgiveness and taking leave of the dead are still blocked. In the legal arena, Supreme Court jurisprudence is not binding for future cases, so the newly emerging doctrine could be reversed or applied only in a few cases and not in others. Further, the military courts still have jurisdiction over most cases and a bill in August 1998 to remove the Army auditor-general from the Supreme Court has yet to be considered.

In the political arena, further attempts to legislate an end to justice may be made. In December 1998, the Senate's Commission on Human Rights, Nationality, and Citizenship attempted to do just that. It proposed that courts should be allowed to investigate human rights cases indefinitely, but it also protected those who testified from ever being prosecuted, much like the Aylwin and Frei proposals of 1993 and 1995. The proposal failed, due to opposition both from the military and from victims' groups, but future attempts could be successful.

As far as Pinochet himself is concerned, although the Chilean government argued that the general should be judged at home and therefore returned to

Chile, he is still defended by many and by the law. He has great influence within the military and parts of the right. He has immunity as a member of the Senate. He can take legal action under the State Security Law against his critics, as he has done in the past. The amnesty law protects him; and if he ever were tried, he would probably be taken to a military court composed of men previously under his command. He is even defended by those favoring human rights. Former president Aylwin was one of those who voted against his impeachment in January 1998. On 14 November 1998 the Supreme Court voted by a majority against a government request to appoint a special judge to deal with the suits against Pinochet; the investigations had gone nowhere. Judge Guzmán Tapia is thus still handling the cases against the general; and in November 1999 it was reported that he might seek to lift Pinochet's immunity. This would have to be authorized by the Supreme Court, in accordance with Article 58 of the Constitution on parliamentary immunity. It is possible, however, that the military courts could claim jurisdiction over these cases and automatically absolve the general.[52]

Society is also divided. A December 1998 MORI poll indicated that 44 percent felt the arrest was a good thing, while 45 percent thought it was bad. The fact that two-thirds considered Pinochet guilty of the crimes he is accused of, is an ambiguous finding. After almost ten years of truth disclosure, it is significant that the number was not higher. Most analysts emphasize that "only" 29 percent thought he should not be tried, but this is a large percentage of the population. On the other hand, the same poll indicated that 57 percent felt it would be best if he were tried. Another poll by *Qué Pasa* in the same month indicated that the issue was ranked only fourth among those of importance, and almost half considered it personally unimportant. It seems, then, that people do not find the issue of justice for violations a top priority. Moreover, although 59 percent wanted Pinochet tried by Chilean courts, this may have been as much a nationalist reflex as a desire for justice. It certainly does not guarantee that society will mobilize to ensure that he is tried.

At the same time, although the basis of "reconciliation" and *convivencia* as conceived of to date has taken a beating, the CPPD still has some way to go. The presidential proposal in June 1999 to reform the Constitution has gone nowhere, because the government has done little to push it forward. Previous attempts at reform on 12 January 1993 and 11 April 1996 failed, and on 17 June 1997 the government was unsuccessful in passing a reform bill in the Senate to eliminate the designated senators.[53] When constraints are challenged, the results are often ambiguous. On 20 April 1999 coalition deputies presented a bill to abolish article 30 of the State Security Law and some provisions of Article 6 (b). It was the first time this law had been challenged, but the outcome of that reform has not been very positive. The provisions of 6 (b) were essentially incorporated into the penal code, and a proposed amendment may make the new situation as repressive as the previous one. Laws to protect journalists and freedom of information have been stalled since 1993.

What is more, in some ways Chile's democracy seems to be as tied up (*amarrada*) as ever. Pinochet immediately took up his lifetime office of senator, amid expressions of support from the right, the business community, and the military. The Organic Law of the Armed Forces has remained untouched due to right-wing opposition. The military is still full of violators, since, except for a mini-purge of the Investigating Police (Policía de Investigaciones, PI) in the early 1990s under General Toro, it has refused to purge its ranks.[54]

On the positive side, on 7 March 1997 the government did manage to change the composition of the Constitutional Tribunal, making it more democratic and facilitating constitutional reform in the future. On 10 March 1998 General Pinochet retired after twenty-five years as commander-in-chief of the Army; and his replacement, General Ricardo Izurieta, was widely regarded as a professional, apolitical military officer. The last of the commanders involved in the military regime, the commander-in-chief of the Navy, Jorge Martínez Busch, retired on 11 March 1998. Furthermore, it is notable that it is in Chile that impunity is most constrained. The amnesty law has led to the closure of court cases investigating 170 disappearances, one-sixth of the total.[55] Yet Chile has far more human rights violators in jail than any other country in the Americas. Overall, in the last year, five generals, including a former member of the military junta, and approximately thirty active-duty and retired officers have been arrested and jailed for human rights crimes. There are currently an estimated eighty cases pending in the courts, affecting 261 victims. And unlike Eastern Europe, where attempts to do justice have often been accused of violating due process, none of the court cases in Chile have been flawed on this count.

In January 2000, PS-PPD presidential candidate Ricardo Lagos won the elections for the CPPD, beating Joaquín Lavín (former mayor of the Las

Condes district where the Pinochetist wealthy live), who led the right-wing Alliance for Chile (Alianza por Chile). In his opening campaign speech, "Contract with Chile: Growing with Equality," delivered on 20 September 1999 in Curanilahue, Lagos stated that there would be no interference with the work of the courts or with government action to find the disappeared and promote a dialogue between the two sides. Since his victory, Lagos has reaffirmed this position. Lavín has also taken a positive stand on human rights, apologizing on 26 July 1999 for rights violations, supporting investigations, and asserting that Pinochet is a citizen like any other and can therefore be tried. Although there is no guarantee that the new CPPD government will not pass a law to limit the pursuit of justice, a Socialist president will find it hard to justify such a course of action.

Meanwhile, the international dimension has acquired a new importance, as efforts to seek truth and justice now transcend national boundaries. Like other states in the region, Chile has become party to international and regional conventions and protocols that limit national sovereignty where human rights are concerned. For the most part, such treaties convey negative duties with respect to human rights; states are called upon not to do anything that may threaten those rights. However, the right to compensation and the truth are positive rights that require state action. Thus, the Chilean government, like others in the region, has been pressed by the regional human rights system to get rid of amnesty provisions or to ensure the right to truth in order to comply with its international obligations. At the same time, because of these universal obligations, victims of repression have been able to resort to an outside source of recognized authority to challenge the authority of national executives or judiciaries. Prosecution efforts have been advanced by mixed ad hoc transnational coalitions, which include exiles, judges, and church and human rights nongovernmental organizations. National agents have gained hope and confidence through this evidence of transnational support. It is thought, for example, that the accusation of genocide against Pinochet presented by Gladys Marín in January 1998 was inspired by Spanish action.

Proceedings and extradition requests have been initiated against human rights violators in various countries other than Spain. They include Argentina,[56] Austria,[57] Belgium,[58] Canada,[59] Denmark,[60] France,[61] Germany,[62] Italy, [63] Switzerland,[64] Sweden,[65] the United Kingdom,[66] Uruguay,[67] and the United States.[68] Of these, Belgium, France, and Switzerland actually requested the extradition of Pinochet.[69] The Chilean government is also under pressure from regional and international human rights organizations, and from their national counterparts, which have sought to exploit the national ratification of human rights laws. Chilean HROs have presented twenty-three denial-of-justice suits to the Inter-American Human Rights Commission (IAHRC), which ruled in October 1997 and on 30 May 1998 that the amnesty law was incompatible with Chile's ratification of the Inter-American Convention.[70] It recommended the annulment of the law and the reopening of twenty-two previously closed cases of disappearance.[71] Further, in January 2000 it struck a blow against the national sovereignty argument, ruling in favor of universal jurisdiction for the Soria case with the opinion that the case could be tried in Spain. In the U.N., on 5 May 1999, the Human Rights Committee (UNHRC), which monitors compliance with the International Convention on Civil and Political Rights (ICCPR), also ruled against the amnesty law.

There are other indications that human rights and justice for past violations matter to Chileans inside Chile as well as outside. In a country where a book that sells two or three editions of a print run of two thousand is a best-seller, Tomas Moulián's *Chile Today: Anatomy of a Myth* (*Chile Actual: Anatomía de un Mito*), which deconstructs the Chilean "myth" of reconciliation, went through twenty-four editions. According to one journalist, the unprecedented popularity of biographies or other academic books that delve into the past is due to the fact that "the country has not explored its recent past."[72] The film "Battle of Chile" ("Batalla de Chile"), about the fall of the Allende regime and the first months of the coup, is a best-selling video. Another film, "Chile: Obstinate Memory" ("Chile, memoria obstinada"), which shows how people have become estranged from the past and are also quickly drawn back into it as if it were not the past at all, is also a best-seller.[73]

The building of commemorative sculptures or monuments also shows a social awareness and need to deal with the past. The former DINA secret detention center, Villa Grimaldi, is now "Peace Park" (Parque de la Paz); and a Wall of Names (Muro de los Nombres) was inaugurated there on 21 December 1998, bearing the names of 230 disappeared persons and the inscription, "forgetting is full of remembering" ("el olvido está lleno de memoria") by the Uruguayan novelist, Mario Benedetti. The symbolically charged date of 11 September, the day of the military coup, has been a focus for public celebration. In a victory for those who have long repudiated the date, the government finally annulled it as a national holiday in 1998. It is common for references to the past to be used to legitimate allies, discredit political opponents, create loyalties, and justify political options. This has been apparent in the current electoral campaign. The position candidates adopt with regard to the events that led to the breakdown of democracy and the ensuing repression is part of the language that legitimates or discredits presidential hopefuls.[74]

In sum, the struggle for justice in Chile does not have a clear path ahead; but it is far from over. Chileans have fought to give expression to their passion for dealing with the past since 1973. In pursuit of that aim since 1990, they have had to wrestle with a tendency to premature "reconciliation," a euphemism for the acceptance of a limited democracy with authoritarian enclaves. They have also had to confront real obstacles in the form of a powerful military and right wing, as well as legal limitations of a kind not found in any other democratized country of the region. The law has been both an obstacle and a source of new opportunities. And *fortuna* (exploiting the hubris of a dictator who would not suffer constraints on his foreign traveling) has lately forced Chileans to look at their past again, and to consider where they want to go next with it. It is likely that the past will remain in the present as long as there are HROs, courts, and international allies to conjure it up. It is, indeed, as Benedetti says: "el olvido está lleno de memorias."

Endnotes

1. I would like to thank Alan Angell for the very useful comments on another draft of this chapter. In addition, I would like to acknowledge extensive use of the web site (http://www.fasic.org) of the Foundation for Social Assistance of the Christian Churches (Fundación de Ayuda Social de las Iglesias Cristianas, FASIC) for updated information about court cases.

2. My use of the terms "passion" and "constraint" was inspired by Stephen Holmes in his *Passions and Constraint: On the Theory of Liberal Democracy* (Chicago: University of Chicago Press, 1995). However, the definition of constraint here is not the same as his, since his concern is with positive constraints on passions in the form of liberal democratic checks and balances and other such instruments to limit absolute power.

3. The use of the term "law" does not refer to actual laws, but rather to the world of law, including legislation, courts, legal procedure, and jurisprudence, as well as the judiciary as a political actor.

4. *Fortuna* (fortune) as a determinant of politics looms large in the thought of Macchiavelli.

5. Comisión Nacional de Verdad y Reconciliación, *Informe de la Comisión Nacional de Verdad y Reconciliación* (Santiago: Ediciones del Ornitorrinco, 1991). For analyses of the Commission, see Mark Ensalaco, "Truth Commissions for Chile and El Salvador: A Report and Assessment," *Human Rights Quarterly* 16/4 (1994): 656–75; Lucy Taylor, "Human Rights in the Processes of Democratization: Chile's Rettig Report," Occasional Paper 55 (University of Glasgow: Institute of Latin American Studies, 1993); and David Weissbrodt and Paul W. Fraser, "Review of the Report of the Chilean National Commission on Truth and Reconciliation," *Human Rights Quarterly* 14/4 (1992): 601–22.

6. Comisión Nacional de Reparación y Reconciliación, *Informe sobre calificación de víctimas de violaciones de derechos humanos y de la violencia política* (Santiago: CNRR, 1996).

7. This figure is very low, when compared to the US$900 million paid out to victims by the Argentine government by the same date.

8. On 15 March 1994 six of the last nine prisoners of the dictatorship had their sentences commuted to exile, and in 1995 the three remaining prisoners still awaiting sentencing had their cases reviewed and were released.

9. The amendments included lowering the threshold for amendments to a simple three-fifths majority vote in both houses for most laws, increasing civilian representation in the National Security Council (CSN), and diluting the CSN's powers. It also entailed an amendment to Article 8, prohibiting all Marxist and left-wing movements, in order to prevent antidemocratic acts or violence. The powers of the legislature were increased and those of the presidency reduced (it lost the power to dissolve Congress, to exile by executive decree, or to censor the press during states of emergency). The number of senators was increased from thirty-six to forty-eight to dilute the power of appointed senators. In addition, the abrogation of habeas corpus under states of emergency was forbidden and the ratification of international and regional human rights instruments ensured.

10. So called because they "tied up" or constrained the nascent democracy.

11. These are appointed by the president, the Supreme Court, and the CSN, which means that each branch of the military gets to appoint one senator.

12. A good account of military "guardianship" over democracy may be found in Brian Loveman, "Protected Democracies and Military Guardianship: Political Transitions in Latin America," *Journal of Inter-American Studies and World Affairs* 36/2 (1994): 105–75.

13. In 1990 and 1992 Socialist Party deputies tabled proposals to interpret the amnesty law, in order to prevent impunity for certain crimes and ensure that investigations to locate the dead could proceed. All of these proposals failed due to right-wing opposition.

14. There is a significant literature on the human rights movement. See, for example, Pamela Lowden, *The Vicariate of Solidarity: Moral Opposition to Authoritarian Rule* (Oxford: Macmillan Press, 1996); Hugo Frühling, *Justicia y violación de derechos humanos en Chile* (Santiago: CED, 1987); Patricia Orellana and Elizabeth Hutchinson-Quay, eds., *El movimiento de derechos humanos en Chile, 1973–1990* (Santiago: CELA, 1991); and Eugenio Ahumada et al., *La memoria prohibida: Las violaciones de los derechos humanos en Chile, 1973–1988* (Santiago: Pehuen, 1989).

15. Edgardo Boeniger, *Democracia en Chile* (Santiago: Ediciones Andrés Bello, 1998), cited in Human Rights Watch, *When Tyrants Tremble: The Pinochet Case* (New York: Human Rights Watch, 1999).

16. The FPMR was formed by the PCCh when the latter declared its commitment to armed struggle in 1980 to fight the dictatorship.

17. Overall, about twenty mass graves were found in 1990 alone.

18. At about the same time, an arrest warrant was issued for an active-duty colonel, Fernando Laureani, for participation in human rights violations, which also increased military nervousness. Until then, only one—laughable—indictment had been obtained for human rights violations. On 3 January 1991 a military court had found Army Captain Pedro Fernández Dittus guilty of negligence in the 1986 burning of two people by a military patrol. He was sentenced to three hundred days of remitted imprisonment. Rodrigo Rojas had died as a result of the burns and Gloria Quintana had been permanently scarred over sixty percent of her body. In December 1994 the Supreme Court decided to increase the sentence to an equally risible six hundred days for the burning, following an appeal by the family. For this case, see Patricia Verdugo, *Rodrigo y Carmen Gloria: Quemados vivos* (Santiago: Editorial Aconcagua, 1986). For the Contreras case, see *Labyrinth* by Eugene Propper and Taylor Branch (London: Penguin, 1982), in which Propper, a Colombian attorney, describes his investigation into the crime; and John Dinges and Saul Landau, *Assassination on Embassy Row* (London: Publishers and Readers Publishing Co., 1980). The Chilean government had already awarded damages of US$2.6 million to the families of Moffitt and Letelier in January 1992, according to the decision of a five-member panel of international arbitrators.

19. In September 1990, Augusto Pinochet Hiriart, the general's son, came under investigation for receiving Army-issued checks worth approximately US$3 million and dated 4 January 1989, during the purchase of a company that manufactured weapons for the Army. After over forty CPPD deputies had signed a petition to the Ministry of Defense requiring more information about the checks, the Army garrisoned its troops on 19 December 1990. The conclusions of the report by the congressional investigating committee had been negotiated with the Army, which issued a statement reaffirming complete loyalty to the commander-in-chief. After El Boinazo, Frei ordered the prosecutors' office to close the investigation in July 1995, appealing to the national interest.

20. For the Pisagua case, see the book by René García Villegas, a lone, heroic judge who was disbarred for his defense of human rights under the dictatorship: *Pisagua! Caín, qué has hecho con tu hermano* (Santiago: Editorial Emision, 1990).

21. Human Rights Watch, *Unsettled Business: Human Rights at the Start of the Frei Presidency* (New York: Human Rights Watch, 1994), 18.

22. The ruling was confirmed by the Supreme Court on 9 July 1998.

23. See below for the Tucapel and Albania cases.

24. For new literature that shows the importance of the courts here and in Argentina, see Carlos Acuña, "Transitional Justice in Argentina and Chile: A Never Ending Story?" (paper presented at the Mellon Seminar on Transitional Justice, Columbia University, 15 December 1998); David Pion-Berlin and Craig Arceneaux, "Tipping the Civil Military Balance: Institutions and Human Rights in Democratic Argentina and Chile," *Comparative Political Studies* 31/5 (1998): 633–51; and Robert J. Quinn, "Will the Rule of Law End? Challenging Grants of Amnesty for the Human Rights Violations of a Prior Regime: Chile's New Model," *Fordham Law Review* 62/4 (1994): 905–60.

25. The reform meant that appeals on criminal cases were thenceforth heard exclusively by a specialized criminal court, the Sala Penal.

26. This armed movement was active under Allende and was reactivated after the establishment of military rule.

27. The Convention affirms the duty to respect the rights of prisoners during wartime and to ensure their physical integrity.

28. Since 1990 two newspapers and three weekly magazines with a history of opposition to military rule have closed: *La Época* (1998), *El Fortín Mapocho* (1990), and *Cauce, Análisis*, and *APSI*. In October 1998 the Christian Democratic *Hoy* folded. See Human Rights Watch, *When Tyrants Tremble*.

29. The most famous cases concern the book by Francisco Martorell, *Impunidad Diplomática*, and that by Alejandra Matus, *El Libro Negro de la Justicia Chilena*. On 4 May 1993 Gerardo Roa Olivares filed a legal suit against Francisco Martorell and the newspaper *El Siglo*, which had published it chapter by chapter. The book alleged that Olivares had covered up the disappearances. On 14 April 1999, the book by Matus was impounded by a court order, following a suit filed by Servando Jordán, former president of the Supreme Court. It had been launched only one day before and its circulation is now prohibited. The case is currently under consideration by the Inter-American Human Rights Commission (IAHRC).

30. A few examples will suffice. In October 1996 secretary general of the PCCh, Gladys Marín, was jailed for two days for calling Pinochet a "blackmailer" and "psychopath who came to power on the basis of intrigue, treason and crime." In June 1997 Pinochet threatened a suit against members of Congress who had criticized the role of the Army in handling the death in suspicious circumstances of conscript Pedro Soto Tapia earlier that year. On 21 January 1998 journalists Paola Coddou and Rafael Gu-

mucio were jailed for libeling Supreme Court judge Servando Jordán, whom they accused of having a "murky past."

31. This refers to an operation whereby the DINA coordinated an international campaign of repression. The Letelier assassination in Washington, the Prats murder in Buenos Aires, and the attempt on the life of Bernardo Leighton in Rome were all part of this operation. See Stella Calloni, *Los años del lobo: Operación Condor* (Buenos Aires: Ediciones Continente, 1999).

32. Spanish prosecution efforts came about partly as a result of an earlier failed investigation in Chile into the case of Carmelo Soria. On 16 November 1991 the Chilean Supreme Court overruled a civilian court judge, sending the case of Soria to a military court. The Supreme Court finally reopened the case in April 1994 under strong pressure from the Spanish government, but on 23 August 1996 it was closed. A denial of justice suit was presented to the IAHRC in 1999, and the ruling is still pending. In 1996, the Association of Progressive Prosecutors (Asociación Progresista de Fiscales, AFP) filed an *acción popular* suit (a procedure permitting persons other than the direct victims to sue) against Pinochet for the disappearance of seven Spaniards, including Soria, supported by the long-time work of the Salvador Allende Foundation and Joan Garces, former Allende advisor and lawyer. There is a fast-growing body of literature on this case. For a legal view see Curtis Bradley and Jack L. Goldsmith, "Pinochet and International Human Rights Litigation," *Michigan Law Review* 97/7 (1999): 2129–84, and Richard Wilson, "Prosecuting Pinochet: International Crimes in Spanish Domestic Law," *Human Rights Quarterly* 21/4 (1999): 927–79. For a more political analysis see Ricardo Lagos and Heraldo Muñoz, "The Pinochet Dilemma," *Foreign Policy* 144 (1999): 26–39, and Arturo Valenzuela, "Judging the General: Pinochet's Past and Chile's Future," *Current History* 98/626 (1999): 99–104. For a domestic and international political perspective, see Alexandra Barahona de Brito, "The Europeans, the Latin Americans, the Chileans and their General," *Revista Estratégia* (in press).

33. This may not be the last word on the case. In September 1999 relatives of victims of the Pinochet regime also filed a suit against the United Kingdom with the European Court for Human Rights, arguing that the failure to bring full charges against the general violates various national obligations contracted by subscription to the European Convention on Human Rights.

34. José Zalaquett, "Human Rights Violations Committed by Former Governments: Principles Applicable and Political Constraints," in Alice Henkin, ed., *State Crimes: Punishment or Pardon* (Maryland: Aspen Institute for Peace, 1989), 26–65; "International Human Rights Symposium: Confronting Human Rights Violations Committed by Previous Regimes," *Hamline Law Review* 13/3 (1990): 623–60; "The Ethics of Responsibility. Human Rights, Truth, and Reconciliation in Chile," Issues on Human Rights Paper 2 (Washington, D.C.: WOLA, 1991); and "Balancing Ethical Imperatives and Political

Constraints: the Dilemma of New Democracies Confronting Past Human Rights Violations," *Hastings Law Journal* 43/6 (1992): 1425–38. Neier wrote a response in the volume edited by Henkin and referred to above. For a fuller appreciation of his arguments, see Aryeh Neier, *War Crimes: Brutality, Genocide, Terror and the Struggle for Justice* (New York: Random House, 1998). A similar, very enlightening debate was held between Santiago Nino, presidential advisor on human rights to the Alfonsín government in Argentina, and Diane Orentlicher, a legal scholar from the United States.

35. Jorge Mera, "Chile: Truth and Justice under the Democratic Government," in Naomi Roht-Arriaza, ed., *Impunity and Human Rights in International Law and Practice* (Oxford: Oxford University Press, 1995), 171–84.

36. Lucy Taylor, *Citizenship, Participation and Democracy: Changing Dynamics in Chile and Argentina* (London: Macmillan, 1998).

37. Manuel Antonio Garretón, "Human Rights and Processes of Democratization," *Journal of Latin American Studies* 26/1 (1994): 221–34.

38. Jorge Correa Sutil, "Dealing With Past Human Rights Violations: the Chilean Case after Dictatorship," *Notre Dame Law Review* 67/5 (1992): 1455–85; and "'No Victorious Army Has Ever Been Prosecuted': the Unsettled Story of Transitional Justice in Chile," in James McAdams, ed., *Transitional Justice and the Rule of Law in New Democracies* (Notre Dame: Notre Dame University Press, 1997), 123–54. Here Correa refers to a combination of hesitation and determination. See also Zalaquett's writings referred to in note 34.

39. Alexandra Barahona de Brito, *Human Rights and Democratization in Latin America: Uruguay and Chile* (Oxford: Oxford University Press, 1997).

40. "Institutionalists" is the name given to the generals who opposed the 1973 coup, and is now used to signify those most committed to the new subordination of the military to civilian authority.

41. Jon Lee Anderson, "Autumn of the Patriarch," *The New Yorker* 78/32 (19 October 1999), 44–57.

42. On 18 March 1998 a suit was filed against Sergio Fernández, minister of interior during the dictatorship and currently a UDI senator, retired Army Generals Raúl Benavides and Arellano Stark, and retired Air Force General Enrique Montero, for the death of two communist militants, Alfonso Carreni and José Luís Baeza.

43. For the Tucapel case, see Rodolfo Sésnic, *Tucapel: La muerte de un líder* (Santiago: Editorial Bruguera, 1985) and Signorelli G. Aldo and Tapia V. Wilson, *Quién mató a Tucapel?* (Santiago: Editorial Ariete, 1986).

44. On 27 May even Pinochet was called on to provide evidence with regard to this case. To date he has not responded.

45. Already on 31 December 1997 the Supreme Court had reversed a military court decision to close the case. On 3 January 1998 it reopened the investigation and called on the DINE to submit documentation to permit the resolution of the case. On 24 March

1998, in a vote of ten to seven, the Court ordered the military court to appoint a special prosecutor for the case.

46. This refers to a contingent of men who traveled around the country executing and making "enemies" disappear with alleged special authority from Pinochet. It is described by Patricia Verdugo in *Los zarpazos del puma* (Santiago: Ediciones Chile América, 1989). This is one of the fifty-five cases filed against Pinochet.

47. Those indicted were retired General Sergio Arellano Stark, retired Brigadier General Pedro Espinoza, and retired Colonels Sergio Arredondo, Marcelo Morén Brito, and Patricio Díaz.

48. Larios was involved in the Letelier murder. He fled to the United States, and was released after a plea bargain that entailed his testifying against Michael Townley, a U.S.-born DINA agent also involved in the Letelier killing. He lives under the Justice Department's witness protection program, but now faces extradition proceedings to Chile.

49. Human Rights Watch, *When Tyrants Tremble*, citing *Qué Pasa* 1477, 31 July 1999.

50. Some lower-ranking DINA agents had already cracked in the early 1990s, including Osvaldo Romo Mena, Alejandra Merino, and Luz Arce. They each caused a flurry of debate and journalistic comment. The first top-ranking officer to talk was retired General Manuel Contreras. In February 1998 he declared that everything he had done as head of the DINA had been under the orders and with the knowledge of Pinochet, renewing intense debate about Pinochet's personal responsibility for human rights violations. Until then Pinochet had always backed Contreras, but following his declaration he disowned him and stated that he had no knowledge of the crimes for which Contreras was responsible. Most reactions to this denial were dismissive or incredulous, with many individuals in the political arena asserting Pinochet's ultimate responsibility for human rights violations.

51. At this time, the outcome of this initiative is unclear, as the military has thus far refused either to apologize fully or to reveal the whereabouts of the disappeared.

52. Not all decisions have been positive, however. On the very day that Pinochet was arrested, the Supreme Court closed a case of a disappeared member of the MIR, ignoring the Geneva Convention as a ground for keeping it open. On 12 November 1998 it ruled to close the case of the disappearance of Eugenia Martinez Hernandez, a member of the MIR, detained by the DINA on 24 October 1974.

53. Six new appointments were made on 23 December 1998, and the new replacements took up their posts in March 1999.

54. In response to the Soria case, Congress proposed that the Army create a commission to purge itself in 1994; but this was the only call for action of this kind, and it was not acted upon.

55. Human Rights Watch, *When Tyrants Tremble*.

56. Enrique Arancibia Clavel, former DINA agent charged with killing General Prats and his wife, is in detention in Buenos Aires and his case is being investigated. In April

1999 the lawyer representing the Prats family in Chile, Pamela Pereyra, requested that the Argentine judge investigating the case, María Servini de Cubría, issue charges against Pinochet and other senior DINA agents (Human Rights Watch, *When Tyrants Tremble*). In November 1999 a suit was filed in an Argentine court against Pinochet, among others, for complicity in Operation Condor.

57. On 14 November 1998 an Austro-Chilean citizen, Osmán Palestro, filed a criminal suit against Pinochet with the Austrian Attorney General.

58. Six Chilean nationals whose husbands were tortured and killed by the DINA in 1973 and 1975 filed suits that same month, leading the judge to issue an international arrest warrant.

59. Investigations were initiated on 19 November 1998 into the torture of various individuals in October 1973, after these had requested the Canadian authorities to initiate proceedings against the dictator.

60. Fifteen Chileans who were tortured during the dictatorship presented cases to the Attorney General, basing their suits on the Convention against Torture.

61. Paris judge Roger le Loire issued two extradition requests in November 1998, in the case of the disappearance of five French nationals in 1973–77. Later that month the family of a French priest shot in Santiago in 1984 presented another suit against Pinochet.

62. Here, prosecutors initiated five suits against Pinochet on behalf of three naturalized Chilean refugees, for alleged crimes committed between 1973 and 1974 in Dusseldorff, Berlin, and Hamburg.

63. Former DINA agent Michael Townley was sentenced to eighteen years in absentia on 11 March 1993, for the attempted assassination in Rome of Chile's former vice president, Bernardo Leighton, and his wife, Ana Fresno, in 1975. On 24 June 1995 it was the turn of General Manuel Contreras and Brigadier Raúl Iturriaga to be sentenced to twenty and eighteen years in absentia for the same crime. After the arrest of General Pinochet, the Attorney General in Milan initiated investigations into allegations of homicide and torture presented by a Chilean national, Vicente Vergara Taquias.

64. Three Chileans have also filed a suit on the murder and kidnapping of family members, and have called for Pinochet's extradition.

65. Pinochet stands accused of the kidnapping and murder of Alexei Jaccard, who disappeared in May 1977 in Buenos Aires.

66. The Medical Foundation for the Care of Victims and the Redress Trust filed a criminal suit against Pinochet on behalf of Sheila Cassidy, a doctor tortured in 1975, and William Beausire, a stockbroker who disappeared in Chile.

67. In November 1998 a Uruguayan court closed the case of Enrique Berrios, a DINA agent implicated in the Carmelo Soria killing who fled to Montevideo in 1991 to escape questioning in the Letelier case. He was protected by members of the Uruguayan military but was mysteriously murdered in 1993. Although closed investigations are in the public domain in Uruguay, the judge has classified the evidence to avoid compromising wit-

nesses in this case (Human Rights Watch, *Chile: Unsettled Business*, 19–20; see also *When Tyrants Tremble*).

68. In the United States, pressure was brought to bear on the administration and Congress by Isabel Letelier, Joyce Horman, Michael Moffitt, and other family members of victims, to adopt a clear position on the case and cooperate with the Spanish investigation. On 3 June 1999 the United States declassified 5,300 documents relating to the dictatorship, the first part of what is known as the Chile Declassification Project. A District of Columbia judge continues to investigate the case, as does the State Department. On 1 September 1999 the Justice Department issued a letter rogatory to the Chilean Supreme Court, which requested the documentation collected by Judge Bañados when investigating the Contreras-Espinoza case, and tapes of conversations between Contreras and Pinochet. Charles Horman, about whom the Costa Gavras film "Missing" was made (based on the book of the same name by Thomas Hauser), and Frank Teruggi were both executed at the National Stadium in Santiago in 1973. Ronnie Moffitt was killed with Letelier in the 1976 car bombing. On the Horman case, see Thomas Hauser, *Missing* (New York: Simon and Schuster, 1978).

69. Judge Garzón has a list of thirty-eight members of the regime who are extraditable in addition to Pinochet himself.

70. Ratified on 21 August 1991.

71. At the time, the government reacted with some severity against the report and the Supreme Court ignored it. That attitude has changed somewhat as events have shown. At the time of writing, the government's response is still pending.

72. Other best-sellers include Hermógenes Pérez de Arce, *Europa vs. Pinochet* (Santiago: Editorial El Roble, 1998); Ascanio Cavallo, *Chile 1990–98: La historia oculta de la transición* (Santiago: Grijalbo, 1998); Patricia Politzer, *El Libro de Lagos* (Santiago: Ediciones Grupo Zeta, 1998); and Elizabeth Subercaseaux, *Gabriel Valdés: Señales de historia* (Santiago: Aguilar, 1998). See Faride Terán, "Floresce en Chile la literatura política," CNN (online), 7 February 1999.

73. Other reminders of the past are not popular. Ariel Dorfmann's play, "Death and the Maiden," about a torturer captured by one of his victims, which was made into a film by Roman Polanski, was not at all well received in Chile.

74. Comment made by Katie Hite, professor at Vassar University, at a roundtable discussion on the Pinochet case held at Princeton University in February 1999.

CHAPTER 10

War, Peace, and the Politics of Memory in Guatemala[1]

Rachel Sieder

Introduction

Since the return to constitutional rule began in Latin America in the early 1980s the constraints of political transition have given rise to a balancing act between truth and justice. Official attempts to deal with the past and engineer "reconciliation" throughout the region have typically involved two elements: commissions of inquiry, generically termed "truth commissions," into past violations of human rights; and amnesty laws that effectively provide immunity from prosecution for those responsible for such violations.[2] Governmental and nongovernmental perspectives on how to address the problem of past violations of human rights have often conflicted: while most transitional regimes have broadly endorsed the view that some kind of truth telling constitutes a valuable contribution to national reconciliation, they have rejected putting those responsible for human rights violations on trial, claiming that this would prejudice the democratic transition.[3] By contrast, many human rights activists have argued that while uncovering the truth constitutes an important form of sanction in itself, alone it is insufficient. From this latter perspective, investigations without at least some measure of legal accountability and punishment of those responsible in effect means the institutionalization of impunity, with detrimental consequences for strengthening the rule of law.[4]

Recent developments in Guatemala have mirrored these familiar arguments and opposing views. My aim here is to explore the broader impact of memory politics in the Guatemalan context. Memory politics is understood to mean the combination of official and unofficial attempts to deal with the legacy of past human rights violations. On the official or government side these include truth commissions, amnesty laws, criminal investigations and prosecutions, and a wide range of institutional reforms aimed specifically at redressing the previous failure of the state to guarantee human rights. Unofficial initiatives developed by civil society actors to confront the past include investigations into human rights violations, legal actions, and different kinds of commemorative acts and exercises in collective memory. Memory politics operate at many levels and involve a range of actors, from local communities and national and international nongovernmental human rights organizations (NGOs), to governments, the media, and—as in the case of Guatemala—the United Nations (U.N.). I argue here that its long-term effects in any national context depend critically on the interaction between official and unofficial efforts to address the legacies of the past. In other words, the extent to which truth commissions and "official" processes of remembering will improve the prospects for overcoming legacies of authoritarianism depends on the degree to which they are linked to and allow for broader social processes. In this respect, the involvement of individuals and communities at the grass roots in wider processes of memory construction is a singular and important feature of the Guatemalan experience.

Focusing on the case of Guatemala, this chapter examines a number of variables central to explaining the nature and impact of memory politics: first, the social legacies of widespread human rights violations, including who the victims and perpetrators were, and the kind of impact human rights violations had on society as a whole; second, the circumstances of the transition itself, specifically the prevailing balance of political forces and the different trade-offs between truth and justice that this engendered; third, the role of local human rights organizations and civil society in general, in particular whether and how they supported and/or contested official attempts to deal with the legacy of past violations of human rights; and fourth, the role played by international governmental and nongovernmental organizations in efforts to uncover the truth about the past and address the consequences of human rights violations. In the light of this analysis, the final section of the chapter considers the impact of memory politics on the wider process of democratization in Guatemala. Such an assessment inevitably raises the complex question of how democratization itself can be assessed. In strictly procedural terms, the shift from an authoritarian regime to an elected civilian government is the most commonly accepted indicator of a democratic transition. However, the transition to elected government in Guatemala in 1985 was orchestrated by the military and followed the worst period of human rights violations, the consolidation of military power over the state and civil society, and the demobilization of opposition movements. It was not until the 1990s, as a negotiated peace settlement began to take shape, that political pluralism became a reality—the left was included in the electoral spectrum only in 1995—and governmental abuses of human rights significantly declined.

Democratization in Guatemala has proven to be long-run and problematic, involving dual processes of elite-led political liberalization and the negotiated settlement to the armed conflict, concluded in December 1996.[5] Given the highly authoritarian legacy of the country's recent past, I suggest here that lasting and meaningful democratization must involve the effective demilitarization of the state and civil society. This involves institutional reforms of the armed forces and the judiciary in order to subordinate the military to effective civilian control and to secure the rule of law. It also implies the creation of a political culture of citizenship based on principles of universal rights and obligations and the nonviolent resolution of conflict. Although truth-telling initiatives in Guatemala to date have not resulted in legal sanctions against individuals responsible for human rights violations, it is argued here that exercises in collective memory have constituted an important variable in the distended and complex processes of demilitarization and developing a political culture of citizenship.

A Legacy of Violence

Guatemala was a counterinsurgency state long before it was engulfed by counterinsurgency war in the early 1980s. Throughout the twentieth century the majority of the population was excluded from the socioeconomic benefits of citizenship, and forms of governance were characterized by intermittent and violent repression and restricted civil and political liberties. Dominant economic elites had long relied on the coercive apparatus of the state to support a particularly exploitative form of rural capitalism. However, following the Central Intelligence Agency (CIA)-backed overthrow of the reformist government of Jacobo Arbenz Guzmán in 1954, recourse by the military to ever-increasing violence to suppress popular demands for change became a defining characteristic of the political system. Between 1966 and 1970, some eight thousand people, most of them civilian peasants, were killed in the east of the country in the first counterinsurgency campaign against the emergent guerrilla movement. By the 1970s the armed forces' dominance over government was undisputed.[6] During the following decade the nature and intensity of state violence was transformed when the military targeted the entire civilian population in an all-out war designed to deprive the guerrillas of a rural support base. In contrast to neighboring El Salvador, direct U.S. aid to the Guatemalan military during the decade was negligible. Military aid had been suspended in 1978 by the Carter administration in protest at human rights violations and by the time it was restored in 1985 the Guatemalan armed forces had all but single-handedly destroyed the popular support base of the Guatemalan National Revolutionary Unity (Unidad Revolucionaria Nacional Guatemalteca, URNG) in a locally conceived counterinsurgency campaign of singular efficiency and brutality.[7]

Under the de facto military regime of General Romeo Lucas García (1978–82), terror tactics became both widespread and random. The armed forces prosecuted an all-out war against left-wing and centrist opposition and many hundreds of students, trade unionists, and community activists were killed or "disappeared" by paramilitary death squads operating in the cities. By the end of the 1970s escalating state repression had forced all civic opposition underground. However, the destructive power of the military was most concentrated in the rural areas, where wholesale massacres were perpetrated against indigenous villagers suspected of sympathizing with the guerrillas. Mass killings were routinely employed as a tactic to terrorize the civilian population, hundreds of villages and hamlets were wiped off the map, and huge numbers of peasants fled their homes to escape the military onslaught; over 200,000 crossed the border to Mexico, and up to half a million people took refuge in the cities or the mountains and jungles of the interior.[8] In total during thirty-six years of armed conflict over 200,000 people were murdered, including up to 50,000 who were made to "disappear."[9]

Guatemalan civil society was radically transformed by the forced integration of the rural Mayan majority into the army's counterinsurgency strategy.

Under the regime of General Efraín Ríos Montt (1982–83), violence against the civilian population reached unprecedented levels.[10] Yet while the massacres continued, an amnesty was declared for those in hiding in the mountains and those who gave themselves up to the army were detained in military-run camps, "reeducated," then subsequently resettled in new "model villages" under close army surveillance. The combination of random violence, mass displacement, and militarized resettlement severely affected indigenous cultural and religious practices. However, perhaps the most destructive element of the armed conflict was the forced involvement en masse of the civilian population in the counterinsurgency violence. The mechanism through which this was orchestrated was the paramilitary civil defense patrols (Patrullas de Autodefensa Civil, PACs), organized under army direction in every rural community throughout the country. The PACs functioned as a front line against the guerrillas in the conflict zones and everywhere as a means of monitoring and control. They numbered some 800,000 men at their height in the mid-1980s and were responsible for numerous grave violations of human rights.[11] Local conflicts over land and other resources took on a lethal edge, and civil patrols from one village were often responsible for carrying out massacres in neighboring communities.[12] In Guatemala state violence was distinguished by this highly localized dimension, and in effect divided the civilian population against itself.

Negotiating Accountability

In contrast to the cases of Argentina, Uruguay and Chile, the official truth-telling process in Guatemala did not accompany a transition to elected civilian government.[13] Instead it occurred over a decade after this had taken place and was both part and consequence of the negotiated settlement to the armed conflict. Following almost eleven years of talks between the government and the URNG, a peace settlement mediated by the offices of the U.N. was finally concluded in December 1996. The nature and mandate of the official commission of inquiry into past violations was defined within these negotiations between the government and the guerrilla forces. Human rights monitoring groups such as the Mutual Support Group (Grupo de Apoyo Mutuo, GAM) and the National Coordinator of Widows of Guatemala (Coordinadora Nacional de Viudas de Guatemala, CONAVIGUA) lobbied hard for a thorough investigation into the fate of their relatives and for those guilty of human rights violations to be brought to account.[14] Given the exceptionally high number of disappeared in Guatemala (some 50,000 individuals), these organizations had long called for effective official investigations. The end of the Cold War and the ascendance of an international discourse of human rights, together with the fact that a number of Latin American countries, including Argentina, Chile, Uruguay, and El Salvador, had already undergone some kind of official investigation into past human rights violations, lent weight to their demands.

However, the circumstances of the peace negotiations did not favor a strong mandate for the official investigating commission. By the mid-1980s the URNG were all but destroyed as a military force. The army considered itself the victor of over three decades of counterinsurgency war and was not economically dependent on external forces for its continued survival. In contrast to the Salvadoran or the Argentine military, the Guatemalan armed forces had not lost the confidence of the domestic private sector. Despite the guided transition to elected government in 1985, party politics in the early 1990s were characterized by division and instability, and economic and political elites remained subordinate to the armed forces.[15] While the balance of power undoubtedly shifted toward civilian power during the course of the peace negotiations, the military remained the most organized and powerful political force in the country. The resulting agreements, concluded in December 1996, were consequently weak on the issue of demilitarization. Nonetheless, formal commitments were secured on a number of important issues, including the formation of a public security force independent of the military; the reduction of the armed forces budget and its troop strength by a third; a program of judicial reform; and the demobilization of the civil defense patrols.[16]

With regard to the thorny question of accounting for former violations of human rights, the Guatemalan army was initially adamant that no such process would take place and repeatedly blocked attempts by the URNG to negotiate a settlement on this point. However, the efforts of the Catholic Church, local human rights nongovernmental organizations (NGOs), and the U.N. ultimately proved vital in securing a mandate for an official truth commission. The Catholic Church, whose members had borne the brunt of military violence in the highlands, was committed to some process of investigation into past violations and since 1987 had played a key mediating role in the peace negotiations. In addition, after 1994 civil society organizations gained a unique and formal role in formulating the terms of the peace;

through sectoral representation in the Civil Society Assembly (Asamblea de la Sociedad Civil, ASC) they were able to put forward proposals to the URNG and the government's negotiating teams on the different topics under discussion.[17] Through the ASC, human rights groups consistently lobbied for an official investigation into past human rights violations. The agreement for a U.N.-sponsored Historical Clarification Commission (Comisión de Esclarecimiento Histórico, CEH) was signed in June 1994 after more than two years of stonewalling by the army. Human rights activists had presented their demands to the talks via the URNG's negotiating team, but were unhappy with the final agreement signed. Their principal complaint was that the commission would not individualize responsibility for abuses, or "name names." In addition, it was given a maximum of just one year in which to investigate over thirty-six years of armed conflict. In the light of Guatemala's long history of state terror and impunity, most human rights campaigners initially rejected the agreement as flawed and unacceptable.

The CEH's remit was to investigate human rights violations committed during the armed conflict, clarify the causes and consequences of that conflict, and formulate specific recommendations to prevent future abuses of human rights. However, it was agreed that its recommendations and report would not have "legal objectives or effects," a clear signal that they would not be linked to judicial prosecutions. In addition, in December 1996 a new amnesty law—the Law of National Reconciliation—was agreed to by the government and the URNG, despite protests from human rights groups who had formed an Alliance Against Impunity precisely to lobby against such an amnesty for the military. The 1996 legislation followed many blanket amnesty laws passed during the 1980s that protected perpetrators from prosecution, and allowed anyone who had committed a political crime or politically motivated common crime related to the armed conflict to be cleared of criminal responsibility. Significantly, however, amnesty was explicitly ruled out for the internationally proscribed crimes of torture, genocide, and forced disappearance, a reflection of a developing international jurisprudence rejecting impunity for crimes against humanity.[18]

Truth without Justice?

The official truth commission was preceded by numerous attempts by civil society organizations and local communities to uncover the truth about past human rights violations and secure some form of compensation and justice. Indeed the widespread involvement of civil society in reconstructing memory is perhaps the single most distinguishing feature of the Guatemalan truth-telling process. While this was partly engendered by the peace accords and the political opening provided by the agreement to form the CEH, the main impetus came from a diverse and dynamic human rights movement that had gained in strength and political independence from the URNG during the 1990s. The cultural specificities of Guatemala were also a factor in the politics of memory; ritual funerary practices to commemorate the dead have constituted a central feature of collective attempts by indigenous communities to deal with trauma and loss. These initiatives have been promoted by many organizations within the heterogeneous Mayan movement that emerged in the wake of the armed conflict.[19]

In addition, the Catholic Church played a decisive role in promoting a grassroots politics of memory as a means to further reconciliation. In April 1998 the first extensive report into human rights violations during the armed conflict was published not by the official truth commission, but by the Human Rights Office of the Catholic Archdiocese. The *Nunca Más* report, product of the interdiocesan project for Recovery of Historical Memory (Recuperación de la Memoria Histórica, REMHI), documented atrocities on the basis of over 6,000 testimonies collected in parishes across the country during the course of three years.[20] It registered over 55,000 victims, including over 25,000 murders, attributing some eighty percent of responsibility to the state security forces and nine percent to the URNG. The REMHI project was originally set up to support the CEH, but had intended to go beyond the official commission's narrow mandate and name those individuals responsible for violations. However, in the event, fears for the safety of those who had given testimony meant *Nunca Más* failed to individualize responsibility in all but a few cases. The armed forces criticized the report for political bias, and many on the right stridently condemned it, accusing the Church of political interests and the promotion of conflict over reconciliation. Just two days after its publication the head of REMHI, Catholic bishop Monseñor Juan Gerardi, was bludgeoned to death at his home in Guatemala City in what few doubted was a political murder orchestrated by a sector of the army. After a year and a half of official investigation efforts, the case remained open, despite considerable national and international pressure for it to be resolved.[21]

The CEH finally published its report, "Guatemala: Memory of Silence," in February 1999, based on over 8,000 testimonies. It included a detailed analysis of paradigmatic cases, such as the burning of the Spanish Embassy by government forces in 1981. It also provided an exhaustive historical analysis of the causes and consequences of the conflict, concluding that political violence in Guatemala was the direct result of acute socioeconomic inequalities and a history of racism against the indigenous majority. The CEH estimated that approximately 200,000 people had been killed or "disappeared" during the armed conflict and documented some 658 individual massacres. In line with its mandate, it attributed responsibility for violations to institutions and not to individuals, stating that ninety-three percent of all cases investigated were the responsibility of the military and their agents and that three percent of those cases were attributable to the URNG. The report also signaled U.S. government and CIA involvement in supporting the structures of repression in Guatemala.

Despite the CEH's relatively weak mandate, its recommendations were far stronger than had initially been predicted. Most significantly, it found that between 1981 and 1983 the state had carried out a deliberate policy of genocide against the Mayan population. On the question of prosecutions, the commissioners emphasized that genocide was not amnestied by the 1996 Law of National Reconciliation and that all those found guilty of nonamnestied, internationally proscribed violations (genocide, forced disappearance, and torture) should be prosecuted, tried, and punished. The CEH also called for significant restructuring of the military and security forces in line with the reforms mandated in the December 1996 Agreement on the Strengthening of Civilian Power and the Role of the Armed Forces in a Democratic Society.[22] Recommendations were far-reaching and included the elaboration of a new military code and doctrine; the abolition of the Presidential General Staff (Estado Mayor Presidencial) and reform of military intelligence; and the strengthening of the National Civilian Police (PNC) and the purging of any PNC members found guilty of human rights violations. Additionally, it called on the government to set up an official commission to review the history of military officers with the aim of removing those implicated in human rights violations, a call which the government rejected.

With respect to compensation for victims, the CEH recommended that the government implement an ambitious program, including psychological and economic assistance through a National Reparations Programme to run for not less than ten years; the investigation of the whereabouts of the disappeared; the location and exhumation of clandestine graves; the establishment of a National Commission for the Search for Disappeared Children to look for children "disappeared," illegally adopted, or illegally separated from their families during the armed conflict; the building of monuments in memory of those killed; and the official acknowledgment by the state of responsibility. It also recommended that victims of human rights violations and their direct descendants be exempt from military service. While many within the U.N. privately viewed the CEH's recommendations for compensation as unworkable in practice, prospects for some form of recompense were strengthened by the fact that both the CEH's mandate and the 1996 amnesty law made explicit reference to the state's obligation to provide compensation.[23] The position of human rights groups on the issue of compensation differed, but most victims' groups continued to insist that it could be no substitute for full disclosure and legal accountability.

Right-wing sectors, including the private sector's Coordinating Committee of Agricultural, Commercial, Industrial, and Financial Associations (Comité Coordinador de Asociaciones Agrícolas, Comerciales, Industriales y Financieras, CACIF), criticized the CEH report as biased. However, neither the government of Alvaro Arzú Yrigoyen (1995–99) nor the armed forces openly criticized its findings. The fact that two of the CEH commissioners, Otilia Lux de Cotí and Alfredo Balsells, were Guatemalans made it harder for the right to level charges of foreign intervention against the U.N.—as had occurred in the case of the Salvadoran Truth Commission. In addition, prior to the publication of the report, President Arzú and Minister of Defense General Héctor Barrios Celada had publicly acknowledged the state's participation in past "excesses" in furtherance of "national reconciliation." While this was criticized by human rights activists as insufficient it stood in sharp contrast to developments elsewhere, such as Chile or El Salvador, where the military have been reluctant to acknowledge their role in past violations of human rights. Nonetheless, the Arzú government rejected most of the CEH's recommendations on the grounds that they were already being carried out by other institutions as part of the peace implementation. The CEH's charges of U.S. involvement in the repression were initially met with a curt response from U.S. ambassador to Guatemala Donald Planty, who insisted that the conflict had been an internal one "between Guatemalans." However, in his visit to Guatemala in March 1999, U.S.

President Bill Clinton set an important precedent by expressing regret at U.S. involvement in human rights violations in Guatemala. The URNG (by now a political party) also publicly asked for forgiveness for the abuses attributed to it by the CEH, characterizing violations committed by its members as "excesses" and "errors."

At the same time as they lent their support to the CEH's preparation of the official report, even before it was published civil society groups in Guatemala were highly active in promoting alternative, "bottom-up" initiatives to secure truth and justice. Since 1993 dozens of mass graves have been exhumed on the initiative of local communities throughout the country and a number of local monuments built.[24] Many Mayans have expressed the need to reconcile themselves with the dead before they can begin to reconcile themselves with the living—although exhumations and burials do not represent punishment of those responsible for violations, arguably they do represent a form of restorative justice for victims' families. However, at the same time as they are developing culturally specific means of reconstructing memory, many people are also demanding justice and economic compensation for their losses. Calls for perpetrators to be judicially sanctioned increased following the publication of the CEH's report. Guatemalan human rights NGOs, including the GAM and the Center for Human Rights Legal Action (Centro de Acción Legal y Derechos Humanos, CALDH), vowed to pursue prosecutions for genocide through the domestic and international courts against high-ranking military officers, including former heads of state Generals Romeo Lucas García and Efraín Ríos Montt.[25] Such claims were strengthened by the efforts of Spanish judge Baltazar Garzón to extradite former Chilean dictator General Augusto Pinochet to Spain to stand trial for human rights violations against Spanish citizens, and to prosecute Argentine military officers for human rights abuses committed during that country's "dirty war."

In December 1999 Nobel laureate and indigenous rights activist Rigoberta Menchú Tum filed charges in a Spanish court against various retired military officers, including former de facto heads of state Romeo Lucas García, Efraín Ríos Montt, and Oscar Humberto Mejía Víctores, for crimes of genocide, terrorism, and torture committed in the early 1980s (including the murder of Spanish citizens). In defense of her petition for a trial in Spain, Menchú argued that the Guatemalan judicial system effectively guaranteed impunity for human rights violators and that those accused should therefore be tried under international law. The case was filed just before Efraín Ríos Montt's party, the Frente Republicano Guatemalteco (FRG) won the 1999 presidential elections and as Ríos Montt was about to take up his post as president of the national congress. Accountability for past violations of human rights promised to be a thorn in the side for the FRG administration of Alfonso Portillo (2000–).

The following section attempts to assess the impact of memory politics on the prospects for democratization in Guatemala, considering both their impact in terms of institutional and legal reforms to ensure that the basic human rights and obligations of all individuals and groups are respected and enforced, and their influence on the construction of a broader political culture of citizenship and tolerance.

Memory Politics and Democratization

Any meaningful process of democratization in Guatemala demands an end to the longstanding militarization of the body politic and the customary impunity enjoyed by the armed forces. In institutional terms this will entail the subordination of the military to a more transparent and accountable civilian authority, together with extensive reform to the judicial apparatus and public security institutions. However, institutional reforms alone will be insufficient to secure a viable democratic order. This is because Guatemala has historically been characterized to a greater or lesser extent by what may be termed "socially constituted authoritarianism,"[26] wherein the arbitrary abuse of power and violence have long been seen as acceptable, or at least normal, by a wide range of political and social actors. Democratization therefore also requires that political elites cease to rely on extrajudicial means to protect their interests and that popular demands find expression through institutional channels—in other words, that conflicts be resolved without recourse to violence or extralegal means. This implies the construction of citizenship aspirations and changes in practices throughout civil society—what might be termed "from the bottom up"—together with changes in the expectations and behavior of elite groups who have traditionally considered themselves to be above the law.

The nature and extent of legal and institutional reform in Guatemala, discussed below, have been framed by the particularities of the transition process. In terms of citizenship construction, memory politics have undoubtedly been important in strengthening a sense of rights and entitlement among many formerly marginalized and victimized sectors of the population, even though their overall effects on elite behavior remain far from clear. Nonetheless, it is important to recognize that the impact of memory politics on democratic consolidation is not a linear process. Irrespective of the nature of official solutions employed to deal with questions of truth and justice in periods of transition, the ways in which past violations of human rights are framed within the public sphere, collective memory is an ongoing process that changes from generation to generation. For example, more than a decade after many had declared transitional processes of truth and justice to be complete in Argentina and Chile, memory politics resurfaced with potentially profound political impacts in both countries.[27] Such developments indicate that transitional processes of truth and justice should be understood as a point of departure, rather than a point of closure. Given the very recent nature of inquiries into memory in Guatemala, it is impossible to be conclusive about their long-term effects on the prospects for democratization; memory may resurface in the future in different ways and with differing political and social effects.

On the whole, legal and institutional reforms in the three years following the signing of the final peace accord were weak, particularly with respect to curtailing the power of the military who remained the most powerful political actor in the country. Progress on the one-third cut in troop size and budget signaled in the peace agreements was uneven, with targets set largely by the army themselves rather than the government.[28] Performance on the commitment to create a civilian police force and remove responsibility for public security from the armed forces was similarly mixed: the civilian police force (Policía Nacional Civil, PNC), hastily set up in January 1997, initially failed to screen new intakes adequately, leading to criticism from many quarters—including the U.N.—that it represented little more than cosmetic reorganization of a police force highly implicated in human rights abuses, corruption, and extortion.[29] Subsequent improvements to the PNC were made, but progress continued to be slow. In addition, the public security crisis that developed in the wake of the armed conflict led to the employment of the army in police patrols and antikidnapping operations to combat the rise in "common crime," raising fears that public security would in effect be remilitarized before the PNC was fully operational. Such limited institutional reforms notwithstanding, significant advances in demilitarization occurred prior and subsequent to the peace settlement. These included the abolition of village military commissioners in 1995 and the demobilization of the civil patrols (PACs) in the first months of 1997, two mechanisms previously central to ensuring military control over rural society. In February 1999 the CEH made detailed recommendations to reform the army and purge it of human rights violators, including the elaboration of a new training doctrine for the armed forces, the reform of military intelligence bodies, and the formation of an official commission to review officers' records with the aim of removing those implicated in human rights violations. However, the Arzú government responded that the army was already being reorganized and purged in compliance with the peace accords, indicating that it would take no action to ensure implementation of the CEH's recommendations in this respect.

Numerous measures to reform the judicial system were included in the peace agreements.[30] Progress was made in some areas: for example, new tribunals were set up in the rural departments and the human rights Ombudsman (Procuraduría de Derechos Humanos, PDH), created in 1985, also extended its network of offices throughout the country. Pilot projects with community courts were initiated in an attempt to incorporate indigenous legal practices, as mandated by the 1995 agreement on indigenous rights, and the U.N. lent its support to the introduction of training programs for legal translators in order to increase access to justice in indigenous languages. In addition, reforms to the penal procedures code, which came into effect in 1994, meant a shift to oral proceedings, strongly promoted by foreign donors and particularly the U.S. Agency for International Development (USAID) as a means to secure more expeditious and transparent proceedings. Nonetheless, the judicial system continued to suffer chronic problems of intimidation and corruption, cronyism and the politicization of appointments, lack of adequately trained personnel, and insufficient provision, particularly in the rural areas. Despite considerable efforts by the U.N. and other international agencies, state investigation and prosecution services remained highly ineffective and subject to pressure from powerful interests. High indices of criminality and lack of public confidence in the judicial system combined with the authoritarian social legacy of the counterinsurgency resulted in people taking justice into their own hands, and numerous mob lynchings of suspected criminals occurred throughout the country.[31] Most significantly, impunity for human rights violations continued; in the vast majority of cases, the military remained immune from prosecution or investigation, even in cases that had gained an international profile such as the 1995 massacre of eleven returned refugees by an army patrol at Xamán, Alta Verapaz, or the 1998 assassination of Bishop Juan Gerardi.[32]

Memory politics in Guatemala has been led by a broad range of civil society organizations increasingly independent from the revolutionary left and supported by a range of international NGOs and the U.N. mission in Guatemala. Human rights activists had long demanded an end to military impunity. However, in the wake of the armed conflict, perhaps precisely because of the limited nature of institutional and legal changes secured through the peace agreements, they have increasingly challenged military power and impunity though a grassroots politics of memory. Civil organizations have developed multiple, unofficial initiatives to uncover the truth and secure justice for victims. In many cases, individuals or civil groups have carried out tasks of legal defense and criminal investigation that are formally the responsibility of the state. For example, in the case of the Xamán massacre, the Guatemalan NGO, the Rigoberta Menchú Foundation, acted as an auxiliary for the prosecution (*querellante adhesivo*) in the trial of soldiers accused of the murder of the refugees. Throughout the country three NGOs, the Human Rights Office of the Archdiocese (Oficina de Derechos Humanos del Arzobispado de Guatemala, ODHAG), the Guatemalan Forensic Anthropology Team (Equipo de Antropología Forense, EAFG) and CALDH have worked exhaustively to meet the demands of local communities to exhume clandestine massacre sites and identify the remains of their relatives.[33] The support of international human rights NGOs and forensic anthropologists proved a vital support to these efforts. In addition, a wide range of NGOs, many financed by international counterparts, are working with communities to try and address the mental health problems generated among the civilian population by years of violence, fear, and denial.[34]

In the ethnically and politically fragmented society of Guatemala, grassroots memory politics have also become a central part of the search for new collective identities in the postwar dispensation. Local processes of organization to initiate exhumations or construct monuments have prompted the formation of new transregional communities of survivors of the violence. Initiatives such as the huge cross built by twenty-eight displaced Q'eqchi'-Maya communities at the village of Sahakok in northern Alta Verapaz in memory of over 900 people killed, or the monument for those massacred in 1982 at Río Negro in Rabinal, Baja Verapaz, have linked groups and individuals across geographical regions and ethnolinguistic barriers. This in turn has prompted new understandings of rights and justice; through local initiatives in memory and with the support of international observers, many rural Mayans have increasingly come to reject military imposition and demand their rights to more autonomous, peaceful, and culturally appropriate forms of development. In many cases this has exposed them to threats and even violence from ex-civil patrollers and others directly involved in the repression. Nonetheless, these local exercises in memory have helped to challenge fear and the extensive militarization of civil society that took place during the counterinsurgency. They have also helped people to understand (although not necessarily to come to terms with) a highly localized violence that divided families and communities.

Memory politics have empowered many previously marginalized sectors of Guatemalan society, particularly Mayan peasants, and as such have contributed to the construction of citizenship "from the bottom up." However, political and economic elites have given little indication that they are willing to submit themselves to the rule of law and cede their historic privileges. Most importantly, the impunity of the armed forces for human rights violations persists. The danger exists that popular frustrations with the justice system and with democracy in general will increase when expectations for justice are not met. However, in the medium term only the combination of pressure from civil society organizations and the international community holds out the prospects of securing the legal and institutional reforms necessary to secure the minimum conditions for democratic viability in Guatemala. In conclusion then, nonofficial initiatives in truth and justice have contributed to a strengthened and radicalized civil society in Guatemala. However, as historical precedent suggests, this alone cannot guarantee democracy.[35] While the cohesion of civilian parties of the right increased during the 1990s, their capacity to channel popular aspirations and the extent of their independence from the military remain open to question. Since 1995 the political spectrum has widened to include left-wing parties, but their ability to respond to popular demands for accountability remains limited in the face of the continuing power of the armed forces. Significant advances have been made in institutional reform and building a culture of citizenship since the signing of the peace accords, but changes in the civil-military balance and in elite political culture have been insufficient to guarantee liberal democracy.

Conclusions

As the above assessment has indicated, the balance of memory politics in Guatemala has been mixed. The state has endorsed the notion of compensation in principle, but not judicial sanctions—despite a high degree of mobilization around these issues by civil society organizations. In a context where militarily defeated guerrillas failed to secure significant concessions from the armed forces through peace negotiations, memory politics continues to mobilize a heterogeneous and independent civil society in the wake of the armed conflict. The U.N.'s mandate to strengthen local civil society organizations has contributed to this, as has strategic collaboration between domestic human rights NGOs and their international counterparts.

Evidently memory politics cannot by themselves guarantee a genuinely inclusive and democratic political system. Indeed the danger exists that popular mobilization around truth and justice issues may give way to widespread disenchantment and frustration if demands for justice and compensation are not met. However, while widespread social mobilization around issues of historical memory and justice is in itself no guarantee that democracy will endure, a memory politics that demobilizes and disempowers civil society does not bode well for deepening democracy. As has been emphasized here, memory politics are not linear, and transitional truth and justice processes should be understood as points of departure rather than points of closure. The rule of law and liberal democracy are far from being realized in Guatemala; indeed the country is perhaps better described as an "illiberal democracy," where electoral alternation of power coexists with the absence of basic civil rights guarantees of citizenship for the majority of the population.[36] Impunity for powerful military and civilian elites persists and access to justice for the majority of the population remains limited. Yet, supported by the active involvement of civil society, efforts at truth telling have contributed to reconstituting a less authoritarian social order in the wake of civil conflict and state violence. Such processes have permitted the re-elaboration and reworking of social memory among those affected by war and violence and throughout the country have made important contributions to demilitarizing state and society, challenging traditions of military impunity and political cultures marked by denial and fear. To the extent that they have emphasised the idea of accountability and the rights and obligations of all groups and individuals within society, memory politics have begun to promote a culture of citizenship. For the victims themselves, the opportunity to give testimony and commemorate their dead has strengthened their perception of themselves as individuals and communities with rights. In some cases, initiatives in memory have contributed to the building of new collective and individual identities in the postconflict political dispensation, leading to the reconfiguration of new "communities of belonging." The commemoration of the victims of political violence also implies the symbolic revalorization and inclusion of those who were previously excluded from the national polity, and as such represents an attempt to rework the moral and political community of the nation-state. Officially recognizing the wrongs perpetrated against those historically marginalized, oppressed, or demonized is a necessary first step toward their inclusion as citizens. Ultimately then, exercises in memory politics cannot secure or consolidate democracy, but in the wake of widespread and systematic violations of human rights by the state they are an essential first step toward its constitution.

Endnotes

1. This chapter is based on another work analyzing the politics of memory in "Guatemala, El Salvador and Honduras," which appears in Paloma Aguilar, Alexandra de Brito, and Carmen González, eds., *The Politics of Memory and Democratization* (Oxford: Oxford University Press, 2001). I would like to thank the editors of that volume, together with Carlos Flores, Rachel Holder, and Tracy Ulltveit-Möe for their incisive and helpful comments on earlier versions of this analysis.

2. For an overview of truth commissions, see Patricia B. Hayner, "Fifteen Truth Commissions—1974 to 1994: A Comparative Study," *Human Rights Quarterly* 16/4 (1994): 597–655, and "Commissioning the Truth: Further Research Questions," *Third World Quarterly* 17/1 (1996): 19–29.

3. The most celebrated exception was the transitional government of Raúl Alfonsín in Argentina (1983–90), which put leaders of the former military junta on trial for human rights abuses. See Alison Brysk, *The Politics of Human Rights in Argentina* (Stanford: Stanford University Press, 1994).

4. See Juan Méndez, "Accountability for Past Abuses," *Human Rights Quarterly* 19 (1997): 255–82.

5. For an analysis of the relationship between the transition to elected civilian government and the peace process in Guatemala, see Dinorah Azpuru, "Peace and Democratization in Guatemala: Two Parallel Processes," in Cynthia Arnson, ed., *Comparative Peace Processes in Latin America* (Washington, D.C. and Stanford: Woodrow Wilson Center and Stanford University Press, 1999), 97–125.

6. On the 1954 overthrow of Arbenz, see Piero Gleijesis, *Shattered Hope: the Guatemalan Revolution and the United States, 1944–54* (Princeton: Princeton University Press, 1991), and Stephen Schlesinger and Stephen Kinzer, *Bitter Fruit: The Untold Story of the American Coup in Guatemala* (New York: Doubleday, 1992). For an analysis of Guatemalan politics after 1954, see George Black, *Garrison Guatemala* (London: Zed Books, 1984) and Jim Handy, *Gift of the Devil: A History of Guatemala* (Toronto: Between the Lines, 1984).

7. U.S. military aid to Guatemala in 1985 was $0.5 million, and never reached more than $10 million in any single year prior to the signing of the peace agreements in 1996 (in James Dunkerley, *The Pacification of Central America* [London: Verso, 1996], 145).

8. On the violence see Oficina de Derechos Humanos del Arzobispado de Guatemala (ODHAG), *Guatemala: Nunca Más*, 4 vols. (Guatemala: ODHAG, 1998), published in English as REMHI/ODHAG, *Guatemala: Never Again!* (London: Catholic Institute for International Relations and Latin American Bureau, 1999); Comisión de Esclarecimiento Histórico, *Guatemala: Memoria del Silencio* (Guatemala: United Nations, 1999); Ricardo Falla, *Massacres in the Jungle: Ixcán, Guatemala, 1975–1982* (Boulder, Colorado: Westview Press, 1994); Robert Carmack, *Harvest of Violence: the Mayan Indians and the Guatemalan Crisis* (London: University of Oklahoma Press, 1988); David Stoll, *Between Two Fires in the Ixil Towns of Guatemala* (New York: Columbia University Press, 1993); and Andrés Cabanas, *Los Sueños Perseguidos: Memoria de las Comunidades de la Población en Resistencia de la Sierra* (Guatemala: Magna Terra Editores, 1999).

9. ODHAG, *Nunca Más*; Comisión de Esclarecimiento Histórico, *Memoria del Silencio.*

10. Ríos Montt's seventeen-month period as de facto head of state was the period in which most killings and disappearances took place. One database comprised of over 37,000 documented cases of murder and disappearance attributed forty-three percent of the violations to Ríos Montt's government; see Patrick Ball, Paul Kobrak, and Herbert E. Spirer, *State Violence in Guatemala, 1960–1996: A Quantitative Reflection* (Washington, D.C.: American Association for the Advancement of Science, 1999).

11. Procurador de los Derechos Humanos, *Las patrullas de autodefensa civil* (Guatemala: PDH, 1994); and Margaret L. Popkin, *The Civil Patrols in Guatemala: Overcoming Militarization and Polarization in the Guatemalan Countryside* (Washington, D.C.: Robert Kennedy Memorial Center for Human Rights, 1996).

12. For the notorious case of Río Negro in Baja Verapaz, see Equipo de Antropología Forense de Guatemala, *Las Masacres en Rabinal: Estudio Histórico Antropológico de las Masacres de Plan de Sánchez, Chichupac y Río Negro* (Guatemala: EAFG, 1995).

13. On Argentina see Brysk, *The Politics of Human Rights*. For the cases of Chile and Uruguay see Alexandra Barahona de Brito, *Human Rights and Democratization in Latin America: Uruguay and Chile* (Oxford: Oxford University Press, 1997).

14. GAM was formed in June 1984 by family members of assassinated and "disappeared" people to challenge the official practice of forced disappearance in Guatemala. Soon after its formation death squads tortured and murdered its founders Hector Gómez Calito and María del Rosario Godoy de Cuevas. It was not until 1988 that CONAVIGUA was formed by indigenous widows throughout villages in the highlands to campaign for widows' welfare and the exhumation of clandestine graves.

15. In April 1993 gridlock between the Presidency and Congress prompted President Jorge Serrano's unsuccessful attempt to dismiss both Congress and the Supreme Court. This proved to be an important turning point; civil sector organizations mobilized against Serrano and the army ultimately supported the ruling of the Constitutional Court that the president's actions were illegal, committing itself to upholding the 1985 Constitution. However, the episode also underlined the comparative weakness of civilian political elites in Guatemala. For a thorough discussion of the events surrounding Serrano's failed *autogolpe*, see Rachel M. McCleary, *Dictating Democracy: Guatemala and the End of Violent Revolution* (Gainesville: University Press of Florida, 1999).

16. Jack Spence et al., *Promise and Reality: Implementation of the Guatemalan Peace Accords* (Cambridge, Mass.: Hemisphere Initiatives, 1998).

17. The ASC has been criticized for failing to engage the grassroots members of its constituent organizations in a truly participatory and democratic consultation process. However, despite the weaknesses of the process, in comparative terms the formal inclusion of civil society organizations in the elaboration of the peace agreements was a distinguishing feature of the Guatemalan process. For a critical view see Tania Palencia, "Advocates and Guarantors: Establishing Participative Democracy in Post-War Guatemala," in Jeremy Armon, Rachel Sieder, and Richard Wilson, eds., *Negotiating Rights: The Guatemalan Peace Process, 1987–1996* (London: Conciliation Resources, 1997), 28–35, and William Stanley and David Holiday, "Everyone Participates, No One Is Responsible: Peace Implementation in Guatemala," draft manuscript prepared for the Stanford Center for International Studies and Arms Control and the International Peace Academy's Project on Peace Plan Implementation (August 1999).

18. For further discussion see Méndez, "Accountability for Past Abuses," and Margaret Popkin and Nehal Bhuta, "Latin American Amnesties in Comparative Perspective: Can the Past be Buried?" *Ethics and International Affairs* 13 (1999): 99–122.

19. On the cultural specificities of loss and trauma in Guatemala, see Judith Zur, *Violent Memories: Mayan War Widows in Guatemala* (Boulder, Colorado: Westview

Press, 1998); Linda Green, *Fear as a Way of Life: Mayan Widows in Rural Guatemala* (New York: Columbia University Press, 1999); and Kuldip Kaur, "The Reconstruction of Mayan Female Identity Through the Politics of Loss and Retrieval" (master's thesis, University of London, 1998).

20. ODHAG, *Nunca Más*.

21. See Francisco Goldman, "Murder comes for the Bishop," *The New Yorker*, 15 March 1999, 60–77. In October 2000, the case remained unresolved.

22. For more on this agreement, see Jack Spence et al., *Promise and Reality*, and Jennifer Schirmer, "Prospects for Compliance: the Guatemalan Military and the Peace Accords," in Rachel Sieder, ed., *Guatemala after the Peace Accords* (London: Institute of Latin American Studies, 1998), 21–32.

23. Following the signing of the peace agreement, the government had already begun to explore options for compensation; see Marta Altolaguirre, "Alcances y Limitaciones de la Comisión para el Esclarecimiento Histórico de las Violaciones a los Derechos Humanos y los Hechos de Violencia que Han Causado Sufrimiento a la Población Guatemalteca," in Sieder, *Guatemala after the Peace Accords*, 151–72. During 1998 and 1999 the government's Peace Secretariat (SEPAZ) set up pilot projects in three communities affected by the conflict: Rabinal in Baja Verapaz, San Andres Sacbajá in El Quiché, and San Martín Jilotepeque in Chimaltenango.

24. For one of the best-known cases, see Equipo de Antropología Forense de Guatemala, *Las Masacres en Rabinal*; Ecumenical Program on Central America and the Caribbean/Center for Human Rights Legal Action (EPICA/CHRLA), *Unearthing the Truth: Exhuming a Decade of Terror in Guatemala* (Washington, D.C.: EPICA, 1996), and Guatemala Solidarity Network, *Guatemala: A Place for Memory* (London: Guatemala Solidarity Network, 1999).

25. In December 1999 some 165 Guatemalan cases were pending before the Interamerican Human Rights Court (IAHRC), including the 1982 massacre at Dos Erres in the northern department of Petén, and the 1995 massacre of eleven former refugees at Xamán, Alta Verapaz. In January 1998 the IAHRC convicted Guatemala for the first time of human rights violations and ordered the government to pay compensation to the family of Nicholas Chapman Blake, an American journalist murdered by civil patrollers in the department of Huehuetenango in 1985. A second conviction was secured in the same year when the court ordered the government to compensate victims of the "Panel Blanca" death squad. The squad operated out of the Treasury Police between 1987 and 1989 using a white van without numbered plates, and was responsible for the abduction, torture, and murder of at least ten people (*Central America Report*, 19 February 1999).

26. I am grateful to Brandon Hamber for this term.

27. In Argentina an association of children and grandchildren of the Mothers of the Plaza de Mayo (Madres de la Plaza de Mayo) publicly denounced ex-military officers responsible for human rights violations during the "dirty war" of the 1970s, despite the

fact that most of those officers had received a presidential pardon in 1990. In 1998 state prosecutors jailed two former Argentine generals for their involvement in the kidnapping of children of disappeared people during the dirty war—a crime not amnestied under current Argentine law. The arrest of former Chilean dictator General Augusto Pinochet in London in October 1998 on charges of murder, torture, and genocide brought by a Spanish court contributed to a reexamination in Chile of the reasons leading to the overthrow of constitutional government in September 1973, the violations of human rights subsequently committed by the military, and the nature of the transition overall. For an eloquent discussion of the Chilean "irruption of memory," see Alex Wilde, "Irruptions of Memory: Expressive Politics in Chile's Transition to Democracy," *Journal of Latin American Studies* 31/2 (1999): 473–500.

28. See Schirmer, "Prospects for Compliance."

29. See Rachel Garst, *The New Guatemalan National Civilian Police: A Problematic Beginning*, Briefing Series on the Guatemalan Peace Process (Washington, D.C.: Washington Office on Latin America, 1997).

30. For more detail on recent changes to the judiciary, see Washington Office on Latin America (WOLA), *La reforma judicial en Guatemala, 1997–1998: Una guía básica sobre los problemas, procesos y actores* (Guatemala: WOLA, 1998).

31. Human rights organizations raised the possibility that such summary justice may be deliberately provoked in order to justify tougher policies on law and order.

32. In August 1999, following a three-year legal battle, a Guatemalan court convicted twenty-five soldiers of manslaughter in the killing of eleven people at Xamán. Human rights organizations and victims' relatives were outraged at the light sentence of four to five years, commutable by a payment of $0.67 per day. Fifteen of the soldiers were subsequently acquitted by an appeals court, and only ten soldiers were sentenced to prison (commutable by fines) on the lesser charge of manslaughter. In December 1999 the Rigoberta Menchú Foundation announced that in the light of the acquittal, the case would be pursued at the Interamerican Court of Human Rights in Costa Rica.

33. The REMHI program identified over three hundred mass graves throughout the country, the majority of which have yet to be exhumed. Demand for exhumations far exceeds the capacities of the various NGO forensic teams, yet the government has done little to support this work, despite being mandated to do so by the CEH.

34. In Guatemala, where huge numbers of peasants were forced to kill each other by the army during the counterinsurgency war, many of the material authors of atrocities are also victims who remain unable to acknowledge the past. By explaining and contextualizing the violence, it is hoped that mental health programs, together with national truth-telling exercises such as the CEH and REMHI, can constitute a first step toward providing a context in which these perpetrator-victims can begin to construct their own truth of what happened during the armed conflict.

35. See Deborah Yashar, "The Quetzal is Red: Military States, Popular Movements,

and Political Violence in Guatemala," in Douglas A. Chalmers et al., eds., *The New Politics of Inequality in Latin America: Rethinking Participation and Representation* (Oxford: Oxford University Press, 1997).

36. On "illiberal democracies" see Fareed Zakaria, "The Rise of Illiberal Democracy," *Foreign Affairs* 76/6 (1998): 22–43.

CHAPTER 11

Restorative Justice in Social Context: The South African Truth and Reconciliation Commission

Charles Villa-Vicencio

In the world of political transition, compromise is inevitable. It can be the beginning of a process that ultimately delivers far more than what the initial steps suggest. Political decisions about the future are not made in a vacuum but on the basis of historical reality. We can build a house only with the bricks available at the time. The South African Truth and Reconciliation Commission (TRC) needs to be assessed in this light. It has provided a somewhat fragile foundation that needs to be reinforced by a range of other nation-building initiatives, on which a strong and enduring structure can one day emerge. The Promotion of National Unity and Reconciliation Act, No. 34 of 1995, identifies "peaceful coexistence" as a first goal of the Commission, highlighting the need to understand the "motives and perspectives" of all involved in the conflicts of the past, as the beginning of a process that can ultimately lead to national reconciliation.

This need has resulted in the affirmation of a form of restorative justice that is grounded in both the struggle against apartheid and the need for nation building. As such, the TRC was a transitional mechanism designed, in the words of the Interim Constitution, to

. . . provide a historic bridge between the past of a deeply divided society characterised by strife, conflict, untold suffering and injustice, and a future founded on the recognition of human rights, democracy and peaceful coexistence and development opportunities for all South Africans, irrespective of colour, race, class, belief or sex.[1]

The Context

In South Africa the resolution of conflict—the first step toward reconciliation—was through negotiation, not through victory on the field of battle nor through the collapse of the old regime. Inevitably, negotiation involves a search for consensus and this includes compromise. When the partners in the negotiation process considered how to deal with human rights violations committed during the apartheid era, three options were proposed. First there was blanket or general amnesty. This was strongly urged by the former government led by F.W. de Klerk, as well as the military and the police. This option was rejected.

Then there was the option of trials and prosecutions. There were many, particularly in the liberation movements, who strongly supported this. It was espoused for many years by the African National Congress. Thabo Mbeki, deputy president of South Africa, put it this way:

Within the ANC the cry was to "catch the bastards and hang them"—but we realised you could not simultaneously prepare for a peaceful transition while saying we want to catch and hang people, so we paid a price for the peaceful transition. If we had not taken this route I don't know where the country would be today. Had there been a threat of Nuremberg-style trials over members of the apartheid security establishment, we would never have undergone peaceful change.[2]

Kader Asmal, a formative influence in the writing of the South African constitution and the formation of the TRC, who is the presently minister of water affairs in the South African cabinet, spoke in 1987 of South Africa's need for Nuremberg-type trials at the Children's Conference in Harare. However, in his inaugural lecture as professor of human rights law at the University of the Western Cape in 1992, he spoke differently. "Each country," he suggested, "will deal with the past in its own way. We will not follow the pattern of vengeance shown in some European countries today where people are being persecuted for their past."[3]

The option of prosecution was a serious ingredient in the thinking of the liberation movements in South Africa. Suffice it to say, there are still many who would argue that, had the antiapartheid struggle ended in the defeat of the South African regime, this would have been the preferred option. Ironically, it was the forced compromise between the forces of liberation and the forces of apartheid that provided an alternative way to dealing with the atrocities of the past.

The third option was a truth commission and it was this that gained majority support. Here the goal was to seek the truth concerning victims and perpetrators, a restoration of dignity for victims and survivors, a limited amnesty and a search for healing and reconciliation. Justice Richard Goldstone put it this way:

> The decision to opt for a Truth and Reconciliation Commission was an important compromise. If the ANC had insisted on Nuremberg-style trials for the leaders of the former apartheid government, there would have been no peaceful transition to democracy, and if the former government had insisted on a blanket amnesty then, similarly, the negotiations would have broken down. A bloody revolution sooner rather than later would have been inevitable. The Truth and Reconciliation Commission is a bridge from the old to the new.[4]

Timothy Garton Ash argues that there are three ways of dealing with past atrocities: trials, purges, and history lessons. "I personally believe a third path, that of history lessons, is the most promising," he writes.[5] Michael Marrus, in turn, identifies the difficulties inherent in criminal trials, which undermine the quest for an historical account of the past.[6] The historic compromise that characterized the TRC involved a belief that future developments cannot be properly dealt with, unless there is a conscious understanding of what happened in the past.

The Possibility of Reconciliation

The TRC sought to promote both truth and reconciliation via three steps that constitute the foci of its three committees: amnesty, victim testimony, and reparation and rehabilitation.

Amnesty

To the disappointment of many—not least from a reconciliation perspective—the Act governing the TRC and the amnesty process did not require anyone to show remorse for their past actions, to apologize, to be repentant, or to take any responsibility for the consequences of what they had done. All that was required was that the deed for which amnesty was requested be politically motivated, and that full disclosure of it be made. In the words of the Archbishop Tutu, "[Y]ou are able to tell the amnesty committee that you are proud of what you did, albeit that it constitutes an offense under law." There are many moral arguments—not least theological ones—for the importance of contrition. It is, however, a difficult condition to impose. At best an insistence upon it would have implied a rather idealistic notion of what could be accomplished within the time constraints of the TRC; and at worst, it could have inhibited some of the more resolute and proud perpetrators from making any disclosures, undermined the integrity of those disclosures that were made, and thus obscured the deepest convictions of those responsible for past gross human rights violations.

This having been said, the fact is that the amnesty process did allow those who have committed gross violations of human rights to walk away free—without taking any responsibility to even endeavor to put right the human suffering and social destruction caused by their actions. Further, amnesty extends not only to criminal acts, but also covers the grantee against civil charges. Further still, it does not exclude agents of the apartheid state from public office—as have the "lustration" (purification) measures adopted in Eastern European countries—and there is no obligation on the recipient of amnesty to make any compensatory contribution to society.

It is for these reasons that some suggest the South African amnesty process has amounted to little more than impunity. This kind of response is understandable—but it is also wrong. Although it did not require applicants to show contrition and take responsibility for the suffering of their victims, the TRC did require them to make full disclosure in a public hearing under cross-examination. This did not constitute simple or crass impunity. It did not involve either personal or political amnesia.

It is true that there is something seemingly satisfying about retribution—and, more specifically, about punishment. I had a conversation once with an elderly Jewish man at the gallows where Rudolph Hess was hanged in Auschwitz. He stood in silence for a long time before commenting, "You've got to have a bit of blood in order to have reconciliation." Many victims the world over would concur. Numerous South Africans are asking for no less, despite the work of the TRC. There is indeed a powerful case to be made that perpetrators who have not applied for amnesty should face criminal trials now that the work of the TRC is finished. The establishment of a permanent International Criminal Court is premised on the need for retribution. At a recent seminar in London titled "Going Home: Problems of Returning Refugees," a spokesperson from Amnesty International came out in support of such a court with a mandate to investigate and prosecute all crimes against humanity; but, at the same time, she insisted that the proposed court should leave space for the exercise of national sovereignty concerning such matters. National needs and historic opportunities should never be overruled by unbending legal imperatives.

Context determines what is possible. It is interesting to note that Babu Ayindo, writing on the International Criminal Tribunal for Rwanda, suggests that Western notions of criminal justice undermine the commitment to communal reconciliation that lies at the heart of most traditional African justice systems, which aim to reintegrate both the offender and the victim into society. He poses the question of retribution or restoration for Rwanda,[7] as follows:

> [I]nstead of salvaging the weak links of relationships to bolster recon-
> ciliation, the [retributive] court process heightens adversity. . . . There
> are questions to which the victim badly needs answers, in the absence
> of which he will conjure up his own. For instance, the witness/victim
> badly needs and wants to know why particularly his wife, father, daugh-
> ter, to mention a few, were maimed or killed. . . . At the end of the day,
> the success of the tribunal will be determined not by how much healing
> has taken place in the Central African Nation, but by how fast cases
> would have gone through the International Criminal Court.

Ayindo proceeds to suggest that the Truth and Reconciliation Commission in South Africa, despite its apparent lack of a comprehensive reparations program for apartheid victims, serves as a more sure path for the restoration of relationships.

The TRC Act spoke of restorative justice as the guiding principle that underpinned both its truth-seeking and reconciliation processes. This justice seeks to reincorporate the perpetrator into society, while restoring the dignity and well-being of the victim. But did the TRC provide the necessary incentive for this to happen? It did provide space within which victims and survivors could tell their stories—which clearly went a long way toward their self-vindication. The reparation of victims through the Rehabilitation and Reparations Committee, however incomplete, further advanced their healing. Restorative justice, however, demands more. It requires not only society as a whole, but offenders in particular, to take responsibility to endeavor to put right past wrongs. The Act governing the Commission did not require perpetrators to take this responsibility; but the jury is still out on whether the amnesty process has been able to apply sufficient moral pressure to persuade them to do so. While it would be naïve to expect all of them to have been so persuaded, a few significant cases could, nevertheless, make a lasting contribution to the process of national reconciliation. "The world is watching," writes Howard Zehr. "The TRC process is flawed, opportunities have been missed, but the importance of this undertaking—not only in South Africa, but for the world—must not be underestimated. It is a bold step on an unchartered path."[8]

The Commission's realizable goals were simple coexistence, a reduction in revenge killing, and the creation of a climate where former enemies can sit down together and negotiate (sometimes in anger) the creation of a better society for all. It aimed at a political climate within which conflicts are moderated by the awareness that everyone has to live together. To have accomplished this would be an important step toward reconciliation.

Victim Testimony

A second and related step in the reconciliation process of the TRC involved the public testimony of victims of gross violations of human rights. This was the flip side of the amnesty process—the stories of victims and survivors as opposed to the explanations of perpetrators. Such testimony was seen in the Act to be an exercise in "restoring the human dignity" of those who had suffered most.

Suffice it to say that some anecdotal evidence suggests that testimony before the Commission has assisted some individuals and their families.[9]

Dan Stein has written that "arguably social structures can theoretically exert a more important influence on post-traumatic reactions than individual psychotherapy interventions."[10] Public testimony assists the victims to feel exonerated in situations where they have been falsely accused or belittled in the community, providing them with what Dumisa Ntsebeza, the head of the TRC's Investigative Unit, has called "a public opportunity to salvage what is left of their human dignity."[11] It provides a basis for what Martha Minow calls the necessary taming, balancing, and recasting of anger and desire for revenge, as a first step in the process of reinterpreting one's life and future options for living in a morally ambiguous and socially complex society.[12]

The media presentation of victims' testimonies captured the worst of the apartheid regime's brutality. The world was told of the killers of Vlakplaas,[13] the poisonings that resulted from South Africa's experiments in chemical and biological warfare, and the chain of shallow graves containing the remains of abducted activists who had been brutalized, tortured, and ultimately killed. Eugene de Kock, the Vlakplaas commander, was labeled by the media "prime evil." Jeffrey Benzien, a Western Cape Security Branch policeman, who demonstrated his notorious "wet bag" method of torture before the Amnesty Committee, was seen on television screens and captured on the front page of most newspapers in the country. He and his henchmen were portrayed as psychopaths, human aberrations, and societal misfits. De Klerk called them "rotten eggs," unrepresentative of the other disciplined, professional security force members. Steven Robins has argued (perhaps a little too zealously) that all too often the public representation of perpetrators before the TRC conformed to the Hollywood stereotype—"evil-looking Nazis with thick Afrikaans accents."[14] In this way, South Africans have been allowed to escape the banality of evil all too easily.

The stories of less spectacular violations of human rights have not made it onto television screens with the same impact as these more horrific events. The vast majority of victims who either made statements to the Commission, or who appeared at a public hearing of the Human Rights Violations Committee to tell their stories of suffering, simply did not receive the same level of public attention. The outcome has often been the undermining of the ability of ordinary South Africans to identify themselves with the perpetrators, to recognize that there is a "little perpetrator" in each one of us. Indeed, the size of this perpetrator, and his capacity to do harm, is considerably a matter of the circumstances in which we find ourselves. Nevertheless, as

Jean-Paul Sartre reminds us, each one of us is "condemned to be wholly responsible" for our own actions.[15] To understand the source of evil does not mean to condone it. To recognize the possibility of evil in each of us, is to highlight the importance of taking responsibility to ensure that the evil of the past does not recur in the future.

Of course, the primary importance of the TRC's human rights violations hearings was their impact on the victims themselves.[16] However, a further question needs to be asked of these hearings in relation to the more inclusive healing or reconciliation process. The full significance of victims telling their stories before the TRC has not always been grasped. To what extent has it provoked a general introspection and acknowledgment that have the potential to contribute to national renewal and reconciliation—even if individual perpetrators (and indeed some victims) remain unmoved in their enmity?

It is a process, I submit, that has scarcely begun. Each story of suffering—whether eligible for media sensationalism or not—has contributed to a more complete picture of gross violations of human rights in South Africa. The nation must learn from these stories as a means of sharpening its moral conscience to ensure that never again does it gradually atrophy to the point where personal responsibility is abdicated. The challenge is to wake up the national memory—not only of gross violations of human rights, but of everyday life under apartheid—to ensure that we do not again become complicit in the banal ways that lead, step by modest step, to atrocious deeds.

More stories need to be told—stories of the direct and indirect involvement of ordinary people in the atrocities and sufferings of the past. Luc Huyse suggests that memory constitutes the ultimate form of justice. It needs, however, to be a rich and inclusive memory (sometimes called "thick memory") that captures the gradations of responsibility for the past. "Truth," Huyse asserts, "is both retribution and deterrence, and it undermines the mental foundation of future human rights abuses."[17] It is this that justifies the focus on victim testimony in the TRC, and accentuates the importance of the telling of more and many stories. It is only through "the widest possible compilation of people's perceptions, stories, myths and experiences . . . [that we] can restore [the past] to memory and foster a new humanity," writes Antjie Krog. This wide truth, she suggests, is "perhaps justice in its deepest sense."[18] Memory must be allowed to flow where it will, giving rise to bitterness and anger as well as life and hope. It is at the same time important to recognize that the "politics of memory" can be abused by politicians to fuel the fires of hatred—as seen in the case of the Anglo-Boer war, in Northern Ireland, and in the former Yugoslavia. This makes it important to include in the nation's repertoire stories that look forward toward restoration, as well as those that look backward to injury. Memory that is engaged in doing justice is partly about victims working through their anger and hatred, in order to rise above their suffering and get on with life with dignity.

An 81-year-old Afrikaner lady from Bredasdorp, who had been loyal to the National Party all her life, responded to the growing impact of the stories told by victims by commenting, "Ek het nooit geweet dat my mense sulke vreeslike dinge kon gedoen het nie" ("I did not know that my people could have done such terrible things"). It is this sense of shame that needs to be transformed into responsibility, if the stories of victims are to be really heard. A recent publication by the Dulwich Centre of the Aboriginal Health Council of South Australia suggests that for stories to be therapeutic, they need to be seen to be capable of changing things.[19] Many politicians on both sides of the South African divide, spokespersons for its many factions, and glib exponents of what the nation or some section of it needs to do, have yet to acquire the insight and grace of that elderly Afrikaner woman. Of course, more is needed than the shame she admitted; but that is an important start, and it is one that the TRC has facilitated.

Reparation and Rehabilitation

The TRC's reparation and rehabilitation policy is an integral part of the healing process. If amnesty provides a basis for truth telling and the reintegration of the perpetrator into society, victim testimony together with reparation and rehabilitation are designed to provide balm for the wounds of the victims.

There has been a huge debate concerning the form and nature of rehabilitation. Ought it to occur at a communal or an individual level? How ought the needs of those who testify before the Commission be balanced against the needs of the nation as a whole? The TRC opted, after extensive consultation, primarily for individual reparation—while making extensive recommendations about reparation at communal level.

This is not the place for a full exposition of the TRC's reparation and rehabilitation policy, nor of the response of the government to the TRC's proposals. Suffice it to say, that whatever one's views may be on this policy, the fundamental critique of Mahmood Mamdani, professor of African studies at the University of Cape Town, goes a long way to completing the cycle of both personal and communal rehabilitation and national reparation.[20] He says that for true reconciliation to happen, the nation's attention ultimately needs to shift away from the perpetrators of human rights violations to the beneficiaries of apartheid—requiring all who have benefited from apartheid to contribute to the material restoration of those who have suffered from it. Although not part of the mandate of the TRC, this important dimension of national reconciliation needs to be recognized as a basis for promoting moral responsibility and accountability in the nation as a whole. To fail to do so would be to fail to acknowledge the extent of the social and economic readjustment required to ensure true reconciliation.

The responsibility for reconciliation extends to all South Africans. It involves a break with, and indeed the reconstruction of, the usual sequence of injury and revenge.[21] It involves enemies becoming co-workers for the common good—maybe even (but not necessarily) friends. It involves the willingness of those who have suffered most to abandon the demand for retribution—a task made even more difficult when some perpetrators show no sign of remorse, let alone compassion, toward those they have injured. It involves the wealthy, but also ordinary middle class citizens who struggle to pay the bills, being willing to have less, in order that others may have a little more. The yawning gap between rich and poor in South Africa simply must be bridged in order for there to be meaningful reconciliation. United Nations Development Programme figures show that the standard of living of white South Africans is comparable to the twenty-fourth most wealthy nation in the world, coming after Spain. The standard of living of black South Africans is one hundred and twenty-fourth in the world, after the Congo. Judge Richard Goldstone suggests that this maldistribution can be redressed in one of two ways: "by bloody revolution which would bury the wonderful advances we have experienced in the past few years," or "by the use of the law—and that requires the co-operation of the whole body politic."[22]

The primary function of the TRC was to address the moral, political, and legal consequences of the apartheid years. The socioeconomic implications of apartheid have been left to other institutions—including the Land Commission, the Gender Commission, the Youth Commission, and a range of reform processes in education, social welfare, health care, and housing. Nevertheless, insofar as the work of the TRC was intended to include reconciliation, it should at least have stimulated a process of economic reform.

Perhaps the most serious weakness of the legislation governing the work of the TRC was its authorization of the Commission to grant amnesty to perpetrators, but only to recommend reparations to victims. The Commission failed in a number of ways to meet the needs of victims. It has been justly criticized for failing to prioritize counseling, to adequately inform victims of the findings of the Commission, or to publicly promote the need for reparations. The government, in turn, has failed to respond to the recommendations made by the Commission concerning reparations. The net result is that those who suffered most during the apartheid years have been asked to suffer yet again. The political consequences of this development are likely to be felt for some time to come.

Broadening the Base: Collective Liability, Communal Responsibility, and National Reconciliation

For extensive and lasting reparation to happen, a sense of collective liability among the beneficiaries of apartheid, corporate responsibility among all South Africans, and an inclusive sense of national commitment to healing is required. Clearly not all South Africans, not even all those white South Africans who did not rise in rebellion against the apartheid state while enjoying the benefit of its fruits, can be equally blamed for the atrocities of the past. We need at the same time to take seriously what Ronald Aronson calls a "spiral of responsibility," which links the actions of those on the lower echelons of the spiral to those on the higher ones.[23] The mere clerk who made the phone call or filed the letter, and the technician who maintained the computer—postwar Germans called them "desk criminals" (*Schreibtischtäter*)—are never entirely exonerated. Even white South Africans who grudgingly gave only minimal consent to a fundamentally oppressive government (by paying taxes and living within the boundaries set by apartheid) are involved in the spiral of responsibility. If many in South Africa have sought to deny this kind of complicity, a former security police spy, Major Craig

Williamson, appearing before the TRC's public hearing on the armed forces, made the case against them forcibly:

> Our weapons, ammunition, uniforms, vehicles, radios and other equipment were all developed and provided by industry. Our finances and banking were done by bankers who even gave us covert credit cards for covert operations. Our chaplains prayed for our victory and our universities educated us in war. Our propaganda was carried by the media and our political masters were voted back into power time after time with ever increasing majorities.[24]

The argument can be taken further. All those who chose not to actively oppose the prevailing system, or to try to create a climate contrary to that which benefited whites over blacks, can scarcely insist on having clean hands. At the very least, their level of involvement is at the level of negative or passive culpability—a situation which can, of course, be extended to most allied nations, business corporations and individuals, who verbally condemned apartheid while sustaining the system through diplomatic, political, economic, and other forms of strategic support.

It is true that most responsible governments have not tried to bring to legal account those who provided this kind of low level or indirect support for an oppressive system. The Nuremberg Tribunal never sought to prosecute ordinary conscripts or "desk criminals." The legislation governing the TRC, in turn, defined gross violations of human rights in a specific manner. While it included acts of killing, torture, abduction, and certain kinds of severe ill treatment committed by foot soldiers and others, it did not extend legal culpability to those who maintained the system within which these acts occurred. Bluntly stated, the TRC Act did not hold all those involved in maintaining and promoting apartheid legally culpable of gross violations of human rights. It did, however, seek to identify "political accountability" and "moral responsibility" to the extent that it required the Commission to determine the "nature, causes and extent of gross violations of human rights, including the antecedents, circumstances, factors, context, motives and perspectives which led to such violations." As such, it implicitly ascribed a kind of responsibility to people other than direct perpetrators. This point takes on poignant meaning when considered in relation to the need for the Commission to make recommendations to the president to ensure the nonoccurrence of the violation of human rights in the future.

The emergence of a responsible society committed to the affirmation of human rights presupposes the acceptance of individual responsibility by all those who either supported the previous oppressive system of government or simply allowed it to continue to function. The need to identify moral responsibility for the gross violations of human rights has as much to do with the future, as it does with the past. To recognize the many-layered spiral of interrelatedness in modern society is a prerequisite for the emergence of a "new" society. Karl Jaspers' celebrated essay, written shortly after the institution of the Nuremberg Trials, spoke of the need to recognize different levels of guilt as a basis for what he called "the new world waiting to be built." "Unless," he warned, "a break is made in the evil chain, the fate which overtook us will overtake the victors—and all mankind with them."[25] This is a break that moves beyond mere anthropological pessimism to responsible citizenship.

The pertinent question here concerns the extent to which individual South Africans can be regarded as responsible for the premises and presuppositions upon which apartheid was built. The kindest answer is that history suggests that most citizens are inclined to lemming-like behavior, which involves them in thoughtless submission rather than thoughtful accountability. It is this inclination that needs to be addressed in order to ensure that the future is different from the past. This reminds us that the most penetrating inquiry into the past involves more than a witch-hunt. It involves laying a foundation against which the present and all future governments are to be judged—guaranteeing that the new society provide space within which critical moral reflection is valued and promoted. The highest form of citizenship and the surest antidote to systematic gross violations of human rights as witnessed in South Africa, is nourished by what Jürgen Habermas refers to as "our understanding of freedom," which is related to "how we understand ourselves as persons and how much we expect from ourselves as political actors."[26]

Conclusion

The long journey to reconciliation in South Africa has only just begun. But it has begun. There is a national will (at least among most South Africans) to live together. A more complete sense of political and socioeconomic reconciliation is a goal that still lies ahead.

Reconciliation involves hard work. It is a process on which the future of the nation depends. As Archbishop Tutu has said to a white audience: "Your ultimate survival depends on it."[27] It involves redressing the squalor of poverty that apartheid has left in its wake. It involves a commitment to rehabilitation and reparation. It also involves the creation of a society within which the chances of the recurrence of the kinds of gross violations of human rights that occurred in the past are reduced to a minimum.

Reconciliation also takes time. As Colleen Scott[28] has suggested, it would not have been even remotely decent for a non-Jewish person to have suggested to the Jews that they ought to become reconciled to the Germans immediately after World War II. Coexistence precedes reconciliation.

Reconciliation involves a different kind of justice—a form of restorative justice that does not seek revenge, but that also does not countenance impunity. This kind of justice allows both for the capacity for evil and for the capacity for good that resides within humanity. It accepts moral and political responsibility for redressing the needs of victims, as well as the need to ensure that perpetrators become responsible members of society.

Finally, reconciliation requires that all South Africans accept moral and political responsibility for what in South Africa is something new—a culture of human rights within which political and socioeconomic conflicts can be addressed both seriously and in a nonviolent manner.

Endnotes

1. Postamble to the Interim Constitution (Act No. 200 of 1993), after section 251.

2. *Cape Times*, 24 February 1992.

3. Kader Asmal, "Coping with the Past: A Truth Commission in South Africa," press release, 3 October 1993.

4. Richard Goldstone, The Hauser Lecture, New York University, 22 January 1997.

5. Timothy Garton Ash, "The Truth About Dictatorship," *The New York Review of Books*, 19 February 1998, 40.

6. Michael Marrus, "History and the Holocaust in the Courtroom" (paper presented at the Searching for Memory and Justice: The Holocaust and Apartheid conference, Yale University, 8–10 February 1998).

7. In *Africa News*, January 1998.

8. Howard Zehr, "Restorative Justice: When Justice and Healing Go Together," *Track Two* 6/3–4 (December 1997): 20.

9. *Truth and Reconciliation Commission of South Africa Report*, vol. 5 (Cape Town: Juta, 1998), 350f.

10. Dan Stein, "Psychiatric Aspects of the TRC in South Africa," *British Journal of Psychiatry* 173 (July 1998): 456.

11. Dumisa Ntsebeza, press conference, Cape Town, 21 June 1997.

12. Martha Minow, *Between Vengeance and Forgiveness: Facing History after Genocide and Mass Violence* (Boston: Beacon Books, 1998), 12.

13. Vlakplaas was a security police center used to deploy death squads.

14. *Cape Times*, 6 August 1997.

15. Jean-Paul Sartre, *Being and Nothingness*, quoted in Ronald Aronson, "Responsibility and Complicity," *Philosophical Papers* XIX/1 (1990): 57.

16. Some outside observers have suggested that the hearings have made many people more embittered. "It opens the patient up and then walks away," Tom Winslow at the Cape Town-based Trauma Clinic tells us. "In some ways, [those who testify] feel they are just being used as a public spectacle" (*New York Times*, 17 July 1997). These harsh words need to be taken seriously. They remind us of our responsibility to those who continue to carry the wounds of the past within them. Nevertheless, there are many who have testified before the TRC who bear witness to the cathartic nature of the experience, regarding it as having contributed to the restoration of their human and civil dignity.

17. Luc Huyse, *Young Democracies and the Choice Between Amnesty, Truth Commissions and Prosecutions* (Leuven: University of Leuven, 1998), 7.

18. Antjie Krog, *Country of My Skull* (Cape Town: Random House, 1998), 16.

19. In *Reclaiming Stories, Reclaiming Our Lives* (Melbourne: Dulwich Aboriginal Health Council, 1996).

20. Mahmood Mamdani, "Reconciliation Without Justice," *Southern African Review of Books* (November/December 1996).

21. See Colleen Scott's lecture on reconciliation at the DasArts Academy in Amsterdam, 14 March 1996.

22. Richard Goldstone, Andries Van Riet Address to the 30th Annual Convention of the South African Property Owners' Association, June 1997.

23. Aronson, "Responsibility and Complicity," 62.

24. Memorandum submitted to the TRC at the Armed Forces hearing in Cape Town on 9 October 1997.

25. Karl Jaspers, *The Question of German Guilt* (New York: The Dial Press, 1947); originally published as *Die Schuldfrage: Zur Politischen Haftung Deutschland* (Heidelberg: Verlagen Lambert Schneider, 1946).

26. Jürgen Habermas, "On the Public Use of History: Why a 'Democracy Prize' for Daniel Goldhagen?" *Common Knowledge* (December 1997): 9.

27. Archbishop Desmond Tutu, speech to the Cape Town Press Club, 21 October 1997.

28. Scott, DasArts Academy lecture on reconciliation.

CHAPTER 12

Rwanda: Dealing with Genocide and Crimes against Humanity in the Context of Armed Conflict and Failed Political Transition

Stef Vandeginste

Introduction

Rwanda has been the scene of the some of the worst atrocities ever committed. The events that took place between April and June 1994 were of an unprecedented intensity, and their orchestration of an unprecedented efficiency. Hundreds of thousands, possibly up to one million, members of the Tutsi ethnic minority and moderate Hutu were slaughtered by the army, by government supported militia, and by their (civilian) neighbors, relatives, and friends. The genocide and crimes against humanity were part of a project of an almost exclusively Hutu regime to retain political power, and, indirectly, access to resources and wealth. This chapter describes the almost exclusively judicial approach that Rwanda has taken to dealing with its past; and, at the same time, it will highlight some of the inherent limitations of such an approach. Indeed, the massive scale of the human rights violations has most seriously affected the social tissue of Rwandan society itself. Dealing with the past in such a context cannot solely be a judicial issue; it is a political challenge and a challenge for society as a whole. This challenge is all the more important in a situation where the past and the present are sometimes hard to distinguish. As the next section will indicate, at the time of this writing, Rwanda had not yet attempted to make peace after civil conflict. Unlike many other countries which have gone through a transitional justice process, Rwanda continues to be actively involved in armed conflict that started as an internal conflict but has become a regional war. Further, Rwanda has not yet successfully conducted a political transition process aimed at power sharing, inclusiveness, and better governance. Further still, the country remains the scene of gross human rights abuses, committed by remnants of the former government army and its militia, and by the current government.

Rwanda 1990–99: Armed Conflict, Political Transition, Genocide, and Other Massive Human Rights Violations

To present the context in which Rwanda is trying to deal with its past, developments over the last ten years in three different but interlinked areas need to be summarized: the armed conflict, the failed political transition, and the genocide and other crimes against humanity. Expectations of the judicial response to genocide and other crimes have been very high; and the judicial approach, at both the international and the national levels, is of extreme importance in itself. Nevertheless, in order to attain the more long-term objectives of peace, reconciliation, and a context conducive to sustainable human development, to which the judicial response is expected to contribute, an appropriate and integrated answer will also need to be found to the two other problems.

The Armed Conflict: From Internal to Regional

The invasion by the Rwandan Patriotic Front (RPF) of Northern Rwanda on 1 October 1990, was the start of an internal armed conflict between the nearly exclusively Hutu regime and army and a Tutsi-dominated armed rebellion, predominantly made up of members of the exiled Tutsi "old case load" refugee community in Uganda (who had fled the country prior to Rwanda's independence in 1962). Throughout the civil war, the front remained situated in the northern part of the country; but in Kigali and elsewhere Tutsi civilians, perceived as allies and spies of the rebel forces, as well as other political opponents of the one-party regime, were victims of arbitrary arrest and other serious human rights violations.[1] A negotiation process began in 1992 and, on 4 August 1993, the Arusha Peace Accords were signed. These included protocols on the integration of the armed forces, the repatriation of refugees, and the resettlement of displaced persons. The internal armed conflict had seemingly come to an end.

The implementation of the Arusha Peace Accords met with strong resistance. The shooting down of the presidential airplane and the assassination of President Habyarimana on 6 April 1994 not only triggered the start of the genocide and of a massive number of other rights violations, but also sparked the resumption of the war. The parallel chronology of both events may have seriously misled international observers in the initial days and weeks of the events: whereas the international community was hoping for an immediate cease-fire to stop the massacres (and as a consequence needed the interim Hutu government as one of the negotiating parties), the reality was that the majority of massacres did not occur as a consequence of the war but as part of the implementation of a well-orchestrated genocide. As far as the military aspects are concerned,[2] it took several weeks for control over the capital to be firmly established. The RPF continued to recruit new soldiers, including Tutsi survivors of genocide. The interim Hutu government of Prime Minister Jean Kambanda was forced to retreat, first to Gitarama, then to Gisenyi, on the Rwando-Zairean border. The establishment of a new government in Kigali on 19 July 1994 coincided with the movement of more than one million refugees, crossing the border into Zaire and Tanzania; these included a large number of former government army soldiers (the ex-FAR or Forces Armées Rwandaises) and extremist Hutu "Interahamwe" militia members. Again, following the military victory of the RPF rebellion, the armed conflict had seemingly come to an end.

However, cross-border raids into the northwestern part of the country continued to create insecurity, initially on a relatively low scale, but gradually, throughout 1995 and 1996, more intensively. The lack of willingness of the Zairean government to control these armed activities, conducted from Zairean territory, was seen by the new government in Kigali as a long-term source of internal instability. The armed invasion of Zaire in November 1996 by the RPA (Rwanda Patriotic Army), the new government army, to dismantle the refugee camps and thereby the military bases of the new Hutu rebellion, was supposed to put an end to this insecurity. Meanwhile, the launching of the AFDL[3] rebellion under the leadership of Laurent-Désiré

Kabila led to the fall of the Mobutu regime, and Zaire became the Democratic Republic of Congo (DRC). However, the source of the ongoing insecurity in the northwest soon turned out to have been "internalized."[4] Again, the armed conflict had not come to an end.

The ongoing security threats and cross-border movements of Hutu insurgents were among the reasons why a second so-called "rebellion" was instigated by Rwanda and Uganda. The RCD (Congolese Rally for Democracy) was launched in August 1998. What initially seemed to be a replay of the first rebellion, soon acquired an unprecedented regional dimension. In fact, several countries, including Angola and Zimbabwe, decided to send in armed forces in support of President Kabila. The number of players involved and their (political, but also financial) interests have increased dramatically and this makes a solution much more difficult to attain. It remains highly uncertain whether the July 1999 Lusaka Agreement, which provides for a cessation of hostilities, a withdrawal of all foreign forces from DRC territory, and the disarmament of all armed groups, including the ex-FAR, will effectively contribute to the ending of what started as an internal armed conflict but, after nearly nine years, has turned into a regional war.[5]

In summary, it is important to note that Rwanda has been subject to continuous armed conflict since October 1990. Therefore, it cannot be seen as a typical postconflict situation and this has a serious impact on the potential use of both international, nation-state, or indigenous justice and reconciliation mechanisms. Whether the ongoing war is seen as an attempt to prevent genocide or as an act of aggression and attempted annexation of part of the DRC by Rwanda,[6] the reality is that Rwandese citizens are sent to a foreign country to fight other Rwandese citizens. The genocide (April-June 1994) may rightly be isolated from an international and domestic legal perspective, but the ongoing regional violence that has a direct impact on many families certainly makes it much more difficult for Rwandan society to come to terms with the violence of the past.

Political Transition: A Long Road Ahead

Following the Franco-African summit at La Baule in July 1990, President Habyarimana announced the introduction of multipartyism in Rwanda. By early 1991, four opposition parties had been created in addition to the

MRND (Mouvement Révolutionnaire National pour le Développement).[7] In March 1992, the extremist Hutu party CDR (Coalition pour la Défense de la République) was set up; it had close connections with the now famous RTLM (Radio Télévision Libre des Mille Collines)[8] radio station and *Kangura* magazine, and would play a key role in the preparation and implementation of the genocide. Prunier has summarized the main difficulty of democratization in Rwanda as coming from "the conjunction of two forces: the obdurate resistance of the power structure to any type of genuine democratization and the selfish greed of a large part of the opposition leadership."[9] There is a further element that should be added here and which would constitute a real challenge for any regime: How does a government respond to a situation of internal armed conflict and, at the same time, implement a donor-driven democratization program?

The Arusha negotiations process in fact had to respond to both challenges, that is, not only reaching a peace agreement to put an end to the internal armed conflict, but also consolidating the internal democratization process, including the RPF as a political party. After several ups and downs during the negotiations process, the Arusha Accords included a protocol of agreement on power sharing, with a nominative distribution of portfolios within the transitional government (article 56) and a numerical distribution of seats in the transitional National Assembly (article 62). The Accords reflected a tripolar political situation, the three poles being the MRND regime, the armed rebellion, and the internal opposition. However, as mentioned above, the agreement was not implemented. The erosion of the tripolar nature of the political landscape was among the main reasons for this failure. In the context of ongoing political killings and massacres of civilians, but also of the assassination in October 1993 of the first democratically elected Hutu president of Burundi, Melchior Ndadaye, the internal opposition parties were subject to increasing internal splits into pro-regime and pro-rebellion factions. Within months of its signing, the tripolar Arusha agreement no longer corresponded to the bipolar political reality.[10]

On 17 July 1994, the victorious RPF announced the installation of a transitional government and a transitional National Assembly along the lines of the Arusha Accords, which would continue to form part of the country's Fundamental Law.[11] A five-year[12] transitional period was declared, which, in line with the Accords, was to result in free and democratic elections. Given the tremendous human and material losses of the country, and given the military victory of the RPF, this option for institutions that combined strong RPF representation with the inclusion of the former internal opposition seemed most reasonable. Since July 1994, the power base of the regime has narrowed down instead of becoming broader and more inclusive. Several leading politicians—nearly all Hutu—have left or have been forced to leave the government, the national assembly, senior administration posts, or the justice system.[13] The army has remained an almost exclusively RPA and Tutsi bastion. Human rights violations are committed against human rights activists, journalists, or other real or perceived political opponents (including members of the Catholic Church). No political party other than the RPF is allowed to conduct the usual political party activities, regardless of their representation in the National Assembly. The political opposition in diaspora is excluded from participating in the design of Rwanda's future political project.[14] The local elections held early in 1999 at the level of the lowest administrative units under a no-party system have been seen by some observers as a first step in a genuine bottom-up democratization process;[15] but they have also been strongly criticized for their lack of freedom and fairness.[16]

The political challenges Rwanda was facing in July 1994 (and is still facing) have been very well summarized by Mamdani: "To break out of this notion of the state as a representation of a permanently defined majority. . ." and "How to move from an order based on conquest to one based on consent. . . ."[17] In other words, neither a system of majoritarian democracy, where a demographic majority holds full and exclusive political power, nor a minority military regime, can offer a durable political framework for Rwanda. The role of ethnicity as a politically relevant element, and the existence of ethnic or otherwise defined groups in Rwanda, has been extensively debated. Mamdani states that

> [P]ower-sharing will not be durable without a reform of the structure, so that majority and minority are not permanent artefacts institutionalized in the structures of the state and confirmed by the political processes set in motion by that state. In other words, while the recognition of the Bahutu and Batutsi identities needs to be the starting point for a process of reconciliation, the point of the process must be, not to reproduce these dualities, but to transcend them.[18]

One technique of acknowledging, incorporating, defusing, and, finally, transcending group differences that has been successfully applied in different instances of a plural society is called "consociational democracy." Elaborating on this concept is beyond the scope of this chapter. However, when applying Arend Lijphart's favorable conditions for consociational power sharing[19] to the Rwandan context, we found the prospects rather grim.[20]

In summary, the political transition process that Rwanda apparently embarked upon in 1990 has certainly not come to an end, and even seems to have become a lower priority on the new regime's agenda. Nevertheless, the importance of political power sharing for the promotion of justice and reconciliation in a postgenocide context should be stressed. The kind of reconciliation needed transcends the micro level of local communities and also that of victim–offender or community–offender reconciliation. It also involves the way in which power over people and resources is exercised—in a monopolistic manner or through genuine power sharing.

Genocide and Other Crimes Against Humanity: Dealing with the Past

The rest of this chapter focuses on the response at the international and national levels to the horrible events that took place in Rwanda in 1994. How these massive human rights violations were planned and implemented is not discussed in detail here. Others, including African Rights and Human Rights Watch,[21] have published extensively on this episode in Rwandan history, and the genocidal nature of the crimes committed is beyond any doubt.

It should, however, be noted that the human rights violations that are currently being investigated and prosecuted are limited to the period ending on 31 December 1994. Unfortunately, as highlighted below, other crimes against humanity have since been committed by Rwandese against fellow Rwandese. To highlight one such instance, reference can be made to the over 200,000 persons who remained unaccounted for after the violent dismantling of the Hutu refugee camps in Eastern Zaire by the RPA and AFDL forces. These acts were categorized as crimes against humanity (and possibly, subject to further investigation, genocide) by a special investigative team of the U.N. Secretary General.[22]

Justice, Reconciliation, and Reparation after Genocide and Crimes against Humanity

In this section, the response by the international community and the government of Rwanda[23] to the genocide and crimes against humanity is briefly described. Current proposals by the Rwandan government to establish *gacaca* tribunals as an alternative means of bringing to account those suspected of certain levels of responsibility for genocide are also introduced.

Response of the International Community

The international community's political decision to consider the events taking place as a genocide had, according to international law,[24] to be followed by the establishment of an appropriate forum to prosecute the alleged perpetrators, many of whom were no longer on Rwandese territory and were consequently beyond the direct reach of Rwanda's national judicial system. The International Criminal Tribunal for Rwanda (ICTR) was therefore created by U.N. Security Council Resolution 955 of 8 November 1994. Interestingly, the ICTR is not only expected to render justice by determining guilt for the horrific crimes committed, but also, in accordance with one of the preambular paragraphs in the ICTR statute, to "contribute to the process of national reconciliation and to the restoration and maintenance of peace."

At the time of this writing, roughly five years after the adoption of the U.N. Security Council Resolution establishing the ICTR, six high-ranking political leaders, senior government administrators, and businessmen (including the prime minister of the interim government, Jean Kambanda) have been convicted and sentenced to prison terms. Thirty-three others are being held in pretrial detention in Arusha.[25] From the perspective of international criminal law and international human rights law, these achievements are highly remarkable. The ICTR experience will also be invaluable for the future International Criminal Court. However, in certain respects, which are not dealt with in detail here, the ICTR must be evaluated less positively. These are related to internal factors, such as poor management and various operational problems that are inherently linked to its ad hoc structure, but also to four factors that have a direct bearing on the possible contribution of the ICTR to a national reconciliation process in Rwanda.

The first factor is "justice delayed is justice denied." For justice to be seen to be done, trials should be held within a reasonable period of time. Victims' organizations have been complaining that the ICTR proceedings simply take too long and that this in itself undermines the objective of justice.

The second factor is that Rwanda has been faced with ongoing gross violations of human rights that are not in the ICTR's mandate (which, *ratione temporis*, is strictly limited to acts committed in the year 1994).

Third, this limitation of the mandate is seen as an additional indication that the ICTR is rendering justice on behalf of the victor, that is, the militarily strongest party. This perception is also fed by the lack of investigation into war crimes committed by the RPF, which do fall within the ICTR mandate.

Fourth, the involvement of victims in the judicial process is almost completely lacking and the possibility of victims obtaining reparation or compensation through the ICTR is nonexistent.[26] Moreover, privileged eyewitnesses have denounced the enormous (mental) distance between the population and the ICTR:

> They are incapable of approaching those who have experienced the genocide. They do not know how to ask the right questions. They have a behavior and opinions which hurt people. The Rwandans had placed great hope in the ICTR. They are very disappointed.[27]

In addition to the establishment of the ICTR, trials against suspected perpetrators under national judicial systems in countries other than Rwanda are also part of the international response. The direct exercise of universal jurisdiction through the conduct of trials in domestic institutions, has, as far as criminal prosecution is concerned, thus far been limited to one case: Fulgence Niyonteze, a former mayor of Mushubati, was sentenced to life imprisonment by a Swiss military court in April 1999.[28]

Response of the National Judicial System

The prosecution of perpetrators of mass human rights violations was one of the major stated objectives of the new Rwandan government that came to power in July 1994. Fighting impunity is seen as the key instrument of rendering justice and an essential precondition for reconciliation in Rwanda. At the level of the national judiciary, the Rwandan government chose to combine two objectives: the rehabilitation of the justice system, which, in terms of both human and material resources, had been brought to a nearly complete standstill by the war and genocide; and the organization of genocide trials within the same judicial system. The main steps taken to enable the organization of genocide trials and results to date are summarized below. In addition, some elements of evaluation are provided.[29]

Legal and Institutional Reforms

Although Rwanda ratified the 1948 Genocide Convention, the previous regime had failed to incorporate it into domestic legislation.[30] This was eventually done through the "Organic Law of 30 August 1996 on the organization of prosecutions for offenses constituting the crime of genocide or crimes against humanity since 1 October 1990." One of its main characteristics is the categorization of suspects (article 2). Category 1 includes the planners, organizers, and leaders of the genocide; persons acting in a position of authority; "notorious murderers"; and persons who committed acts of torture. Category 2 is made up of all others who committed homicide. Persons who committed other serious assaults against persons fall into category 3. Category 4 includes persons who committed offenses against property. The Organic Law also establishes a confession and guilty plea procedure. This was seen as an instrument to overcome the main obstacle for the prosecution of genocide suspects: the lack of evidence. Although there was some written evidence of the involvement of top leaders in the planning of genocide—for example, lists of arms distributions, documents about the training of Interahamwe militia members, radio broadcasts, and newspaper articles—there was hardly any evidence to substantiate the involvement of the large majority of "ordinary" killers: most eyewitnesses had been killed or had left the country. It was soon realized that this would be the major problem for the preparation of legal case files by the prosecution department. Therefore, a confession and guilty plea procedure was introduced, offering a considerable penalty reduction for perpetrators who confess and provide evidence that can be used against other suspects.[31] As of 30 June 1999, and according to Ministry of Justice figures, more than 15,000 detainees have reportedly confessed.[32] In accordance with the general criminal procedure, the Organic Law allows for the participation of victims in the criminal proceedings as civil claimants (*parties civiles*). The tribunals have jurisdiction to award civil damages, even to victims who have not yet been identified.

Given the massive number of criminal offenses that had been committed, in combination with the nearly complete breakdown of the law enforcement and justice system after the genocide, a huge number of people had been arrested illegally, that is, not in accordance with the relevant legal provisions. Many suspects had been arrested by ordinary soldiers who did not have the legal authority to carry out arrests, and virtually no arrest had been submitted for a judicial review and confirmation within the period prescribed by the Code of Criminal Procedure. On 15 September 1996, the date of its publication in the *Official Gazette*, the Law relating to Provisional Modifications to the Criminal Procedure Code entered into force retroactively from 6 April 1994. Its objective was the regularization of tens of thousands of illegal arrests and detentions that had taken place since the new government came to power. The Rwandan government explicitly referred to the derogation clause in Article 4 of the International Covenant on Civil and Political Rights to justify these modifications to the Criminal Procedure Code. However, the adopted derogations were excessive[33] and, as could be expected, the deadlines for regularizing the detentions were not met in a large number of cases. Consequently, in January 1998 an additional modification to the Code of Criminal Procedure was published to extend the "regularization" period by another two years until December 1999. Even if this new time limitation is respected—which is extremely unlikely—some suspects will have spent over five years in pretrial detention without a judicial review. This situation is not only contrary to international human rights norms; it has obviously also been conducive to large numbers of arbitrary arrests, mainly by military but also by administrative authorities, often on the basis of poorly substantiated denunciations and in the context of a settlement of personal scores.[34] In October 1998, the minister of justice announced that 10,000 pretrial detainees without legal case files would soon be released. A public campaign was set up by IBUKA (the main genocide survivors' organization) to denounce this measure.[35] As of 15 June 1999, only 3,365 had been released.[36]

The problem of the legal representation of defendants before domestic genocide tribunals was exacerbated by the absence of Rwandan lawyers willing to take up the defense of genocide suspects. A number of lawyers had been assassinated, and others had participated in the genocide and had either left the country or been arrested. Most, if not all, of the remaining lawyers were themselves victims of the genocide, having lost relatives or property, and some of them were unwilling to represent genocide suspects. Others were intimidated and abstained from intervening due to fear of reprisals. Although not an immediate solution to the lack of defense lawyers, the establishment of a bar (or law society) in Rwanda for the first time ever was nevertheless an important step in the reconstruction of a functional judicial system. On 30 August 1997 forty-four Rwandan holders of a university degree in law were admitted to the bar. The law establishing the bar also provides for a corps of judicial defenders, who are not law graduates, but who, after six months' training, are entitled to assist and represent parties at the level of the Tribunals of First Instance. In practice, a significant number of the lawyers (Rwandese and international), representing either the accused or the civil claimants, have operated under the Attorneys without Borders (Avocats sans Frontières) project.

Reference should also be made to the creation of Specialized Chambers within the existing Tribunals of First Instance with exclusive jurisdiction to handle genocide cases, and also to the training of a remarkable number of judges, prosecutors, judicial police inspectors, and administrative personnel. However, a proposal to call upon foreign judges—albeit on a temporary basis—was unfortunately rejected by the National Assembly. The participation of foreign experts would have helped to raise the legal quality of trials, as well as the perception of independence and impartiality of the justice rendered.

Results to Date

Domestic genocide trials started in December 1996. According to the official figures of the General Prosecutor's office of the Supreme Court, some 304 persons were judged in 1997 and some 864 persons in 1998. During the first six months of 1999, 634 persons were judged.[37] The total number of accused who had been judged (in the first instance), as of 30 June 1999, therefore amounts to 1,802. Given the number of pretrial detainees, estimated around 122,000,[38] it may, statistically speaking, take over 200 years to complete the genocide trials. This in itself is the most convincing indication that the one-track criminal justice approach for which the Rwandan government has so far opted, is insufficient to deal with the past.

In the early stages of the national trials, various violations of fair trial standards and other criticisms were reported. These were related to the lack of defense lawyers, severe limitations of the normal appellate rights, intimidation of defense witnesses, and so on.[39] Generally speaking, the quality of trials has considerably improved: the number of defense lawyers has dramatically increased (where Attorneys without Borders was active in 1997 and 1998, some fifty percent of defendants were assisted by a defense lawyer), relatively inexperienced judges have benefited from on-the-job training, convictions are generally better substantiated, and so forth. Some of the major problems remaining are (1) the large number of pretrial detainees, a large majority of whom remain without a regular judicial review of their detention;[40] (2) the one-sidedness of the investigations,[41] and threats that continue to be made against defense witnesses;[42] (3) rearrests of persons who have been released (prior to their trial or following their acquittal); (4) the lack of legal assistance during the pretrial investigation stage;[43] (5) and cases of sexual crime remain, for various reasons, largely uninvestigated and tried.[44] Reports about corruption, which were virtually nonexistent in the early months of the trials, have increased. Earlier this year, IBUKA denounced the "early release of suspects by corrupt judges for 50,000 Rwandese Francs" (approximately US$150). This is directly linked both to the fact that, for the truly innocent who are held in pretrial detention without a judicial review, bribes may turn out to be the most efficient way of obtaining release, and to the extremely low salaries of the judges and other judicial personnel. However, victims rightly refuse to accept these practices as just. In a number of cases, this seems to have led to popular revenge and so-called "disappearances" of suspects after their return home.[45]

As far as criminal sentences are concerned, the number of death penalties as a percentage of overall sentences has decreased. For the years 1997 and 1998, death penalties were pronounced in some 232 (or 18.2 percent) of all sentences; for the first semester of 1999, this amounted to only 9 percent of sentences. Twenty-two convicts, some of whom had not benefited from assistance by a defense lawyer, were publicly executed in Kigali in April 1998. Life imprisonment was imposed in 32.1 percent of cases. The number of acquittals rose significantly: on average, 18 percent of all defendants were acquitted in 1997 and 1998 (21 percent for the first semester of 1999).[46] Statistically speaking, on the basis of the latter percentage, over 25,000 persons (21 percent of 122,000) have been detained despite their innocence.

Needless to say, prison conditions in severely overcrowded prisons, especially in municipal detention centers, often amount to cruel, inhumane, and degrading treatment.

Elements of Evaluation

The Rwandan government has been remarkably successful in rehabilitating the state and its structures, including, for example, local and national administrative structures, the education system, a completely new communal police force, and road infrastructure. The justice system is another example of this successful effort: in a relatively short period of time, some important legal reforms have been carried out, essential structures (such as the Supreme Court, the Supreme Council of Magistrates) put in place, court buildings repaired, human resources trained, and new judicial personnel appointed. The Rwandan government should be commended for its strategy of combining both the organization of trials for genocide suspects and the rehabilitation of the "normal" judicial system. In the long term, this will definitely enhance the sustainability of donor support in this region. In the short term, looking at the bare figures, the number of national trials (and judgments) exceeds by far the number of ICTR judgments.

In spite of these major achievements, and in addition to the abovementioned violations of fair trial standards, there is an important problem concerning not only the army, the communal police, and other parts of the administration, but also the judiciary. This problem does not so much affect the technical performance of the judicial system (where rendering justice is an objective in itself), as it does jeopardize the role of the justice system as an instrument of peace and reconciliation. Many Rwandans outside and inside Rwanda (and not only those in prison) do not sufficiently recognize the state and the justice rendered as theirs. It is a widely shared perception—whether fully accurate or not—among Hutu (including the so-called "moderate" ones) that victor's justice is being done. This is a major problem, given the principle that justice must not only be done, but must also be seen to be done: even if the reportedly predominantly Tutsi judiciary were to act evenhandedly and fairly (which is an enormous challenge in itself), the perception of bias would remain.[47] The refusal to incorporate experienced Hutu judges and prosecutors who remained in the country or who returned after the RPF's victory, as well as the arrest, assassination, or departure into exile of a number of them, only exacerbated the problem.[48] Furthermore, efforts to end the culture of impunity would require the systematic prosecution of RPA military responsible for human rights violations. In cases where such abuses have caused international concern (such as the large-scale massacres of Hutu refugees in Eastern Congo), the official RPF line has been that those responsible would be prosecuted and punished. However, despite some reports that the transparency and efficiency of the military justice system are improving,[49] prosecution and punishment seem to remain the exception rather than the rule.

Rendering justice to victims is one of the major stated objectives of the government's justice policy. Judgments establishing guilt and innocence and the punishment of convicts are in themselves important instruments of recognizing victims' sufferings. However, as far as the position of victims and their reparation rights are concerned, several problems can be identified, not only (as mentioned above) in obtaining payments of compensation, but also before and during the trial proceedings. Despite radio messages announcing forthcoming trials, victims are often unaware that court hearings are taking place. The process of identifying the victims, of obtaining the necessary official certificates, and of estimating the damage is extremely cumbersome and expensive compared to average victims' incomes. Establishing a causal link between the criminal act and the damage done may be difficult in many cases. But the major difficulty remains with the actual payment of compensation. Full civil compensation of all damages, given their magnitude, is not possible. As of May 1999, the compensation awarded to civil claimants by the Tribunals of First Instance amounts to some US$90 million. This raises the more general issue—which is not further developed here—whether and how, especially in instances of transitional justice after massive human rights violations, a collective settlement of reparation claims can go hand in hand with a case-by-case approach.[50]

The principal conclusion, however, is that mainly because of the magnitude of the problem and the still limited capacity of the judicial system, the judicial approach of individual criminal trials alone will not suffice. It should be noted that probably no other criminal justice system in the world would be able to deal with such a large number of cases in a satisfactory manner, that is, within a reasonable period of time and with due respect for all human rights norms. As a consequence, the entire process is generally perceived as being extremely slow. As Attorneys without Borders, in its latest report, states: "There is a clear progress and justice is at work, but this justice does not convince [*la justice ne convainc pas*]."[51] This conclusion raises the question of which supplementary, alternative solutions might be available. An alternative approach might consist of the establishment of a national or international truth and reconciliation commission for Rwanda. From an international law perspective it can be argued that in the case of genocide, there is no alternative to the criminal prosecution of all individual perpetrators.[52] Some authors have examined the opportunities for and constraints upon the establishment of a national truth and reconciliation commission in Rwanda,[53] arguing that

> Unless an independent institution is developed that provides the opportunity for victims to tell their stories and for those who are guilty of human rights violations to confess, Rwandan society will continue to live under the shadow of division, tension and violence. . . . This body need not replace criminal prosecutions or grant amnesties. In fact, international law prohibits the granting of amnesty for the gross violations of human rights that have occurred in Rwanda. The Commission should instead complement other activities already under way in Rwanda, serving as a forum in which victims can tell of their suffering and be heard and acknowledged, and so regain their dignity.[54]

Proposed Establishment of Popular Gacaca Tribunals

At the time of this writing, the Rwandan government is proposing the establishment of popular *gacaca* tribunals. This section will first describe the traditional concept of *gacaca*, before presenting in more detail the current proposal. This is obviously an important innovation in Rwanda's strategy to deal with the past, because among other things, the proposed *gacaca* tribunals would deal with the large majority of suspects.

Gacaca

Defining *gacaca* is a hard thing to do. As a society-rooted phenomenon, it is more appropriate to describe than to define it: its precise form strongly depends on the community in which it operates.[55] A *gacaca* is not a permanent judicial or administrative institution, but rather a meeting convened whenever the need arises and in which members of one family or of different families or all the inhabitants of one "hill" participate. There are no generally applicable rules or criteria to determine the number of participants in the proceedings, which are chaired by family elders. The *gacaca* intends to "sanction the violation of rules that are shared by the community, with the sole objective of reconciliation."[56] The "modern" distinction between judges, parties, witnesses, and audience is hardly applicable: given the disruption of social order, all members of society are affected and are, as a consequence, party to the conflict. The objective, therefore, is not to determine guilt or to apply state law in a coherent and consistent manner (as one expects from state courts of law), but to restore harmony and social order in a given society, and to reincorporate the person who was the source of the disorder. The outcome of the *gacaca* may therefore not at all be in accordance with the state laws of the country concerned.[57]

Generally, the types of conflict dealt with by the *gacaca* are related to land use and land rights, cattle, marriage, inheritance rights, loans, damage to property caused by one of the parties or by animals, and so on. Most of these conflicts would therefore be considered to be of a civil nature when brought before a state court of law. However, conflicts amounting to criminal offenses (generally of a minor kind, such as theft) may also be settled here, although they will not result typically in a criminal sanction such as imprisonment, but in some sort of civil settlement—for instance, an amount of compensation, possibly exceeding the damage incurred. The sentence has a double objective: it should be a sanction that allows the person concerned to understand better the gravity of the damage caused, but at the same time it should allow the same person to reintegrate into the local community. As a consequence, a prison sentence is unknown under the *gacaca* system.

A sociological inquiry conducted in 1996 by a group of experts of the Institut de Recherche Scientifique et Technologique (IRST) found that people generally felt that genocide should not be dealt with by the *gacaca* but by the highest political authority, that is, the state (which, in a system of the separation of powers, should be understood to be the judiciary). Once guilt is established, it was felt that the killer (or one of his family) should also be killed. This would enable forgetting and forgiveness and lead to a reconciliation of the families involved.[58] Similarly, under the traditional *mwami* (king) justice, cattle thieves were very often sentenced to impalement and died of their injuries.

Following the war and the genocide that devastated the country, there were (and still are) a very large number of legal and other conflicts to be settled. At the same time, the capacity of the national justice system was extremely limited, even more than was already the case before 1990. In its Action Plan on Justice of August 1994, the new Rwandan government hoped for a reactivation of the *gacaca* in order to promote a peaceful settlement of disputes and in order to reduce the number of cases submitted to the formal judicial structures. However, in order for the *gacaca* to be operational, some preconditions need to be fulfilled. As a traditional, community-based mechanism for the settlement of disputes, it is grounded on certain common values and norms of reciprocity. It has been rightly argued that the genocide and other crimes against humanity have not only caused an exceptionally high number of deaths, refugee movements and internal displacements, and destruction of existing communities, but that these events have also destroyed the fundamental value structures that formed the basis for the *gacaca*. As one author says of the report of an inquiry into this matter: the report "confirms that the *gacaca* can no longer function today, because custom was based on fundamental values of respect for the human being which today are no longer in existence."[59] This illustrates how a conflict can fundamentally alter or even reduce the availability of existing traditional mechanisms for reconciliation and dispute settlement. The abovementioned IRST study has shown that, in many villages, the *gacaca* has been reactivated spontaneously, partly because of the lack of functioning state courts (*tribunals de canton*). However, its nature has been fundamentally altered due to the new circumstances, including the new composition of the local population after the genocide.

Proposed Gacaca Tribunals

It is extremely important, in light of the current proposals by the government of Rwanda, to note that the role and functioning of the *gacaca* as described above was based on the common understanding of the members of a given family or community, and not on a decree adopted and imposed by any (traditional or state) political authority whatsoever. However, on the other hand, when looking at the stated objectives that the Rwandan government hopes to attain through the establishment of *gacaca* tribunals, there are some clear similarities with the indigenous mechanism: the proposal aims at increasing popular participation in the organization of genocide trials through some process of "truth telling" at the local level, and at promoting concord, . harmony, and reconciliation.

The relatively complicated structure of this new, parallel *gacaca* justice system is briefly summarized below, based on the most recent available official document, which dates to 8 June 1999. This document forms the basis of ongoing discussions and consultations and was submitted for debate in the National Assembly in June 2000.

Structure of Proposed Gacaca Tribunals

The pyramidal structure of the proposed *gacaca* system (to be established at four different levels) is strongly linked with the structures of Rwanda's public administration. All adult inhabitants of one "cell" (the lowest administrative unit) will, through an election process and on the initiative of the chief of the cell, choose twenty persons of "high integrity" who will compose the bench of the *gacaca* tribunal at cell level. The bench will choose its own coordinating committee of five persons. Similar elections will take place at the levels of the sector, the commune, and the prefecture.[60]

At the level of the cell, the general assembly of all the inhabitants will provide testimonies and other possible elements of proof of the crimes of the suspected perpetrators. The assembly will also assist the bench in drawing up a list of victims and perpetrators within the cell's territory. From this perspective, the proposed *gacaca* tribunals can be seen as yet another attempt to collect evidence, which has been one of the main constraints on the ongoing criminal trials. The bench of the cell *gacaca* tribunal will conduct investigations on the basis of the testimonies and classify the suspects in categories in accordance with the Organic Law. The bench can request assistance from persons of high integrity with legal expertise. It will judge the category 4 suspects. No appeals against its rulings are possible. The coordinating committee will supervise the activities of the general assembly and the bench, and will record the judgments, which will be kept in a special ad hoc register.

At the level of the sector, the *gacaca* tribunal will judge the category 3 suspects. At the level of the commune, category 2 suspects will be judged. Appeals against sector *gacaca* tribunal decisions will also be brought before the bench of the commune *gacaca* tribunal. The prefecture *gacaca* tribunal, which does not have jurisdiction in the first instance, will hear appeals against the commune *gacaca* tribunals. Category 1 suspects will continue to be judged by the regular state Tribunals of First Instance.

Overall control will be exercised by a new *Gacaca* Tribunals Department within the Supreme Court and by the Ministry of Justice.

Jurisdiction and Powers of Gacaca Tribunals

As a general rule, the government proposal specifies that the *gacaca* tribunals will have the combined powers of the "ordinary" tribunals and the public prosecution department.[61] More specifically, they will be able to summon anyone to appear and testify (and transfer to the public prosecutor anyone who refuses to appear or gives false witness); issue search warrants and conduct house searches; confiscate goods and order the return of confiscated goods to those defendants who have been acquitted; impose criminal sanctions; and request the public prosecution department to clarify case files and past investigations.

As far as punishments are concerned, category 1 genocide suspects will continue to be judged by the Tribunals of First Instance and will be liable to the death penalty. This penalty will remain the same as in the current system. Category 2 genocide suspects (under the jurisdiction of the commune *gacaca* tribunal) who refuse to confess and plead guilty will be liable to a prison sentence ranging from a twenty-five-year prison term to life imprisonment. This is obviously one of the best illustrations of the nonindigenous nature of the proposed tribunals, and, at the same time, the most worrisome feature from a human rights perspective. Those who confess after an indictment will be liable to a prison term of between twelve and fifteen years. A new element in the execution of punishment is being proposed: eight years of the sentence will have to be served in prison, the remaining part being spent outside the prison compound and converted into public service work. Those who confess prior to an indictment will be liable to a prison term of between seven and eleven years, with possible conversion after a three-year prison term. Especially for category 2 suspects who have very good reasons not to confess, but, as a consequence, will be liable to life imprisonment, it might be preferable to use the current, "ordinary" trial system, where the usual fair trial guarantees are better respected than may turn out to be the case in the *gacaca* tribunal system. Category 3 genocide suspects (under the jurisdiction of the sector *gacaca* tribunal) will be liable to prison terms as determined by the Organic Law of 30 August 1996. Irrespective of their confession (and the timing of the latter), half of the prison term will be spent outside the prison compound and converted into public service work. Category 4 convicts (under the jurisdiction of the cell *gacaca* tribunal) will repair the damage they caused or carry out works considered equivalent to the damage done.

Evaluation

It is obviously premature to present a thorough evaluation of the possible contribution of the proposed *gacaca* tribunals to the attainment of the objectives of justice, reconciliation, and reparation in Rwanda. The proposals are still at a preliminary stage and will, without any doubt and similarly to the Organic Law of 30 August 1996, be the subject of lengthy debates in the National Assembly. However, some provisional comments can be made in evaluation.

Some of the most salient features of traditional justice systems, as summarized in an excellent publication by Penal Reform International,[62] do not only apply to the traditional *gacaca*, but also to the proposed *gacaca* tribunals. The proposed role of the *gacaca* general assembly in opening up participation to all adult citizens reflects both the traditional widespread involvement of the population in the process and the traditional objectives which go beyond rendering justice in the strict sense. The "decentralization" of justice to the cell level may have an overall positive impact, not only on the active participation of the population, but also on the perception that justice is being done and on the acceptance of verdicts.[63] Further, the possibility of the conversion of part of the prison sentence into public service work indicates a shift from a purely retributive approach to a jointly restorative and retributive one.

There are, however, some very important differences between the typical traditional justice system and the proposed *gacaca* tribunals. The most striking differences include, first of all, the establishment of the tribunals by the state legislator and the determination of their composition, functioning, and jurisdiction by state law. Second, the *gacaca* tribunals will be expected to apply state law, which is contrary to the traditional approach and which, in itself, underscores the need for legal knowledge (and, logically, also the need for professional legal assistance). The execution of prison sentences will be secured through state law enforcement agents and in state prison buildings. Finally, the strongly pyramidal and centrally steered and funded (by the Supreme Court and the Ministry of Justice) nature of the *gacaca* tribunal system is also atypical. In summary, whereas social pressure is at the heart of a typical informal and traditional justice system,[64] here state coercion—the ultimate feature of a formal state justice system—may turn out to be the ultimate engine for the proposed *gacaca* tribunal justice.[65] Among the reasons for the importance of the state's involvement, two should be mentioned. First of all, state involvement may have a significant impact on the genuine acceptance of the process by the local communities and their participation in it. This in itself has an important bearing on the reconciliatory effects of the justice rendered. Second, it may also have an impact on whether the usual human rights norms (e.g., fair trial standards) operate in the *gacaca* tribunal system.[66]

Some survivors groups have expressed fears that the current proposals amount to a form of disguised amnesty. However, although in some instances the prison sentence may indeed be significantly reduced, neither the penalization of the acts committed, nor the determination of individual guilt are put into question by the proposed legislation. Concerns have also been raised that the acts of genocide will be trivialized through the proposed justice system, and that it may be used to settle personal scores through some form of collusion or "conspiracy of silence" between defendants and elected bench members. Further, there is no possibility of being involved as civil claimants (*parties civiles*) in the hearings, which, at least in theory, diminishes the opportunity for active involvement in the trials. On the other hand, it may be physically easier for victims to participate than under the current system. It should also be noted that through the conversion of prison sentences into public service work, the de facto reparation (through restitution or compensation) might be greater than under the current system.

The proposed *gacaca* tribunals would dramatically increase the overall capacity to try suspects. This in itself would make more likely the speedy treatment of individual cases, which, in turn, would reduce the overall period of pretrial detention. The proposed introduction of this parallel system, however, should by no means be used as an excuse not to release the remainder of the pretrial detainees without case files (as announced by the government in October 1998) and to seriously reactivate the council chambers. The proposed system, with its possibilities for the conversion of prison sentences, would also result in the early release of a number of convicts who are willing to confess. Investigation, indictment, prosecution, judgment, and sentencing would be done by one and the same institution, raising serious concerns from the perspective of fair trial standards and other human rights norms. Further, if the proposed *gacaca* tribunal system is primarily perceived as a state law institution and not as an indigenous, community-based mechanism, it may very well be seen as an instrument of state power and oppression.[67]

Concluding Remarks

The general atmosphere in Rwanda with regard to dealing with the past remains extremely tense. Through a preliminary field study conducted in 1998 in three communes in southern Butare, the Programme Santé Mentale Communautaire of Dr. Simon Gasiberege inquired into the views of the population about responsibility for the rehabilitation of goods and persons after the war and genocide. The researchers found, first of all, that Rwandans are extremely suspicious of inquiries on this subject. Moreover, social coexistence in Rwanda is made more difficult due to the antagonism[68] between two categories of the population: genocide survivors and their families versus genocide suspects and their families.[69] Obviously, the situation in particular communities may differ to an important extent from these general conclusions. In some communities, there may be a general willingness to participate in an open discussion about truth, responsibility, guilt, acknowledgment, and punishment. However, the prevalence of extreme suspicion and social antagonism in other communities may make any top-down attempt at imposing collective truth telling and the restoration of social harmony extremely difficult. For justice to be rendered, especially through the proposed *gacaca* tribunals, and for the latter to have the desired restorative and reconciliatory effect, people will need to own the process, and this in itself will require a high degree of freedom of speech and a political spirit of openness and room for dissenting opinion.

In addition to these features of today's Rwanda at local community level, the challenges at the national political level are different from many other post-conflict, transitional justice situations. The number of crimes, victims, and perpetrators is much greater. The ongoing conflict situation and lack of political power sharing constitutes a major difference between Rwanda and, for example, South Africa, where the question of political power sharing came first and where the instrument to deal with the past was agreed upon only at a later stage in the negotiations process.[70] Further, despite a possible overall consensus regarding the need to eradicate impunity, perceptions of the current approach vary significantly. Victims perceive it as amounting to ongoing impunity because only a small percentage of the total number of perpetrators have been found guilty. Others perceive it as resulting in massive political (and even ethnic) oppression, because tens of thousands of families are affected by the detention of one of their members, despite the fact that they should be considered innocent until proven guilty.

Mahmood Mamdani has written that

> [A]fter 1994, the Tutsi want justice above all else, and the Hutu democracy above all else. The minority fears democracy. The majority fears justice. The minority fears that democracy is a mask for finishing an unfinished genocide. The majority fears the demand for justice is a minority ploy to usurp power forever.[71]

One of the ways forward is to overcome the apparent dichotomy between the two concepts of justice and democracy, and to find ways of combining them. Genuine reconciliation at the community and national levels may be the end result of a lengthy process of acceptance of both justice and democracy (or, to avoid a taboo word, "power sharing"). For justice to be accepted as an instrument of reconciliation, it must meet certain conditions that go even beyond criteria of the independence and impartiality of the judiciary. These conditions include its embeddedness in an overall process toward transparency, political participation, and inclusiveness. At the same time, history has shown that, in the context of Rwanda's plural society, political participation can by no means equal majority democracy, but requires a balanced system of power sharing, including the protection of minority rights and security guarantees.

Endnotes

1. For many Rwandese and a number of foreign observers, this was actually the real start of the genocide, which is generally interpreted as limited to the three-month period of April–June 1994.

2. G. Prunier, *The Rwanda Crisis: History of a Genocide* (London: Hurst and Co., 1995), 268.

3. Alliance des Forces Démocratiques pour la Libération du Congo-Zaire (Alliance of Democratic Forces for the Liberation of Congo-Zaire).

4. In June 1997 the Phases and Security Procedures of the United Nations considered one third of the communes as being "inaccessible" to U.N. personnel, and another third as "requiring a military escort." A 1998 African Rights report lists all operational leaders of the armed Hutu insurgency, known as the Peuple Armé pour la Libération du Rwanda (PALIR): all of them are ex-FAR members who held important positions in Rwanda before July 1994.

5. For a recent overview and comparison of both wars, see F. Reyntjens, *La guerre des Grands Lacs. Alliances mouvantes et conflits extraterritoriaux en Afrique centrale* (Paris: L'Harmattan, 1999).

6. E. Lubala, "Interventions militaires étrangères au Kivu: prévention de génocide ou voie de puissance?," in *L'Afrique des Grands Lacs, Annuaire 1998–1999*, S. Marysse and F. Reyntjens, eds. (Paris: L'Harmattan, 1999), 284-308.

7. These were the MDR (Mouvement Démocratique Républicain), the PSD (Parti Social Démocrate), the PL (Parti Libéral), and the PDC (Parti Démocrate-Chrétien).

8. Literally, Independent Radio and Television of the Thousand Hills. This was the extremist Hutu radio station; the television station was never operational.

9. Prunier, *The Rwanda Crisis*, 131.

10. In *Les antécédents politiques de la crise rwandaise de 1994* (mimeographed report submitted to the U.N. Tribunal on Rwanda), A. Guichaoua noted that "[T]he kind of alliance to be made with the RPF divides each party. On the one hand, there is the dominant temptation to depend on the military power of the FPR in such a way as to make a complete break with the Habyarimina regime; while on the other hand, a strategy of autonomy and maintaining a central position on the tripolar system of confrontation recommends itself. . . . The strategies of ethnic tension lead inexorably to bipolarization." (Translation by Nigel Biggar.)

11. However, the seats and ministerial posts that would normally have been awarded to the MRND, CDR, and other parties or factions that had played an active role in the genocide, were now to be filled by the RPF.

12. In June 1999, the RPF decided to extend the transition period by another four years. See M.F. Cros, "Le pouvoir s'octroie quatre ans de plus," *La Libre Belgique*, 11 June 1999.

13. For example, Faustin Twagiramungu (MDR Hutu prime minister, who resigned and fled in 1995), Seth Sendashonga (RPF Hutu minister of the interior, who resigned in 1995 and was assassinated in Nairobi in 1997), Augustin Cyiza (Hutu president of the Cour de Cassation, who resigned under pressure in 1998), Faustin Nteziryayo (Hutu

minister of justice, who resigned and fled in January 1999), and Alype Nkundiyaremye (Hutu president of the Council of State, who fled in June 1999).

14. In this context, it should be stressed that not all diaspora organizations, which include both Hutu and Tutsi opponents of the current regime, can be automatically labeled as "génocidaires." Reference should be made, for instance, to the UFDR (Union of Rwandese Democratic Forces), UNAR (Union Nationale pour le Rwanda), CDA (African Democratic Congress), NOUER (Nouvelle Espérance pour le Rwanda), and the RNLM (Rwanda National Liberation Movement).

15. J. Prendergast and D. Smock, *Postgenocide Reconstruction: Building Peace in Rwanda and Burundi* (Washington, D.C.: U.S. Institute of Peace, 1999).

16. "Rwandans prepare for first post-genocide elections," *Integrated Regional Information Network for Central and Eastern Africa* (U.N.: Nairobi, 26 March 1999).

17. M. Mamdani, "From Conquest to Consent as the Basis of State Formation: Reflections on Rwanda," *New Left Review* 220 (1996): 17.

18. Ibid., 30.

19. See A. Lijphart, *Democracy in Plural Societies. A Comparative Exploration* (New Haven and London: Yale University Press, 1977) and "Changement et continuité dans la théorie consociative," *Revue Internationale de Politique Comparée* 4/3 (1997): 679–97. Favorable conditions include a multiple balance of powers, cross-cutting cleavages, overarching loyalties, and external dangers perceived as a common threat by all segments, and so on.

20. For more detail, see S. Vandeginste and L. Huyse, "Approches consociatives dans le contexte du Rwanda," in *L'Afrique des Grands Lacs, Annuaire 1998–1999*, 101–23.

21. See African Rights, *Death, Despair and Defiance* (London: African Rights, 1995), and Human Rights Watch, *Leave None to Tell the Story: Genocide in Rwanda* (New York: Human Rights Watch, 1999).

22. See the *Report of the Secretary General's Investigative Team Charged with Investigating Serious Violations of Human Rights and International Humanitarian Law in the Democratic Republic of Congo* (New York: United Nations, 1998), para. 96: "[T]he systematic massacre of those remaining in Zaire was an abhorrent crime against humanity, but the underlying rationale for the decisions is material to whether these killings constituted genocide, that is, a decision to eliminate, in part, the Hutu ethnic group."

23. For a discussion of the difficulties related to the concurrent organization of trials at the national and international levels, see M.H. Morris, "The Trials of Concurrent Jurisdiction: the Case of Rwanda," *Duke Journal of Comparative and International Law* 7/2 (1997): 349–74.

24. Article 6 of the U.N. Convention on the Prevention and Punishment of the Crime of Genocide states that "persons charged with genocide or any of the other acts enumerated in article 3 shall be tried by a competent tribunal of the State in the territory of which

the act was committed, or by such international penal tribunal as may have jurisdiction with respect to those Contracting Parties which shall have accepted its jurisdiction."

25. For an overview of all ICTR detainees and their current status, see the Tribunal's web site at www.ictr.org/english.factsheet/detainees.htm.

26. In contrast to Napoleonic legal systems (such as Rwanda's), victims cannot constitute themselves "parties civiles" (civil claimants). However, under Rule 106 of the ICTR Rules of Procedure and Evidence, the ICTR Registrar shall transmit to the competent authorities of the state concerned the judgment finding the accused guilty of a crime that has caused injury to a victim. Pursuant to the relevant national legislation, a victim or persons claiming through him may bring an action in a national court or other competent body to obtain compensation. For the purposes of this claim, the judgment of the ICTR shall be final and binding as far as the criminal responsibility of the convicted person for such injury is concerned.

27. A. Sibomana, *Gardons éspoir pour le Rwanda* (Paris: Desclée De Brouwer, 1997), 166. My translation.

28. In addition to criminal prosecution, some states also recognize the rights of the victims to seek (civil) compensation before their own courts. The case against Jean-Bosco Barayagwiza, one of the leaders of the extremist CDR political party, before a New York district court, resulted in the decision in April 1996 to award compensation amounting to US$105 million to the group of survivors who initiated the proceedings.

29. For more detail, see C.J. Ferstman, "Domestic Trials for Genocide and Crimes against Humanity: The Example of Rwanda," *African Journal of International and Comparative Law* 9 (1997): 857–77, and M.A. Drumbl, "Rule of Law Amid Lawlessness: Counseling the Accused in Rwanda's Domestic Genocide Trials," *Columbia Human Rights Law Review* 29/3 (1998): 545–639.

30. Article 5 of the Genocide Convention states that "The Contracting Parties undertake to enact, in accordance with their respective Constitutions, the necessary legislation to give effect to the provisions of the present Convention, and, in particular, to provide effective penalties for persons guilty of genocide or any of the other acts enumerated in Article 3."

31. In fact, for a confession to be admissible under the Organic Law, a detailed description must be given of the offenses that the applicant committed, including the date, time, and location of each act, as well as the names of victims, witnesses, accomplices, and instigators (Article 6).

32. Avocats Sans Frontières, *Justice pour Tous au Rwanda. Rapport Semestriel: 1er Semestre 1999* (Brussels: Kigali, 1999), 14.

33. According to René Degni-Ségui, Special Rapporteur of the Commission on Human Rights, this clause cannot be invoked in such cases (*Report on the Situation of Human Rights in Rwanda*, U.N. Document E/CN.4/1997/61, 20 January 1997, para.112).

34. Following accusations by IBUKA (the main genocide survivors' organization)

against Elysée Bisengimana, a newly appointed RPF member of parliament from the Cyangugu prefecture, even RPF Secretary General Charles Muligande denounced these arbitrary denunciation practices: "The FPR is committed to help the government find ways and means of combatting this tendency to accuse people falsely of participation in genocide and massacre" (*Le Verdict*, May 1999, 13). (Translation by Nigel Biggar.)

35. See also P. Massenet, "La libération des détenus sans dossier doit continuer," *Le Verdict*, June 1999, 7.

36. "Les 'sans dossiers' accusés de génocide continuent d'être libérés," *Le Verdict*, July 1999, p. 14.

37. Avocats Sans Frontières, *Justice pour Tous*, 22. This increase is mainly due to the increased "group trial" approach: for instance, the Tribunals of First Instance of Butare, Gikongoro, Byumba, Nyamata, and Rushashi together judged 249 defendants in twenty-two trials in the first six months of 1999.

38. Although official figures may not fully correspond to the real number of detainees, the Ministry of Justice recently counted approximately 120,000 pretrial detainees and approximately 1,500 convicts. According to the Attorneys without Borders' recent report, an estimated 86,292 suspects (including 4,104 women) are held in civilian prisons, 33,327 in communal detention centers, and 3,208 in other lockups, which amounts to a total number of 122,827 pretrial detainees. The number has decreased by some 2,200 compared to the December 1998 figures (125,028). See Avocats Sans Frontières, *Justice pour Tous*, 14.

39. See Amnesty International, *Rwanda, Unfair trials: Justice denied* (London: Amnesty International, 1997).

40. The activities of the council chambers (*chambres de conseil*), where pretrial detentions are supposed to be judicially reviewed, remain unacceptably limited, which is one of the major concerns from a human rights perspective. As of May 1999, approximately twenty percent of detainees had had a judicial review of their pretrial detention in a council chamber (Avocats Sans Frontières, *Justice pour Tous*, 14).

41. Under Rwandan law, the public prosecutor has to investigate a case *à charge* and *à décharge*: both evidence of guilt and evidence of innocence should be taken into account. Very often, however, defense witnesses are not heard by the public prosecutor.

42. It should be noted that prosecution witnesses, albeit in a less "official" manner, have also received threats.

43 Rwandan law (Code of Criminal Procedure) limits the right to legal counsel to the hearings in council chamber and to the trial hearings in court. No legal assistance is permitted during the investigative stage (when the case is in the hands of the prosecution department).

44. M. Schotmans, "Violences sexuelles pendant le génocide: les femmes réclament justice," *Le Verdict*, August 1999, 18.

45. See, for instance, J.P. Remy, "Une justice à risques au Rwanda," *Libération*, 10 June 1999.

46. Acquittals are often barely accepted by certain parts of the population. This has contributed, in a minority of cases, to a certain reluctance to release the acquitted, which is obviously extremely worrisome (Avocats Sans Frontières, *Justice pour Tous*, 6).

47. Although sociological field research would be necessary to give a more scientific character to this assertion, it is worth referring to a study conducted by Gerard Prunier who made an "ethnic count" of senior civil servants. According to his estimate, at the end of 1996, 15 of the 22 cabinet directors, 16 of 19 director generals, 6 of the 11 prefects, 80 percent of mayors and 95 percent of all soldiers, gendarmes, and police officers were Tutsi (Prunier, *The Rwanda Crisis*, 369).

48. This problem is not necessarily an ethnic matter; it is primarily a matter of inclusiveness. The same concern would apply to a situation where all judicial personnel originate from the same prefecture (a regional bias), or where all judicial personnel are men (a gender bias), or where all judicial personnel are Muslim (bias based on religion), and so forth.

49. Prendergast and Smock, *Postgenocide reconstruction*, 18.

50. For more detail, see C. Tomuschat, "Individual Reparation Claims in Instances of Grave Human Rights Violations: the Position under General International Law," in *State Responsibility and the Individual: Reparation in Instances of Grave Violations of Human Rights*, A. Randelzhofer and C. Tomuschat, eds. (The Hague: Martinus Nijhoff Publishers, 1999), 18.

51. Avocats Sans Frontières, *Justice Pour Tous*, 38. My translation.

52. See, for example, S. Landsman, "Alternative Responses to Serious Human Rights Abuses: Of Prosecution and Truth Commissions," in *Law and Contemporary Problems* (special issue, "Accountability for International Crimes," edited by C. Bassiouni and M. Morris) 59/4 (1997): 148–67.

53. See, for example, J. Sarkin, "The Necessity and Challenges of Establishing a Truth and Reconciliation Commission in Rwanda," *Human Rights Quarterly* 21/4 (1999): 767–823, and S. Vandeginste, *A Truth and Reconciliation Approach to the Genocide and Crimes Against Humanity in Rwanda* (Antwerp: University of Antwerp, 1998).

54. Sarkin, "Necessity and Challenges," 822–23. Interestingly, one of the only provisions of the Arusha Accords that the current government has not implemented relates to Article 16 of the Protocol of Agreement on the rule of law, which states that "the two parties also agree to establish an International Commission of Inquiry to investigate human rights violations committed during the war." Such an international commission might have been a stepping stone to the establishment of an internationally sponsored and staffed truth commission (similar to the one in El Salvador, for instance). Obviously, as follows from Article 16, this would involve looking into human rights violations committed by both parties, irrespective of the military outcome of the war.

55. For a micro-study on *gacaca* in the rural setting of the Ndora commune (Butare

prefecture), see F. Reyntjens, "Le gacaca ou la justice du gazon au Rwanda," *Politique Africaine* (December 1990): 31–41.

56. S. Mbonyintege, "Gacaca ishobora ite kongera kuba inzira y'ubwiyunge bw'aban-yarwanda," *Urumuri rwa Kristu*, 15 August 1995, 15. Translation by C. Ntampaka and S. Vandeginste.

57. The abovementioned study by Reyntjens showed that forty-five percent of the *gacaca* decisions were in accordance with state law, and fifty-five percent were not.

58. Summary of the inquiry by Smaragde Mbonyintege, reported in J. Jyoni wa Karega, *Gacaca, Le droit coutumier au Rwanda: Rapport final de la première phase d'enquête sur le terrain* (Kigali: U.N. High Commissioner for Human Rights, 1996), 29–30.

59. C. Ntampaka, "Le retour à la tradition dans le règlement des différends: le gacaca du Rwanda," *Dialogue* (October–November 1995): 96. This refers to the abovementioned article by Mbonyintege.

60. The country is divided into twelve prefectures, which are subdivided into 154 communes, each representing an average of about 50,000 citizens. Each commune is further divided into (on average) ten sectors and each sector into six cells. Cells total 8,987. Statistically speaking, one cell represents an average of 830 citizens.

61. Nevertheless, the proposal reaffirms the powers of the public prosecution department to continue its usual investigation activities. The case files on individual suspects and related elements of proof will be transferred to the relevant *gacaca* tribunal level (Article I.2.5).

62. Penal Reform International, *Traditional and Informal Justice Systems in Africa, South Asia and the Caribbean* (London: Penal Reform International, March 1999).

63. Similarly, the judgments pronounced by roving Specialized Chambers of the Tribunals of First Instance, where hearings are held closer to the people involved, are reported to be better perceived and more readily accepted.

64. Penal Reform International, *Traditional and Informal Justice Systems*, 41.

65. One could ask: Does the abovementioned explicit penalization of the refusal to testify provide an indication in this respect?

66. Unfortunately, the latter issue, which is somewhat controversial, cannot be further developed here. Generally, it is my position that trials before the proposed *gacaca* tribunals, as a parallel state justice system, do need to conform with human rights norms.

67. Related to this issue of a possibly perceived lack of impartiality is the question of whether and to what extent, an historical record will be compiled of war crimes or other human rights violations committed by the former RPF rebellion through these local hearings.

68. This antagonism was already tangible in early 1996 when the proposed Organic Law on genocide trials was at the heart of the public debate. Genocide survivors did not accept the proposed penalty reductions—because genocide is the crime of crimes, penalties for it should be at least as severe as for similar crimes committed outside the context

of a genocide. Detainees and their families considered this to be a highly irrelevant theoretical discussion; their illegal pretrial detention was seen as the ultimate proof of the severe repression imposed by the new regime.

69. PSMC-UNR (Programme Santé Mentale Communautaire-Université Nationale du Rwanda), *Le rôle de la communauté dans la restauration de la justice: rapport général* (Butare: National University of Rwanda, 1998), 4.

70. See, for example, L. Huyse, *Young democracies and the choice between amnesty, truth commissions and prosecutions* (Leuven: University of Leuven, 1998), 15.

71. M. Mamdani, *When Does a Settler Become a Native? Reflections of the Colonial Roots of Citizenship in Equatorial and South Africa* (Cape Town: University of Cape Town, 1998), 11.

CHAPTER 13

❧

Northern Ireland: Burying the Hatchet, Not the Past

Terence McCaughey

The "Peace Process"

The Belfast Agreement of Good Friday 1998 envisaged the establishment of a devolved assembly and executive in Northern Ireland. It also proposed cross-border bodies to operate in certain named areas of mutual interest to both parts of Ireland, as well as providing for east-west structures that will enable the Republic and Northern Ireland to discuss matters of shared concern, not only with London but also with the new regional administrations in Cardiff and in Edinburgh. No plebiscite on these proposals was held in Great Britain, but referenda in the two parts of Ireland showed that there was very strong support for the Agreement.

Nevertheless, it took more than seventeen months of work, involving the recall of U.S. Senator George Mitchell and another prolonged series of talks and negotiations, before terms for demilitarization and the decommissioning of explosives and weapons could be settled. Only when these matters were agreed could the mechanisms for setting up the structures envisaged in the Agreement be triggered into existence. In the end, it turned out that, notwithstanding a sustained and prolonged cease-fire on the part of the paramilitaries, nothing could happen until there was an undertaking all around to "bury the hatchet."

No one who has followed the progress of this peace process closely, or who is familiar with similar processes elsewhere, will imagine for a moment that the demilitarization of a conflict like the Irish one is simple. Nor will they in this case imagine that the delay in arriving at terms for the Agreement's implementation was due solely to the stubbornness or irrationality of the particular negotiators involved. It was not. Unionists,[1] for their part, have always been affronted by the prospect of sitting down in any administration with people whom they believe to have close links with the Irish Republican Army (IRA); and they have been brought reluctantly and only after a great deal of pressure and persuasion, to agree to do so—at least in the meantime. A majority of unionists have agreed to stay with it, provided there is evidence of decommissioning of arms.

Unionists argue that their position would be the norm in any normal democratic society—and so it would. What they tend not to take on board is the widely held and plausible view that Northern Ireland is not now, and has not been, a normal society. To those who are not unionists, it would appear that the unionists have always been in a position to call upon the armed forces of the state to protect their sectional interests in an emergency. The British Army, the Royal Ulster Constabulary (RUC), and formerly the B-Special Constabulary, were theirs in a special way. The proposals of the Patten Commission[2] for the reform of the RUC and in particular for a change in its title (which would only bring it into line with police forces in the rest of the United Kingdom), have met with unionist opposition. This is less because of serious opposition to the proposals considered on their merits, than because it is felt that any change will probably loosen the unionist hold upon the police force.

On the republican side, it has been clear that, if we really are talking about a negotiated settlement, there can be no question of their agreeing to do anything that gives the impression that republican paramilitaries are "surrendering." Of course, many in the nationalist or even republican[3] part of the population deplored the decision of the IRA to go on the offensive in an "armed struggle" in the early 1970s. Such people would agree that nothing has been gained by the use of force that could not have been gained by other means, and that the loss of many lives could have been avoided. This view cannot, in the end, be proved or disproved. What can be said without fear of contradiction is that, given that there has been an armed struggle which lasted for more than twenty-five years, the Sinn Féin[4] negotiators have had their work cut out for them. They could only have made the progress they have made as long as they negotiated an agreement that allowed their combatant colleagues to hand over arms *voluntarily* to an independent commission.

Here, as in South Africa, agreeing to "bury the hatchet" has in fact happened more or less simultaneously with the setting up of the political structures envisaged in the Agreement. All this has taken an enormous amount of time and patience on the part of those involved. The task has not been made any easier by the fact that the participants did not then and do not yet trust one another, even though they may have come more or less grudgingly to recognize in the "others" a genuine desire for peace with justice and honor—however honor and justice are to be understood in this case. Both sides are nervously committing themselves to a future with others whom long experience has taught them not to trust, but a future without the backup they have traditionally relied on.

In South Africa in 1994 and in Northern Ireland in 1998 both sides were able to sign up to a document which—even if it did not give either side all that they wanted, and even if it involved (in some respects) the abandonment of positions initially regarded as non-negotiable—at least enabled them to consider living in disagreement but in dialogue with one another.

To arrive at such a political accommodation, however, does not mean that either side acknowledges guilt for what happened, or that it forgives anyone. It certainly does not guarantee reconciliation, even though it may well create the conditions of nascent trust under which forgiveness and reconciliation may take place later. The question therefore arises as to what steps have to be taken now by those who have survived the conflict, whether as perpetrators or as victims of human rights violations, in order to open the way for reconciliation in the future.

Public Amnesia or Remembering?

In Chile, Argentina, and South Africa (to name only three countries) the chosen way forward has been via truth commissions. These have been well documented, and it is clear that their various remits and modes of operation have differed considerably. But in all cases, they have been driven by the conviction that transformation simply cannot take place without the opportunity being given to victims to speak of their (often traumatic) experiences, and to perpetrators to tell what they did (and maybe then gain amnesty). Often all that the survivors want is to know what happened to their deceased loved ones and where they are buried. The question of reparations and who is to pay for them is, of course, a universal question; but it must be answered without recourse to what has been called the "wild justice" of revenge.

It must remain an open question to what extent Christian or Jewish-Christian thinking and practice with regard to repentance, confession, forgiveness, reparation, and reconciliation, lie behind the legislation in the various countries that have set up commissions of this sort. What is undeniable with respect to Christians is that their faith does speak of a sequence of events from repentance to reconciliation. Christians have often had a tendency to individualize the process so that it has relevance for the resolution of personal wrongs only, rather than public or collective ones. In the public sphere they have often tended to speak prematurely of forgiveness or reconciliation, without due regard to the claims of justice and reparation to which their tradition and scriptures also witness.

With regard to this individualizing tendency, it is worthy of note that a hundred years ago a seminal text of the New Testament, St. Paul's Epistle to the Romans, was widely understood exclusively in terms of the relationship of the individual to God. In our time, it has come to be read also with reference to the condition of communities and even of the entire human race. This is wholly proper, because the epistle was written in the context of tension between two communities in Rome. Contemporary reading takes it for granted that evil takes institutional forms and that confession, forgiveness, and reconciliation involve institutions, communities, and peoples no less than individuals. Resolution of conflict and the forgiveness of offenses require listening, acknowledgment, and confession at the collective or institutional level as much as at the personal, as a careful reading of Paul makes clear. He understood better than any twentieth-century commentator that evil has a suprapersonal character. Furthermore, he recognized that even those who are not directly involved in injustice may still be complicit in the actions of an oppressive system.

In the wake of the Good Friday Agreement signed in Belfast, we are faced with serious questions as to what might be involved in the transition from its political accommodation to possible reconciliation. What is involved in forgiving? Is it wise, wholesome, or even possible to forget?

In the period immediately following the Irish Civil War of 1921–22, those who were concerned with rebuilding society recognized that compromises were necessary, and that it was going to be essential to work with people whose hands were not clean. On the whole they reckoned that it was not desirable to do anything that might stir up new bitterness, and that simply because something is true does not mean you ought to say it. The Irish political scientist, Professor Tom Garvin, puts it this way:

> For a long time after the end of the Civil War a lot of people didn't like talking about it. A sort of conspiracy was entered into by a lot of people, to ensure that the bitterness of the war was not transmitted to a younger and possibly more innocent generation.[5]

Certainly it is the testimony of some who belong to that generation that this policy and practice met with success. Those who approve of it today point to the persistence of democratic process in the Irish Free State (now the Republic of Ireland), to the fact that the defeated party entered the legislature and in 1932 became the government party, to the existence of an independent judiciary and an unarmed civil guard or police force, and to a number of other healthy features of Irish political life. They claim that these could hardly have occurred, had it not been for the conspiracy of silence and restraint of which Professor Garvin speaks.

However, there is another side to the story. The silence did not in fact subdue the resentment; the fact that wounds are not spoken of does not ensure that they do not suppurate. And it is plausibly arguable that Irish political discourse was stultified for two generations, and that imaginative political action on the question of Northern Ireland was inhibited by the fear of speaking too much or too openly about what had happened in the earlier years of the century. Where the past was spoken of, it was most often used simply as a source for the justification of present political positions. Worse still, blame was often attached to sectors of the population, attributing more or less indelible negative traits to (say) Catholics or Protestants as a group. Unacceptable behavior emanating from one's own side was largely blamed on individuals, if it was acknowledged at all; whereas the unacceptable actions of the "others" was ascribed to their collective nature.

Facing the Past

In contrast, one of the most remarkable features of more recent political history—particularly in South and Central America, and in South Africa—has been a determination to face the past. This has been fostered precisely by a desire to facilitate the process of transition from a state of civil conflict (usually involving state terror and the counter-violence of resistance to it) to a new state of participatory democracy. In Chile where some 3,000 citizens "disappeared," and in Argentina where the equivalent number was about 30,000, the truth commissions set up during the movement to democracy were a response to the demands of families and friends to know what had happened to their loved ones and where their bodies lay. They grew out of the conviction that no new society could be built as long as the fate of the disappeared remained shrouded in lies or hidden in sealed records, and as long as those who knew what had really happened were indefinitely condemned to carry about in themselves the terrible truth. The truth commissions of South and Central America were a response, not to an irresistible historical voyeurism, but to a sensed need to set future society on a sound moral basis.

In South Africa, in particular, it had come to be recognized by 1994 that the "new country" had to hold up a mirror to the old protagonists (passive and active) of apartheid, to show them their actions by the light in which these were seen by the majority of the people of South Africa, and indeed by most people in the world. The aim of the Truth and Reconciliation Commission (TRC) was to help people move away from the discredited regime's version of the past, so as to build a new and shared and ceaselessly debated memory of that past. A general recognition on the part of those who reflected on these things was emerging: that only when the past is spoken of, heard, and acknowledged is there any chance that it will cease to poison the present and instead become simply the past.

It is important to recognize that the legislation which established the TRC (The Promotion of National Unity and Reconciliation Act) was itself the result of political compromises arrived at in the two-year process of negotiation leading to the interim constitution in 1994. In fact an impasse had been reached in the first week of December 1993 when the then-president, F.W. de Klerk, demanded amnesty for all servants and agents of the apartheid regime. After the election of 1994, a wide spectrum of civil society began to put the question sharply as to how such amnesty could possibly be granted unless victims had first had an opportunity to tell it the way they saw it.

But some inducement had to be offered to the perpetrators. That inducement was the prospect of possible amnesty. It can be argued that the enabling act was, in the end, too perpetrator oriented. However, it can be said in response that this was the price that had to be paid. The TRC was the result. It consisted of seventeen members divided into three working groups: a committee to investigate gross violations of human rights, an amnesty committee, and a committee to propose policy on rehabilitation and reparation. In addition to these committees and servicing them, there was a much larger investigative unit, consisting of sixty members, with equal numbers of persons from the international community, organizations drawn from civil society in South Africa, and persons belonging to the South African police services. The TRC was also granted the authority to organize protection for those giving evidence at the Commission's hearings.

A Truth Commission for (Northern) Ireland?

Those who would argue the case against the establishment of a truth commission for Northern Ireland—or for Ireland as a whole—usually point to the fact that the conflict itself, its duration, and the casualties inflicted, are on a small scale compared with similar conflicts in South and Central America, Africa, or Asia. The number of the "disappeared" in the Irish conflict, 27, is small compared with approximately 3,000 in Chile, and 30,000 in Argentina or South Africa. In this context, it should be pointed out that the population of Northern Ireland is a mere 1.5 million, and the whole of Ireland, 5 million. So the proportion of the population killed since 1969 (i.e., more than 3,000) is larger than it might first appear. Figures for the number of people who have been threatened or, fearing "punishment" by paramilitaries, have had to leave Northern Ireland, are not available but may well be higher than is commonly reckoned. These, too, are victims who should be assured that they can come home safely. Furthermore, the violence from 1969 to the present may be seen as merely the most recent outbreak in a conflict that has erupted from time to time over a period of at least 350 years, and has done so most often because people on all sides have repeatedly supposed that there was unfinished business yet to be done.

On balance, however, it would appear from the Bloomfield report that Northern/Ireland is not likely to get a TRC for the foreseeable future—if at all.[6] Sir Kenneth Bloomfield, who was presumably writing his report at about the time of the Good Friday Agreement or just before, spoke of a commission being possible "only in the context of a wide-ranging political accord." So does his statement mean that, now such an accord is in place, we should proceed to establish a commission? Bloomfield thinks not, because the heat of the debate between those who favor amnesty and the early release of prisoners on the one side, and those who favor "condign punishment for perpetrators" on the other, render a truth commission problematic if not seriously unthinkable. Besides, even if a TRC were sought and set up, it would at best only be one of the steps to be taken on the road to reconciliation.

The Requirements of Reconciliation

So, if we are not likely to get a TRC, what should we aim at—*faute de mieux*? Or (to put it differently), whatever structures we look for, what basic requirements should we have? What must we look for, if we are to bury the hatchet, and if we are to remember and eventually forgive, and even forget?

Certainly, we must seek to unscramble the past better than we have, for the plain fact is that in the Northern Ireland conflict (as much as in any other, and more than in most) it is not and has not been easy to answer questions like these: Where does the power lie in this society? Who is defending what, against whom? Who started the violence? Who has profited from the violence? Who still profits, now that it is over? Who has suffered? Who has suffered the most?

When we seek to understand any conflict, we habitually seek to do so by applying models. Our Irish conflict (whether the Irish-English one or the internal Irish one) is of very long standing. Edgar Gutierrez, speaking at the "Burying the Past" conference in Oxford in September 1998, pointed out how various groups and generations in Guatemala differ in saying exactly how far back their conflict goes.[7] The same is true with us. Perhaps it is its long duration that makes our situation susceptible to so wide a variety of interpretative models. It has been seen as religious (an untiring replay of the seventeenth century wars of religion); a racial-linguistic conflict between native and incomer; a straightforward colonial or neocolonial situation; and a class conflict, often obscured or "mystified" by the rhetoric of religious and racial hostility. Now, if one settles for only one of these to the exclusion of the others, then it is going to be much easier to confidently identify the perpetrators and the victims.

But unless one can do that with at least some confidence, it will not be possible to see clearly enough whom to forgive or whose forgiveness to ask for. However, the fact that unionists, nationalists, republicans, and Marxists may each to their own satisfaction identify the villains at work, should not lead us into cynicism. We cannot allow ourselves simply to conclude that one side is as bad as the other. Donald Shriver, in the course of his treatment of President Richard von Weizsäcker's presidential address to the German people on 8 May 1998, lays it on the line like this: "Politicians . . . have a responsibility for accurately identifying the past, including the past that the enemies of their people are the first to call 'evil.'"[8] That responsibility must not be evaded in the alleged interests of harmony or not "rocking the boat" or out of respect for a painstakingly constructed political accommodation.

The most intractable aspect of the problem for us in Ireland, as I have already suggested, lies in the fact that our past is made up, not of one conflict only, but rather of a complex of conflicts each with its own quota of victims and perpetrators. The latter do not recognize themselves as such, and the victims have often themselves become the perpetrators of terrible human rights offenses.

At this stage and for a long time to come, it is too much to expect that we will "reconcile" our memories to such an extent that we may come to share a common memory of the past. What we can do, first, is begin to respect the integrity of those who have an idea of how we got to where we are that differs from our own. Our own view may gain the right to be respected once we have begun painfully to acknowledge the shaming truth in theirs. Second, we can resolve not to start now, at this stage, to rewrite the story in a way that flatters us.

Part of the reason why the Omagh bomb in August 1998 touched so many hearts was that it killed so indiscriminately people from both "communities," and even young visitors from Spain. It was not aimed at, nor did it kill, people from only one side. The stark simplicity of individual suffering and death drew everyone together. The "Real IRA" who planted the bomb were seen by no one as representing any cause that people could in general remotely identify with.

However much we may be inclined (particularly when viewing from a distance) to lump all acts of violence together, we cannot in good conscience do so; for example, we cannot equate Bloody Sunday in Derry (30 January

1972)[9] with paramilitary shootings or bombings elsewhere that killed more or less the same number of people. From the viewpoint of the bereaved, of course, there is no difference. But, the significance of what happened in Derry on that day is that the shooting was done by the army of the state. How far up the ladder went the succession of orders that led to the shooting, we do not know yet, although we may find out in the coming months. It appears that it went pretty high—and that an attempt was made by senior figures in the judiciary to cover it up. The then prime minister, in briefing the lord chancellor and chief justice, reminded them that they were engaged, not only in a military war, but also in a propaganda war.[10]

As we seek to rebuild while we begin the task of reconstruction, we must know the facts about this. People cannot be expected to believe in or to respect the law, or to join in building a participatory society, until we do and until appropriate steps are taken to identify and discipline those culpable. It is sobering to reflect that it was Bloody Sunday and the Widgery Tribunal[11] that attracted the young Martin McGuinness, like hundreds of others, into the IRA, since it was the only response they could think of to the cowardice and lack of moral integrity of the state. In this case, it will not be enough to limit the inquiry to what happened on that particular day: attention must also be paid to the orders that led to the deployment of troops and their dispatch to Derry in the seventy-two hours or so before 30 January.

Whether we eventually have a TRC or not, I suspect that in our situation and with our tendency to the "Yes, but what about such and such?" response to any accusation, we would do well not to begin with the atrocities of the white noise torture at the Castlereagh interrogation center or of the paramilitary beatings.[12] Too much emphasis, too soon, on these would only encourage those who wish to distance themselves, to do so even more and put the blame on others: "It was them: the psychopaths, the scum!" Instead, we should start with the complicity spectrum so well delineated by the Asmals and Suresh Roberts in their book on reconciliation in South Africa,[13] and which includes the tacit kind of complicity in sectarianism that I grew up with as a Protestant in the North. The fact is that it can remain tacit only until the going gets rough, when (suddenly) you discover it has covered you like a rash.

Nor was this complicity limited to the Protestant population. The tiny, nervous Catholic middle class and more importantly the leadership of the

Roman Catholic Church in the North, while overtly discontented and in some measure discriminated against, was nevertheless increasingly satisfied with the bargain they had struck for the rights of Catholic education. The record shows that they said little if anything about unjust discrimination in jobs or housing. For them, power lay in the control of education, not in jobs, and that was the area where they expended their energy.

Beginning with the complicity spectrum may enable us to make constructive use of what is otherwise rather a dangerous notion—that of collective guilt. The whole phenomenon of anti-Semitism appallingly illustrates how dangerous it can be. It can lead to what Shriver has called the "atrocity myth," whereby we believe (as in Northern Ireland people so readily have) that "they" have certain innate tendencies that incline them to atrocity.

The fact is that there is an important distinction to be made in any conflict, both while it is going on and when it is over, and from one generation to another; namely, between guilt and responsibility. I or my group may well feel guilt about what has happened or been done on my "side" or in my name, even though I myself did nothing or was not alive at the time, or am simply a guilty survivor or beneficiary of the suffering of others. But I am certainly not responsible for what the fathers and mothers did, nor on the other hand should I feel responsible for avenging the wrongs they suffered. As Michael Ignatieff has put it:

> What each side, in the aftermath of civil war, essentially demands is that "the other side" face up to the deaths it caused. . . . Without an apology, without recognition of what happened, the past cannot return to its place as the past.[14]

Reconciliation has little or no chance against the demands for vengeance until we come, as Ignatieff puts it, to "respect the emotions that sustain vengeance, with its intense urge to keep faith with the dead," and to replace that respect with rituals in which communities once at war learn to mourn their dead together.

A tragic example of the failure to come anywhere near doing that is seen in the bomb that was set off some years ago in Enniskillen, County Fermanagh. It was timed to go off in the middle of a ceremony to commemorate the dead of the 1914–18 and 1939–45 wars. The tragedy lay primarily in the fact that the "republicans" who planted it could only see the cenotaph that day as an Orange totem pole. They had not read enough, for instance of James Connolly,[15] to recognize in the (mostly, but not exclusively Protestant) young men whose names were inscribed on it the victims of the very forces which then, as now, regard the lives of young people as expendable in the service of economic and other interests. Such a comprehensive understanding and analysis would have allowed them—if not "to weep with those who weep"—at least to allow the mourners to weep in peace.

The Structural Requirements of Reconciliation

Any movement in the direction of reconciliation, with or without a TRC, will require certain structures.

First, there must be an independent ombud or "champion." The victims' minister appointed by the British government can only be expected to fulfill a facilitative role, because he is himself a government agent.

Second, there must be reparation and restorative justice. This has usually been thought of as being the prerogative and obligation of central government. Certainly, it is questionable whether central government throwing money or even educational bursaries at victims or former prisoners is an altogether appropriate response. For here, compensation or reparation is made from outside, without reference to the fact that a large proportion of atrocities and human rights violations were committed at the local level. In such cases, whatever is done to make amends should be done by ourselves for one another, since it is at this interpersonal level that the injury occurred. The possibility of a "voluntary" tax being paid for the benefit of victims by those who have profited or continue to profit from the conflict, might be considered. The only reparation made directly by central government (in Northern Ireland's case, by London) should be for the suffering caused by internment without trial, by the unacceptable treatment of detainees in interrogation centers, or by the British Army's culpable shootings of innocent citizens. In this way, the British imperial involvement as a primary source of the conflict would be acknowledged unequivocally, as sooner or later it must be.

Third, the possibility of a "forum for the unheard" should be considered. This would be cheaper than the courts and would have the advantage of being nonadversarial.

Conclusion

Of course, what was achieved by the Good Friday Agreement of 10 April 1998 was not forgiveness, much less reconciliation. What was achieved was an agreement to disagree, a modus vivendi. In a situation such as existed in Northern Ireland, that is an enormous step forward, however modest it may sound to outsiders.

Forgiveness will take longer, and reconciliation longer still. I take it for granted that forgiveness requires a prior expression of repentance. The words attributed by Luke to Jesus on the cross, "Father, forgive them for they do not know what they are doing,"[16] do not contradict this assumption. No one should be forgiven for what they have not only not repented of, but are actually not even aware of. The dying Jesus can scarcely have been praying that they should be. In fact, his words are to quite different effect; they point to the eschatological character of forgiveness. Jesus is asking that when those who are executing him do finally come to recognize the enormity of their offense—perhaps far in the future—then they will be pardoned.

Christians, at any rate, are committed to faith in an ultimately moral universe in which there is resolution and reconciliation. In the meantime, they are called on to recognize that the debris with which we have littered the scene is (much of it) too heavy and awkward to clear away, but that nevertheless life can begin again amid it—a kind of "love among the ruins." Furthermore, neither Christian nor humanist should imagine that forgiveness can be demanded or must be granted. Some victims and some survivors have simply been hurt so much that they cannot now forgive and perhaps never will. That is their right, and this means that some perpetrators, however penitent, can only pray for the strength and fortitude to live out their lives with that stubborn fact in eschatological hope.

Perhaps forgiveness is best thought of as an imaginative gift to the imagination. Those who speak, as Christians do, in terms of God, may perhaps want to say that God's forgiveness springs from the fact that God can and does "imagine" those who have hurt one another unpardonably as living together again. Jesus' parable of the prodigal son illustrates this perfectly.[17] The son destitute in the far country, when he "comes to himself," begins to imagine life in the home he abandoned years before. He pictures himself, not as a son and heir, but in the less exalted role of hired servant. He determines to go home and ask to be received as a servant. But on his return, his father who has been watching and waiting for this day in imagination, dismisses his son's imaginative solution, and insists on his own. The prodigal will come back as a son or not at all; and—perhaps as important—he will come back as brother to the other son who stayed at home, and whose imagination the father now challenges to grow beyond its resentful constraints. Jesus does not tell us how the story ended. Did the brothers settle down together? Did they ever speak? He leaves us with the father's imaginative vision dancing before our eyes as the one thing that really matters in the end. Forgiveness and rehabilitation are clearly articulated in the story, but reconciliation belongs to the narrative that the listener is asked to act out.

Endnotes

1. Unionists are those in Northern Ireland who wish for it to remain part of the United Kingdom. They are very largely Protestant.

2. This is the body set up by the British government in 1998 under the chairmanship of Chris Patten, the last governor of Hong Kong and a Catholic, to propose reforms of policing in Northern Ireland. Its report was published on 9 September 1999.

3. Nationalists are those in Northern Ireland who wish it to be incorporated into the Republic of Ireland. They are very largely Catholic. Republicans are nationalists who support the political party, Sinn Féin, and who are sympathetic toward the IRA.

4. Sinn Féin is the political party that represents republicans and is closely linked to the IRA.

5. Although I am quite sure of the attribution, I have not been able to locate the origin of this quotation.

6. Kenneth Bloomfield, *We Will Remember Them: The Report of the Northern Ireland Victims Commissioner*, Sir Kenneth Bloomfield KCB (Belfast: The Stationary Office, 1998), 37–38.

7. In discussion at the "Burying the Past" conference, Oxford, 14–16 September 1998.

8. Donald Shriver, *An Ethic for Enemies* (New York: Oxford University Press, 1995), 107.

9. This is the occasion when British troops in Derry shot and killed fourteen demonstrators.

10. Don Mullan, ed., *Eyewitness Bloody Sunday* (Dublin: Wolfhound Press, 1998), 45–46, 268–71.

11. In the wake of Bloody Sunday, the British government set up a tribunal of inquiry under the Lord Chief Justice Widgery. The tribunal's report, published in 1972, exonerated the troops involved.

12. Castlereagh is on the outskirts of Belfast, and has been the site of a police and army interrogation center. It was due to close at the end of 1999.

13. K. Asmal, L. Asmal, and S. Roberts, *Reconciliation through Truth: A Reckoning of Apartheid's Criminal Governance* (Cape Town: David Philip, 1996).

14. Michael Ignatieff, *The Warrior's Honor: Ethnic War and the Modern Conscience* (London: Chatto and Windus, 1998), 189–90.

15. James Connolly was a labor leader and writer who was executed by the British in 1916. He discouraged Irish involvement in the 1914–18 war on the grounds that it was a capitalists' conflict. The slogan of the Irish Citizens' Army, of which he was a leader, was "Neither King nor Kaiser, but Ireland."

16. The Gospel of Luke 23.34.

17. Ibid., 15.11–32.

PART IV

Conclusion

Concluding Remarks

Nigel Biggar

I conclude with some reflections on seven important topics raised in the course of this book by its contributors: the policy of forgetting, the problem of contested history, the relationship between justice and political "prudence," the significance of South Africa's Truth and Reconciliation Commission (TRC), reconciliation and forgiveness as political categories, the implications of this discussion as a whole for Northern Ireland, and, finally, the bearing of religious ideas on the matter.

The Policy of Forgetting

In this conversation, a policy of forgetting the unjust past *instead* of dealing with it has not received much support. No one has argued that it would have been better had the truth commissions in Latin America or South Africa never happened. Several have warned that a past that has not been properly reckoned with cannot be properly buried, and that, sooner or later, it will rise up and demand just attention. Marie Smyth cites the experience of World War II veterans in general (p. 128), and Donald Shriver mentions the experience of Eric Lomax in particular (p. 29). Rachel Sieder notes that "more than a decade after many had declared transitional processes of truth and justice to be complete in Argentina and Chile, memory politics resurfaced with potentially profound impacts in both countries" (p. 196). Alexandra Barahona de Brito confirms this observation with respect to Chile (p. 163–70). And Terence McCaughey, referring to the argument that the conspiracy of silence that followed the Irish Civil War of 1921–22 was necessary to sustain democratic politics, comments:

> However, there is another side to the story. The silence did not in fact subdue the resentment; the fact that wounds are not spoken of does not ensure that they do not suppurate. And it is plausibly argued that Irish political discourse was stultified for two generations, and that imaginative political action on the question of Northern Ireland was inhibited by the fear of speaking too much or too openly about what had happened in the earlier years of the century (p. 258).

Sieder, referring to Guatemala, also implicitly reminds us that what is "forgotten" at an official, national level, may not be at all forgotten at the local communal one, where many of the actual violations of human rights took place and where rough justice is meted out among neighbors (pp. 196, 197). And this, of course, is exactly what the *Épuration* in post-World War II France was about. These two examples substantiate my own more abstract supposition that whereas some might be able simply to forget, it is not likely that the victims could (p. 8).

There is evidence, then, that the truth about the past will out, and that sooner or later, justice will press its claims. Humans, it seems, are not satisfied with peace in the present. They are constituted by moral as well as political needs.

Nevertheless, to say that the unsettled past cannot be simply forgotten is not to imply that it can all be remembered and resolved in an instant. Nor that it should. Human beings, it also seems, cannot bear too much reality—at least, not all at once. Domestic social life often requires the drawing of discreet veils over difficulties. This may be because there is no obvious solution: the burden of history is sometimes too big and heavy and complex to manage. It will also be because, since the truth can as easily destroy as liberate, it needs to be handled charitably and prudently. Honesty, therefore, makes heavy demands on our resources of courage, patience, resilience, and generosity—and it can be quickly exhausted.

For these reasons at least, in public life as in private, remembering and dealing with the past is likely to be a process rather than an event. We can do it bit by bit over years, and probably generations. This is corroborated by several of our authors. As already mentioned, Sieder points out that in

Argentina and Chile, business declared closed a decade ago has reopened again in recent years. With regard to South Africa's TRC, Charles Villa-Vicencio (pp. 207, 212, 214, 219–20), and more so Brandon Hamber (pp. 135, 136) and Hugo van der Merwe (p. 100), all assert that it should be viewed as the beginning of a long process, and not at all as complete in itself.

Further, not only will the business of dealing with the past be a long process; it may well be a fitful one. That is to say, it may comprise moments of the irruption of memory with periods of not exactly forgetting, but rather "not-remembering." The reason for this is that, for public remembering to be feasible, a certain level of political stability must be assured. This is Tuomas Forsberg's point when he suggests that the standard sequence of truth and reconciliation should be reversed: only on the basis of a measure of reconciliation can the truth be told (p. 65). The parties involved must be sufficiently secure that they are willing to remember what shames them as well as what justifies them—what calls into question the ideology behind their political violence, as well as what supports it. And the achievement of such security may require a period—a decade, a generation—of considerable, if not absolute, silence. This brings us directly to the second topic.

The Problem of Contested History

This is the crucial problem that attends any attempt to do justice in the aftermath of a civil conflict. Each side in the conflict will tell a story that justifies its own violence and delegitimates the other's. There is therefore a basic disagreement about who the guilty perpetrators and the genuine victims really are. In Northern Ireland, as Smyth points out, those who are "genuine victims" from one side's point of view are, from the other's, perpetrators or accomplices who deserve what has been inflicted on them (pp. 109–10). In the absence of any agreement about the identity of perpetrators and victims, there can be no agreement about what justice needs to be done—no Irish republican, for example, would agree for a moment with my claim that a measure of justice has been achieved through the conviction and sentencing of republican paramilitaries (p. 15–16). Thus, the attempt to do justice in one side's terms will be seen by the other side as the continuation or resumption of war by judicial means.

This is why some prefer to abandon any attempt to talk about burying the past in moral terms. Justice cannot be done, because it is a weapon in the hands of political ideology. Far better, then, to operate simply in the honest terms of power politics and look for a mutually acceptable accommodation, forget the past, and get on with building a peaceful future.

The problem with this proposal is that people really do seem to care about truth and justice, so much so that there are points beyond which they will not be prepared to buy political peace at the price of them. The reason for this is that, if the future is not going to risk repeating the past, and so if the new regime is going to win sufficient confidence from its people, a measure of consensus needs to be achieved about what was wrong with the past and how the future should be different. Kader Asmal and his coauthors argue this point very strongly in their book-length apology for the TRC. The main function of the Commission, in their eyes, was to expose the truth about the apartheid regime in order to win support for the new one as something clearly different:

> In these early years of consolidating democracy, there must be a galvanising and self-critical vision of the goals of our society. And such a vision requires a clear-sighted . . . grasp of what was wrong with the past.[1]

Further,

> An important goal of the commission is to act as a catalyst for swift and thorough disclosure of past horrors, in order to . . . end . . . the steady and corrosive drip of past pathologies into the new order.[2]

Accordingly, they dismiss curtly what they call "the lollipop world of superficial and childish evenhandedness" with its "playground relativism"[3]—calling to (my) mind Mary Hawkesworth's telling remark that the oppressed cannot afford the conservative luxury of postmodernist resignation to radical relativism.[4]

On the other hand, Asmal and his colleagues are clearly sensitive to postmodernist concerns. Thus, they take pains to invoke Derrida and Foucault as they protest that what they aspire to is not the establishment of an oppressive, "totalizing" ANC ideology, but "a shared and ceaselessly debated memory" of the past, or "a complex, perhaps contradictory, set of narratives about the past."[5] It appears, then, that what they claim with one hand, they give away with the other; for it is not immediately obvious how "ceaseless debate" resulting in conflicting narratives would achieve the public establishment of "the truth" about the (apartheid) past.

Nevertheless, it could. If debate is ceaseless, then the past must indeed remain contested. But this need not be true about all of the past, only some of it. So ceaseless debate might rage over an ever-narrowing range of topics while consensus expands over the remainder. Alternatively, debate might continue to rage over the same range of topics, while the number of dissenters shrinks. But for consensus to grow at all, there must be certain realities—facts—to which conflicting stories are accountable, against which their veracity can be measured, and to which those who tell them (if they are honest) must yield. It is hardly surprising that a lawyer such as Martha Minow should concur, albeit by implication, when she asserts bluntly: "Some versions of the past are wrong" (p. 82).

It may well be true that the human grasp of historical reality—especially if that grasp operates in moral terms—is bound to be partial, revisable, and so ceaselessly debatable. But, "it does not follow that because a mountain appears to take on a different shape from different angles of vision, it has objectively either no shape at all or an infinity of shapes."[6] In other words, if our stories claim to describe the same past, then *in principle* there is scope for the rational building of consensus about it—a building that might be without secular end, but need not be without proximate success. And there is evidence that such building is possible in practice. One of the considerable achievements of the TRC appears to have been that, under pressure from the victims' testimonies and the perpetrators' confessions, the faith of many white South Africans in the veracity of the apartheid regime's story about the civil conflict has been broken. Charles Villa-Vicencio's Afrikaner lady is a case in point: "I did not know that my people could have done such terrible things" (p. 215).

Justice and Political "Prudence"

The possibility of building consensus about contested history, about who was the real victim and who the real oppressor, holds out the possibility of agreement about what a just burying of the past would be. But such agreement will probably not be achieved for a long time; and in the meantime to pursue "justice" could easily jeopardize the political accommodation upon which peace rests. Therefore, compromise is inevitable, and the price of peace is that justice—especially its retributive dimension—must be allowed to suffer political constraints. Would that it were not so; it is not ideal, and for the victims it may well be painfully frustrating. But, as I have tried to argue in chapter 1, justice here should be conceived in terms that go well beyond retribution (pp. 10–14); in which case the doing of some justice (the several forms of vindicating the victim) may be possible even within the constraints imposed for the sake of keeping the peace.

Moreover, it is a significant oversimplification to think of this compromise as one that sacrifices morality to mere political "prudence." Prudence is commonly understood as a carefulness that is self-interested, and therefore ungenerous and little-spirited;[7] and political prudence accordingly connotes something at best less than noble, at worst timid. But this is unfair. Political leaders have a responsibility to look after the genuine interests of their people—and this is a *moral* responsibility. My point here is the same as Shriver's when he denies that collective interests are subethical (p. 25). Provided that these interests are not understood in too narrow terms, but are conceived as bound up with the interests of other political communities and as including justice as well as material wealth and physical security, then carefulness and circumspection in their promotion is a virtue. Thus, if political prudence in the aftermath of a civil conflict discerns that the prosecution of violators of human rights is likely to destabilize the peace, and that there are other ways of having the future distance itself morally from the past, then it would not be immoral to agree to let the retributive dimension of justice suffer constraints. This is all the more so, when it is remembered that the victims themselves have an interest in a future where their rights will be protected. The need to make compromises is regrettable, but it is a moral as well as a political need. In the secular world of time and space, not all justice can be done; and it belongs to the virtue of political prudence to recognize that.

South Africa's Truth and Reconciliation Commission

The prudence of South Africa's option for a Truth and Reconciliation Commission, rather than Nuremberg-style trials, is somewhat confirmed by the experience of Rwanda. There, according to Stef Vandeginste, the justice being meted out by the International Criminal Tribunal is cumbersome, is distrusted by the Hutu as "victor's justice," involves the victims hardly at all, and is something from which the population that experienced the genocide feels alienated (p. 231). Likewise, the justice done by Rwanda's own judicial system, although more concerned with vindicating victims, also suffers from being seen as victor's justice. Further, even though it is more efficient, it is still very slow; as Vandeginste points out, at the current rate of progress, it could take over two hundred years to complete the genocide trials (p. 234). The problem of the perception of victor's justice, the focus on perpetrators at the expense of victims, and the cumbersome nature of proper judicial process are among the very reasons that Kader Asmal and his coauthors have offered in justification of South Africa's decision against trials and in favor of a truth commission (see p. 21, n. 22).

None of the authors in this book disputes the wisdom of this decision. I, for one, have the TRC to thank for expanding my concept of criminal justice to include the victims' vindication as well as the perpetrators' punishment, and for focusing it on the former, especially its truth-revealing element. Nevertheless, several contributors do criticize the TRC for promising more than it was able to deliver. Van der Merwe makes it clear that the Commission's achievement fell far short of being comprehensive: as a uniform, national process of reconciliation, it barely touched the effects of conflict in its local internecine forms (pp. 94–95). Hamber points out that the process of the psychological healing of individual victims will long outlast it (p. 135). And Villa-Vicencio, himself an office-holder in the TRC, states frankly that it should be regarded as a beginning, not a conclusion, and that it needs to be followed by economic reparations (pp. 215–17).

Political "Reconciliation" and "Forgiveness"

The limitations of the TRC's undoubted achievement raise questions about its goal of "reconciliation." Is this what it has realized? And if so, in what sense(s)? Clearly, given the criticism leveled by Van der Merwe and Hamber, the TRC has left much reconciliation yet to be brought about at the level of local communities and interpersonal relationships. It could hardly have been otherwise, because it had neither the time nor the resources to deal comprehensively with all of the injuries meted out and suffered during South Africa's civil conflict. But what about those cases that it did treat? Did it achieve "reconciliation" there? It gave some victims a public voice. It gave some the truth of what had happened to them or their loved ones—"truth" at least in the sense of the bare facts (who, what, where, when); and where the perpetrators not only confessed but expressed remorse, "truth" also in the fuller sense of an agreed moral evaluation of the facts. And by opening a window onto the covert operations of the apartheid regime, it has advanced its discrediting in the eyes of many who had given it the benefit of the doubt. Insofar as this has helped victims to (begin to) come to terms with what happened to them, the TRC has achieved a measure of psychological "reconciliation." Insofar as it has helped victims to trust the state again, and to look forward to a political future free of severe threats to their human dignity and rights, it has achieved a measure of political "reconciliation." It has achieved the same insofar as it has encouraged some perpetrators and former supporters of apartheid to see the error of their ways, and so to identify themselves more with the new regime.

But what about *interpersonal* reconciliation, which is the paradigmatic kind (and so stands unencumbered with quotation marks)? It may be that the TRC has enabled some victims to be reconciled with their oppressors (as Shriver avers on p. 33), but that only really makes sense in cases where they were known to each other beforehand. As Ulrike Poppe, the dissident twice imprisoned in the former East Germany, remarked during the conference that inspired this book, why should she want to be reconciled with the man who had informed on her and who now lives down the street? She never knew him before, and she doesn't want to know him now. So what could it possibly mean for her to be reconciled to him? Interpersonal reconciliation takes place between former friends and neighbors. It presupposes a prior relationship that has been ruptured. In its primary sense, reconciliation is an intimate business, as is the granting and accepting of forgiveness. Hence the unease rightly felt by many—among them Timothy Garton Ash[8]—at the attempts made to encourage events of interpersonal reconciliation on the public stage constituted by the TRC's hearings. Because this kind of reconciliation was never appropriate as a direct goal of the TRC, it is hardly surprising that it achieved little of it. Still, insofar as the TRC has helped victims feel more secure about the political future, it may well have made it easier for some of them to contemplate granting the forgiveness that concludes the process of interpersonal reconciliation.

The same qualifications need to be made of political "repentance" and "forgiveness," as we have made of political "reconciliation." In the paradigmatic sense, a state cannot forgive. As Joyce Mthimkulu remarked of those who had applied to the TRC for amnesty for their killing of her son,

> They are not asking forgiveness from us, the people who have lost their loved ones. They are asking forgiveness from the government. They did not do nothing [sic] to the government. What they did, they did to *us*.[9]

She was right: only the victims have the authority to forgive, in the paradigmatic sense of that word.

But Joyce Mthimkulu was not entirely right; for in their act of murder the killers of her son had put themselves at odds with the whole community. Through one crime, they had brought upon themselves the suspicion that what they had done once, they might do again—and to someone else. They had set themselves above the community and its agreed structures. They had made themselves outlaws, and in so doing they now presented a general threat. So, in a secondary sense, the state did have something to "forgive"—on behalf of the national community.

In the circumstances, however, it is still not correct to talk straightforwardly of amnesty as a political form of forgiveness—*pace*, perhaps, Jean Elshtain (p. 53) and Tuomas Forsberg (p. 61). Amnesty is an undertaking by a new regime not to prosecute certain people for crimes they have committed. Like forgiveness, it abandons a hostile posture, because it reckons that the perpetrators no longer pose a threat to future peace—and that therefore the community they have offended can "trust" them again. Unlike forgiveness, the general commitment to grant amnesty is undertaken under a certain political duress; and the actual granting of it is not dependent on any expression of remorse on the part of the perpetrators. If these no longer pose a threat to the community, it is not because of any inner transformation or repentance, but only because of a change in their political circumstances. If we speak of amnesty as a kind of forgiveness, we speak strictly by analogy.

What applies to political "reconciliation" and "forgiveness" also applies to political "repentance." What sense does it make for a British prime minister in the 1990s to apologize for the irresponsibility of a British government in the 1840s (see Shriver, p. 29)? How can an Irish cardinal ask forgiveness from the British people on behalf of his own for injuries suffered at the hands of Irish terrorists (see Elshtain, pp. 46–47)? Tony Blair was not responsible for failing to act sufficiently to alleviate the Irish Famine, nor was

Cardinal Daly responsible for the IRA's campaign of violence since the early 1970s. If we have acts of repentance here, we have them only in a secondary, metaphorical sense. Neither Blair nor Daly were taking responsibility for, and repenting of, something that they themselves had done. What Blair was doing was publicly repudiating an instance of culpable negligence by the British state that had become, for many Irish people, symbolic of the British. In his apology Blair was saying, in effect, this:

> Although there is continuity at various levels between the British state today and the British state then, there is discontinuity in the moral evaluation of Britain's handling of the Irish famine (and, given the famine's status as a token, of Ireland as a whole). We British today recognize that we failed to do what we should have done. We therefore publicly accept your judgment upon us, and distance ourselves now from ourselves then. Thereby we hope to assure you that our negligence in the past does not betoken our negligence in the present or in the future.

Likewise, Daly was saying something like this:

> We, the vast majority of Irish people, publicly repudiate what some have perpetrated in our name. We do not want you to confuse us with them, nor the current and future relations between our peoples to be distorted by such confusion. Know that we agree with you in your moral evaluation of republican violence, and that therefore you can trust us.

This deliberate repudiation of deeds done or left undone by *other* members of our people is strictly an expression of regret, rather than one of remorse. It is indeed a political act of apology rather than a personal one of repentance. But it is nonetheless important for that.

Some Implications for Northern Ireland

All of our authors appear to agree that burying the past by discovering the truth about it is important for a peaceful political future. But this is not to say that all the truth must be brought to light straightaway. Indeed, to insist on doing so might well jeopardize the peace, and it might well be fruitless. The opposing sides may simply not be ready to make the concessions necessary for achieving a measure of "reconciliation" between their respective stories; too much may be at stake. This appears to be one reason why McCaughey (pp. 260–61, 262) and Hamber (pp. 143–44) doubt the viability of a truth commission in Northern Ireland—and this view is the one held by most people.[10] It may be that the experience of a period of successful accommodation—or, to use Barahona de Brito's slightly more positive term, *convivencia*—may be necessary to enable the former opponents to feel sufficiently secure to begin to negotiate the truth. Maybe it will only be when unionists in Northern Ireland are assured of their British identity (through, for example, Northern Ireland remaining part of the United Kingdom, albeit in a significantly qualified and ambiguous way), that they will be able to concede that the Troubles would never have happened if Catholics in Northern Ireland had been treated as equal citizens by unionist-dominated administrations. Likewise, maybe it will only be when republicans feel that their Irish identity is secure (through, for example, successful power sharing, measures against discrimination, and governing institutions that can claim to be Irish as well as British), that they will be able to admit the injustices perpetrated by the IRA.

If so, Northern Ireland will have to wait for any significant "reconciliation" of hostile readings of the past, and their forging into a more or less agreed "truth," until a political settlement has enjoyed many years of success. In other words, before truth on this grand scale can out, there must be a period of general not-remembering. But this is not to say that no particular truths should be told. In the meantime, it will be vital that the whole truth about "Bloody Sunday" is seen to be disclosed, if Irish nationalist confidence in what looks likely to remain substantially British government in Northern Ireland, is to be won—that is, if nationalists are to be "reconciled" to continuing British authority in Ireland.[11] It will also be important that particular facts come to public light, enter public debate, and so begin to apply critical pressure to the official stories of both local sides in the conflict. Examples of these can be found in the data that Smyth reports (pp. 114–15, 117–18): the fact that almost fifty percent more Catholics than Protestants have died in the Troubles (so is the unionist story correct to assume that Protestants have been the primary victims, and Catholics the primary oppressors?); and the fact that almost twenty-five percent of Catholics who have died were killed by republican paramilitaries—several percentage points *more* than those killed by the security forces (so how true is the republican story when it claims that the IRA was fighting in defense of Catholics against British oppression?). The gradual emergence of little truths like these is not likely to disturb the "peace process," and it will help to prepare the way for the day when a larger-scale renegotiation of the past is possible.

Thus far my discussion has assumed that a truth commission for Northern Ireland would not be viable. It is arguable, however, that it would not even be appropriate. Truth commissions in Latin America and Africa have been set up to put on public record facts about violations of human rights largely committed by the previous regime. A major part of their raison d'être has been to expose the old, oppressive regime for what it really was, in the hope of putting unambiguous distance between it and the new dispensation. The situation in Northern Ireland, however, is different. It is true that, until its suspension in 1972, the unionist-dominated government in Stormont[12] had permitted various kinds of injustice to be meted out to Catholics—for example, discrimination in housing, jobs, and education; and it is true that the United Kingdom government had done nothing to stop it. It is also true that during the Troubles some members of the security forces have been deliberately involved in illegal killings and torture; and that police fraud has resulted in some unjust convictions. On the other hand, it is widely recognized that the British state has made serious efforts during the past thirty years to combat structural injustice in Northern Ireland.[13] Further, some of the agents of the state responsible for crimes have been convicted and sentenced by the courts; and there is even republican testimony that the judiciary has not acted simply as a weapon of the state against its enemies.[14] Further still, the forces of the state have been responsible for only 10.7 percent of all Troubles-related deaths, whereas republican paramilitaries have killed 55.7 percent and loyalist paramilitaries 27.4 percent (see Smyth, p. 117). My point here is not that the British state's hands are entirely clean, nor that it does not need to tell the whole truth about some of the deeds it has authorized or at least presided over. Rather, my point is that, in this case and in contrast to South Africa, it is the paramilitaries' hands that are the dirtier; and that the state's behavior has not been such as to require the kind of wholesale repudiation that truth commissions are largely designed to bring about.

Burying the Past and Religion

It is not by accident that at least five of the contributors to this volume are Christian theologians, whether by profession or intellectual stance. The task of dealing with a strife-ridden and guilt-laden past, in order to make possible a peaceful future, lies at the heart of Christian religion; and the themes of forgiveness and reconciliation have an accordingly high profile in its traditions of thought. Such themes may not be simply unique to Christianity, but they are, arguably, unique in their prominence. After all, as Elshtain reports (p. 40), it was the Jewish Hannah Arendt who accredited Jesus with the discovery of the political role of forgiveness.[15]

However, as Arendt observed, the fact that political forgiveness was discovered in a religious tradition does not mean that such a notion is so tied to its theological context that it cannot be considered "in a strictly secular sense."[16] This is quite true. One does not have to believe in God, the soul, an afterlife, or a Final Judgment, to see the wisdom of forgiveness. When, in Peter Shaffer's play, "The Gift of the Gorgon," Philip warns his stepmother, "The truth is, you must forgive . . . or die,"[17] there is no need to locate that spiritual death in anything other than a secular context.

Nevertheless, it is easier to see the justice of forgiveness, as distinct from its prudence, against the background of a Christian anthropology. According to this, human beings share an equality, not only of dignity, but of sinfulness. Although some of us may have committed graver, perhaps more heinous sins than others, we belong to the same stock, subject to the same or similar temptations and propensities. This, of course, is Donald Shriver's point when he talks of the need to recognize the humanity of the enemy because "all have sinned" (p. 37); and it is also Jean Elshtain's when she approves of Václav Havel's apology to dispossessed Germans on behalf of the Czech people, because the Czechs, although the original victims, "also knew sin" (p. 49). Such equality in sinfulness, however, should not be taken to imply that no one has the right to "judge" another, and that all wrongdoing—from gross crimes to peccadilloes—should simply be forgiven. Love for our neighbors, whether in the form of actual victims, potential victims, or perpetrators, requires that provisional justice be done, and maybe even that a certain punishment be inflicted. What the concept of equal sinfulness does imply is that those who dare to judge must look upon the criminal as one of their own kind, and not as the righteous upon the unrighteous. While recognizing the necessity of judgment, they must also recognize that, but for divine grace or good fortune, there in the dock they themselves could easily be standing. This, of course, amounts to compassion, rather than forgiveness. But compassion is one of the basic motives behind forgiveness; and it is one that recognizes in forgiveness, not only a means to a good end (reconciliation), but also something intrinsically fair and, in that sense, just.

Still, although the justice in forgiveness is brought out by a Christian anthropology, it is not clear in this respect that anthropology is necessarily theological. For it is possible to acknowledge the common status of human beings as fated and flawed without having to make any reference to specifically religious concepts. It is really only when we look—as we have done on many occasions in this book—upon the severe limitations of the justice that human beings can achieve in history, and when we notice how within the bounds of time and space the human yearning for justice often finds little more than scraps to gnaw on, that reference to things that transcend the secular becomes at all pressing (see McCaughey, p. 266, and Biggar, pp. 17–18). For then the rationality of this yearning, and of the heroic dedication it can inspire, come into question. Why is it that we aspire so deeply, and strive so assiduously, after something that long and wide experience tells us comes only in fragments, if it comes at all? Is it really because of a cosmic joke of sadistic proportions? Or might not our deep and humane yearning for justice in time and space, and our admirable commitment to it, make it reasonable to wager on an eschatological hope that looks far beyond?

Endnotes

1. Kader Asmal, Louise Asmal, and Robert Suresh Roberts, *Reconciliation through Truth: A Reckoning of Apartheid's Criminal Governance* (Cape Town: David Philip; Oxford: James Currey; New York: St. Martin's Press, 1997), 6.

2. Ibid., 26.

3. Ibid., 7.

4. Mary Hawkesworth, "Knower, Knowing, Known: Feminist Theory and Claims of Truth," *Signs* 14/3 (1989): 557.

5. Asmal et al., *Reconciliation through Truth*, 9, 215. McCaughey (p. 259) appropriates the problematic phrase, "shared and ceaselessly debated memory."

6. E.H. Carr, *What Is History?* (1961), quoted in Richard J. Evans, *In Defense of History* (Cambridge: Granta, 1997), 224.

7. My supposition here is confirmed by *The New Oxford Dictionary of English* (Oxford: Oxford University Press, 1998), which gives as its sole illustration of the use of "prudent": "no prudent money manager would authorize a loan without first knowing its purpose."

8. Timothy Garton Ash, "True Confessions," *New York Review of Books*, 17 July 1997, 36–37.

9. Recorded in "Getting Away with Murder," a BBC documentary about the TRC, presented by Michael Ignatieff and originally broadcast on 1 November 1997 as part of the "Correspondent" series.

10. Bertie Ahern, the Irish *taioseach* (prime minister) confirmed this in his address to the South African Institute for International Affairs on 12 January 2000: "The option of having a Truth and Reconciliation Commission has not attracted significant support in Ireland. . . . The reasons have not, in general, been made very explicit, but my assessment is that people feel that, on balance, the potential harm that would flow from disclosure, against the background, in particular of the small size of the society and of local communities, would considerably outweigh the benefit, in terms of establishing the truth or of catharsis for the victims or the bereaved." Cited in "The Irish Peace Process and Beyond," in *New Dialogue News* 82 (February 2000): 5–6. (New Dialogue's web site address is www.newdialogue.org.uk.)

11. See p. 130, n. 21 in this book for a description of "Bloody Sunday." It is possible, of course, that the truth about this event will turn out to be other than what some nationalists and republicans assume—less a vicious tale of stereotypical British malice than a tragic one of military inexperience, extenuating circumstances, and political cowardice. That is to say, it may be that disclosure of the "real truth" will still not be sufficient to win the trust of some.

12. Stormont was the seat of Northern Ireland's devolved government, until it was suspended in 1972. It is the seat of the new Northern Ireland Assembly. It lies just outside of Belfast.

13. Even Catholics in Northern Ireland recognize this. See Fionnuala O'Connor, *In Search of a State: Catholics in Northern Ireland* (Belfast: Blackstaff, 1993), 14, 17. "It is widely accepted that barriers to Catholic advancement have fallen, to a great extent because of the reforms eventually initiated and administered by British politicians" (p. 34). "British rule . . . is not seen as discriminatory against Catholics: or at least, it is not seen in that light by those who have done well out of the reforms of the past decade" (p. 43). Mary McAleese, academic lawyer in Belfast, now president of the Republic of Ireland, said, "For Catholics, direct rule [from London] has been the best form of government we've had. . . ." (pp. 182, 198). O'Connor's book won the George Orwell Prize for Political Writing in 1995.

14. At least one active member of the IRA, Eamon Collins, was so impressed by his fair treatment at the hands of British justice (he was acquitted of charges for a crime that

he had in fact committed, because the evidence brought against him was improperly obtained), that he was moved to abandon violence. He wrote of his reaction to the judge's declaration of acquittal: "[T]he judge's words had sent a real shock through my body. I felt peculiarly emotional about them. The law, that part of the system at least, had revealed its genuine dignity: there could be such a thing as the impartial application of the rule of law. This judge had brought to life for me, even though he loathed the IRA, principles which were important boundaries between civilisation and barbarism. The implied judgement on what I had been doing for the past six years was one that I absorbed, and the contrast with our revolutionary justice was extreme. . . . When the reality had sunk in, I knew I really could abandon violence because the system, for all its manifest injustices, carried within itself the possibility of justice. When British justice worked, when it operated impartially according to its highest principles, it could still represent the highest achievement of a civilized society" (in Eamon Collins, *Killing Rage* [London: Granta, 1997], 339–40). Collins was murdered, probably by some of his former IRA colleagues, in 1999.

15. Hannah Arendt, *The Human Condition* (Chicago and London: University of Chicago Press, 1958), 238.

16. Ibid.

17. Peter Shaffer, *The Gift of the Gorgon* (London: Viking, 1993), 92.

Index

Printed in the United States
3102